Mysteries of the Afterlife

Great Mysteries

Book Club Associates
London

Mysteries of the Afterlife

by Frank Smyth and Roy Stemman

Editorial Consultants:
COLIN WILSON
DR. CHRISTOPHER EVANS

Series Coordinator: John Mason
Design Director: Günter Radtke
Picture Editor: Peter Cook
Editor: Sally Burningham
Copy Editor: Mitzi Bales
Research: Sarah Waters
General Consultant: Beppie Harrison

This edition published 1981 by
Book Club Associates
By arrangement with Aldus Books Limited
First published in the United Kingdom
in 1978 by Aldus Books Limited
17 Conway Street, London W1P 6BS

Printed and bound in Hong Kong
by Leefung-Asco Printers Limited

Introduction

We all have an absorbing fascination
with the problem of what happens after
death. A man or woman dies, and what is
left is a lifeless thing, a corpse that decays
and disappears. But does something
continue? Down the ages there have been
many explanations and theories—that the
spirits of the dead live among their
successors and descendants, that each
individual dies to be born again in a new
shape or form, that this worldly existence
is lived again on a different plane. But in
our own skeptical century the doubts
and the questions grow louder: is there any
life at all after death? If there is not, how
does one account for the continuing human
experience of ghosts and spirits: mysterious
apparitions which appear and disappear
unbound by natural laws, unaccountable
intelligences which communicate
information apparently unavailable by
normal means? Are all the tales of haunted
houses the result of credulous imagination?
Are all the peculiar manifestations in the
seance rooms to be dismissed as clever
tricks played on the gullible? We say dead
men tell no tales—but are there around us
witnesses to a life which continues after the
body is in its grave?

Contents

Chapter 1
Seeing and Believing

Are there such things as ghosts haunting our ordinary world? Do these half-legendary spectral beings really exist? The evidence is tantalizing, baffling, and raises almost as many questions as it answers. Certainly it appears that men have long believed there are ghostly presences stalking through the land of the living. What are these presences? Are they returning spirits, demons in disguise, or unfortunate souls doomed to wander restlessly because they were denied proper burial rites? Or are they simply the result of wishful imagination on the part of a storyteller? There are stories to support all these premises, but the questions linger on.

As a young man living in Boston, the writer Nathaniel Hawthorne often used to go to the Atheneum Library. Among the distinguished men he usually saw in its reading room was the Reverend Doctor Harris, a clergyman in his 80s, who could be found every day about noon sitting in a chair by the fireplace reading the *Boston Post*. One evening, having visited the Atheneum that day and having remembered seeing Dr. Harris sitting in his chair as usual, Hawthorne was astonished when a friend told him that the old man had recently died. He was even more astonished when, on entering the reading room the following day, he again saw Dr. Harris reading his paper by the fire. Hawthorne spent some time in the room, reading and occasionally stealing a glance at the seemingly solid, lifelike apparition. For weeks he continued to see the old man in his chair. "At length," reported Hawthorne, "I regarded the venerable defunct no more than the other old fogies who basked before the fire and dozed over the newspapers." None of these living "old fogies" seemed to see the ghost although many of them had been close friends of Dr. Harris. So it was the more odd that his ghost appeared to Hawthorne, who knew him only by sight. Perhaps, however, the others did see it, but were as reticent as Hawthorne about acknowledging it.

Describing the incident years later in a letter to a friend, Hawthorne marveled at his own reluctance to investigate the phenomenon—to brush against it or try to snatch the paper,

Opposite: a real ghost? This photograph was taken in 1959 in the Australian bush by Reverend R. S. Blance. Although the site had once been used by aborigines for gruelling initiation ceremonies, it was deserted except for the photographer when he took this picture. Technical examination of the film ruled out double exposure. Photographs of apparitions (or seeming apparitions) are very rare, but they provide one piece of evidence supporting the argument that ghosts exist.

"One Day the Figure Was Missing..."

Below: the American novelist and short story writer Nathaniel Hawthorne. The author of many stories dealing with the supernatural, Hawthorne had several encounters with real-life ghosts. The house he lived in in Massachusetts was haunted, but the apparition confined itself to the front yard. "I have often," wrote Hawthorne, "while sitting in the parlor, in the daytime, had a perception that somebody was passing the windows—but, on looking toward them, nobody is there." The ghost Hawthorne saw in the Atheneum Library, however, was less elusive. In fact it sat in the same place for weeks, reading a newspaper.

if it was a paper—out of its hands. "Perhaps," he said, "I was loth to destroy the illusion, and to rob myself of so good a ghost story, which might probably have been explained in some very commonplace way." In time, Hawthorne said, he became aware that the old gentleman seemed to be gazing at him with a certain expectancy. The novelist thought that maybe he had something to communicate, and was waiting for Hawthorne to speak first. "But, if so, the ghost had shown the bad judgment common among the spiritual brotherhood, both as regarded the place of interview and the person whom he had selected as the recipient of his communications. In the reading room of the Atheneum, conversation is strictly forbidden, and I couldn't have addressed the apparition without drawing the instant notice and indignant frowns of the slumberous old gentlemen around me. . . . And what an absurd figure should I have made, solemnly . . . addressing what must have appeared in the eyes of all the rest of the company, an empty chair. Besides," concluded Hawthorne, in a last appeal to the social proprieties, "I had never been introduced to Doctor Harris. . . ."

One day the figure was missing from the chair by the fire, and Hawthorne never saw it again.

What are we to make of this story? Was Hawthorne the writer simply spinning a yarn? Probably not, for as a skilled literary craftsman, he would surely have constructed his fictional ghost story so that it had some development and point. As fiction, the story is a bit flat. As a psychic experience, however, it is first class. This is no vaporous and transparent "gray lady" glimpsed for a few seconds in a darkened hallway by an impressionable person with weak eyesight. Instead, we have an apparently solid figure seen continually over a period of weeks by a man who—although sensitive and attracted to the mystical—was obviously clear-headed. What did he see?

Many people would have had a ready answer: Hawthorne saw the spirit of the deceased Dr. Harris, which for some reason was delayed in its progress into the next world and was temporarily trapped in the place he had "haunted" while alive.

The belief in an afterlife, held by almost all peoples since earliest times, once gave ghosts a legitimacy they lack in our more skeptical culture. Most religions have assumed the existence of a place, or places, where departed spirits go, and have provided rites to ensure the soul's passage into the next world. Still, in varying degrees, people have believed that there was a certain connection between body and spirit, even after death, and that it was most important to bury the body in such a way that the spirit of the deceased would not come back to haunt the living. Some primitive peoples, for example, bind the arms and legs of the corpse to prevent perambulation after death. Traditionally, people have believed that if the person died without receiving the rites, and especially if he died by his own hand or in other violent or tragic circumstances, his spirit might remain earthbound.

One such imprisoned spirit was the object of the first recorded case of psychical research. In Athens, in the 1st century B.C., there was a house reputed to be haunted by a specter of a gray-haired old man whose hands and feet were bound in iron

chains—a style of ghost later immortalized as the chain-rattling Marley in Dickens' *A Christmas Carol*. This ghost was said to have frightened one man to death, and in time the house fell vacant. Eventually the owner of the house, desperate to get some return from his property, reduced the rent to a ridiculously low figure. Hearing of these bargain-rate premises, the philosopher Athenodorus made inquiries, and was intrigued to learn the reason. He promptly moved in to investigate, and on the first night was rewarded by the sound of rattling chains.

In a moment the thin gray figure of the manacled specter appeared in the room and beckoned to him. Athenodorus ignored it. The ghost moved closer, clanking and rattling in agitation and beckoning all the while. Still the philosopher remained motionless. Finally the ghost gave up the effort, turned, and dragged its fetters out into the courtyard where it

Above: in the mid-19th century the new art of photography joined with the new cult of Spiritualism to produce pictures such as this ingenious fabrication. The despondent widower, presumably lost in reminiscences, is visited by the ghost of his beloved wife.

Haunting Their Burial Ground

Ghosts are found in the folklore, art, and literature of all nations.
Below right: a typical Japanese ghost with flowing white gown and disheveled hair, bending over a terrified mortal. Japanese ghosts are often shown without legs, and ghosts of people who led a wicked life are often physically deformed to suggest punishment after death. In Japanese folklore ghosts often visit people to warn them of approaching death. One writer, Inouye, remarks that "they are especially likely to be seen by persons who are out of health or . . . feeble in body and mind, deficient in knowledge and impressionable."

Below: the entrance to an amusement park "spook house" showing the kinds of terrors offered inside. People love to be frightened by make-believe versions of the supernatural, such as ghost stories and vividly hideous papier mache specters that pop out of the dark. Yet most of the well-authenticated accounts of seeing a ghost involve no horror. Usually, the percipient is not even frightened. Many apparitions are so lifelike that they are mistaken as human.

suddenly vanished. Out of the corner of his eye Athenodorus watched it go, and carefully noted where it had disappeared.

The following morning he went out, got a magistrate, and returned to the courtyard. After some digging they discovered a chained skeleton, its bonds covered with rust. The magistrate arranged for it to be given a decent burial, and the ghost was never seen again.

About 2000 years later a similar case of apparent cause-effect haunting came to light in England. Eric Maple, a folklorist and collector of ghostly lore, was interviewing some people in the village of Reculver, Essex, the site of a Roman settlement. The villagers told him about a clump of trees nearby that was haunted by the spirits of some babies, whose piteous crying disturbed the winter nights. Several of Maple's informants swore that they had heard these doleful sounds, and that on no account would they go near the "children's wood."

In the 1960s a major archaeological excavation took place in Reculver during which a number of important Roman remains were unearthed. Eric Maple visited the dig in time to see a collection of children's skulls and bones discovered by the excavators. Analysis of the bones showed them to be at least 1500 years old. They included one complete skeleton of a child who had apparently been ritually murdered and interred in the foundations by the Gaulish soldiers encamped there. Here was evidence that the grisly custom of making a foundation sacrifice to the gods, common in many parts of pre-Christian Europe, had been done surreptitiously after the practice had been officially condemned. The question is: did the discovery of the bones at Reculver give substance to the phenomenon of the crying in the wood, or had the ancient story of the murder created the idea of children crying in the wood?

Pre-Christian Europe was thickly populated with ghosts, spirits, fairies, gods, and goddesses. Christian missionaries tried to discourage the native belief in such beings, but ended by absorbing some of them in altered form into Christian teaching. The grotesque gargoyles that perch on the roofs and towers of

some medieval churches are evidence of the survival of the pagan superstition that a demon could be used to frighten away other demons. This belief was adapted to protect the Christian faithful inside the church.

Ghosts were looked upon with some suspicion by the Church. It was generally assumed that a demon who was unable to find a weak-willed human to possess might create a visible form for himself and appear as a ghost. The Church allowed that some phantoms were those of souls in Purgatory, and that a very few might be saints, but warned its members to treat any specter with caution.

This wary attitude toward ghosts is one of the elements in the plot of *Hamlet*. When he first sees the ghost of his murdered father, Hamlet acknowledges the possibilities of its being evil: "Be thou a spirit of health, or goblin damn'd, / Bring with thee airs from heaven, or blasts from hell, / Be thy intents wicked or charitable, / Thou com'st in such a questionable shape, / That

Below: this gargoyle on the Cathedral of Notre Dame, Paris, is a typical medieval representation of a demon, placed on a church to guard it from other demons. The Church believed that demons could assume the form of ghosts.

Above: in Shakespeare's famous play, Banquo's ghost appears to the terrified Macbeth, who has had Banquo murdered. He cries out to the apparition—which he alone can see—while Lady Macbeth assures the guests that her husband is merely suffering a momentary fit.

I will speak to thee. . . ." Later, although almost entirely convinced of the truth of the ghost's claim that his own brother murdered him, Hamlet hesitates to avenge the murder, partly because he has a nagging doubt as to the ghost's true identity. "The spirit that I have seen / May be a devil, and the devil hath power / To assume a pleasing shape." He arranges a play depicting a similar murder, hoping to trick the king into revealing his guilt and thereby verifying the ghost's accusation.

Interestingly the *Hamlet* ghost is not visible to everyone—just as Hawthorne's ghost was not. Hamlet's friends see it, but his mother does not. When the ghost appears in the queen's room and Hamlet speaks to it, he alarms the queen who sees nothing. Already suspecting that her son is mad, she tells him: "This is the very coinage of your brain."

The queen's interpretation of Hamlet's ghost is the skeptic's interpretation of all ghosts. An apparition—and to the skeptical this word is much preferable to ghost, which implies a surviving personality—is simply a picture conjured up by the person who sees it. Determined scoffers are inclined to believe that anyone who sees a ghost is, at least temporarily, mentally unbalanced. More objective researchers will tend to agree that a ghost is indeed a kind of picture, but that it may not necessarily originate in the brain of the person who sees it. The wealth of evidence accumulated on apparitions and hauntings so far contains many questions that cannot be answered by any one theory.

Even the most thorough skeptics will usually show a reluctance to confront specters, imaginary though they believe them to be. In an introduction to a collection of ghost stories, Bennett Cerf pokes gentle fun at "the greatest skeptic I ever met [who] was asked point-blank if he would sleep alone in a house that had been haunted, according to common belief, for a hundred years or more. 'Not on your life!' said the skeptic. *'Why should I take the chance?'*"

The potentially frightening aspect of ghosts is one reason for their enduring popularity in legend and literature. The psychical researcher may be more interested in cases that have an aura of prosaic normality about them, such as Hawthorne's; but the average person is more likely to be intrigued by ghosts that terrify. Ghostly lore abounds with phantoms that have empty eye sockets instead of eyes, or are missing their heads, or are skeletons. According to a legend of Norfolk, England, every May 31 at midnight a phantom coach that sets out from the village of Bastwick is driven furiously through the countryside by a mad coachman. The coach appears to be on fire, but the sharp-eyed or imaginative observer may catch a glimpse of its passengers—who are skeletons. Eventually the coach crashes into a bridge and the whole thing, including horses, driver, and occupants, plunges into the water. As the story goes, this ghastly conveyance recalls the marriage in 1741 of Sir Godfrey Haslitt of Bastwick Place, and Evelyn, Lady Montefiore Carew of Castle Lynn, a match arranged by the bride's mother with some help from the Devil. The marriage festivities were barely over when the Devil claimed his own—not only the ruthless mother, but also the bride and groom, all of whom lost their lives in a fire that burned down Bastwick Hall.

One of the most horrifying of all kinds of ghost stories concerns premature burial. The possibility of being interred while still alive but in a coma is a very real, and to some extent well-founded, fear. Today such an occurrence is extremely unlikely, although it does occasionally happen. In his book *The Romeo Error*, Lyall Watson cites a case that occurred in New York in 1964. A surgeon was about to perform a post-mortem examination when the supposed corpse leaped up and grabbed the surgeon by the throat. The surgeon died of shock.

Edgar Allan Poe was morbidly fascinated by the idea of premature burial, and this theme recurs in several of his stories. In one of the most macabre, "The Fall of the House of Usher," the master of the house, Roderick Usher, meets his death at the hands of a dead person. His sister, the Lady Madeline, has apparently died after a long wasting illness, and is installed in a vault in the lower regions of the decrepit mansion prior to final interment. Several nights later, in the midst of a violent storm, the deranged Roderick hears from below in the house the rending of her coffin, the creaking of the iron gate of the vault, and her footsteps on the stairs. Leaping to his feet he shrieks, *"'I tell you that she now stands without the door!'"*

At that moment the doors swing open slowly, and "there did

All in the Mind?

Below: a scene from one of the best-loved of all ghost stories, Dickens' *A Christmas Carol*. Here the miser Ebenezer Scrooge is visited by the ghost of his former business partner Jacob Marley. Moaning in anguish for his ill-spent life and present torment, Marley warns Scrooge that he too will be condemned to an afterlife of suffering unless he mends his ways and learns charity toward his fellow men.

Buried Alive?

Below: a humorous treatment of a terrifying subject, the possibility of being buried alive. This 18th-century print depicts an exchange between a juror at an inquest and the coroner. The caption reads: "Juror: 'The man's alive, Sir, for he has opened one eye.' Coroner: 'Sir, the doctor declared him dead two hours since and he must remain dead, Sir, so I shall proceed with the inquest.'"

stand the lofty and enshrouded figure of the Lady Madeline of Usher. There was blood upon her white robes, and the evidence of some bitter struggle upon every portion of her emaciated frame. For a moment she remained trembling and reeling to and fro upon the threshold, then, with a low moaning cry, fell heavily inward upon the person of her brother, and in her violent and now final death agonies, bore him to the floor a corpse, and a victim to the terrors he had anticipated."

In the best tradition of the horror story, the ghastly figure of Lady Madeline can be interpreted in more than one way: as a living woman who has crawled out of her own coffin; as the revengeful spirit of one who has suffocated in the tomb; or as the projection of Roderick's own guilt and fear.

The premature burial theme often appears in the persistent English legend of the moaning nun. The story has many variations, but a popular version concerns a nun who broke her vow of chastity and was punished by being buried alive within the

Far left: this illustration from "Netley Abbey," one of the ghost stories in the *Ingoldsby Legends* written by R. H. Barham, shows a nun being immured.

Left: a picture from the *Illustrated Police News* of 1869 showing the discovery of a skeleton in the vaults of a medieval convent in southern Europe.

convent walls. From this unconsecrated grave, her spirit ventures forth in an endless, futile quest for peace. In fact, many nuns and monks *were* buried secretly—after a natural death—inside the walls of manor houses to which they had fled for protection following the dissolution of the monasteries by Henry VIII. It may be that the legend of the immured nun grew out of stories of such actual cases of clandestine burial.

If so, it would not be the first time that the folk process had created a mythical ghost story around a kernel of fact. This process of distortion and embellishment goes on whenever any story is passed down by word of mouth. An example of the kind of distortion that takes place over the years is related in an article by the contemporary Scottish novelist Gordon M. Williams. While living in a hamlet in Devon, he heard of a local superstition that it is bad luck to die in mid-November. The manager of the local pub told him that "in the old days" dead bodies had to be transported across the moor to the nearest graveyard, a distance of some 50 miles, for there was no consecrated graveyard nearby. Sometimes when the corpse was transported in winter, the carriers got caught in heavy snow on the wild moors and left the body packed in ice until the journey could be completed in spring. Thus, said the tavern keeper, the dead man was left alone, and without benefit of clergy, was the prey of any wandering demon that might pass his way. Inquiring when the last corpse had been transported, Williams was told by the pub keeper that it had happened "in my grandfather's time, or maybe my great grandfather's." Later, on checking the story in the British Museum, Williams found it to be basically true—with the significant difference that the last such corpse transportation had occurred in the year 1138.

In 1915 during World War I, the *Evening News* of London published a story by writer Arthur Machen describing an incident during the terrible retreat of the British army from Mons. Machen quoted an officer who claimed that, as he rode along with two other officers, he became aware of horsemen with longbows in the fields on either side. "So convinced were

Life in Death

In 1878 the daughter of D. J. Demarest, a grocer of Paterson, New Jersey, died apparently of a heart disease. The child died on a Tuesday, and the body was dressed for burial and laid in its small coffin. On Friday, the father left the coffin where he had been kneeling, and went into the next room. There he sank into an armchair, hid his face in his hands, and wept.

Suddenly he heard footsteps outside the door. He raised his head and saw the door slowly swing open. To his astonishment he saw his daughter, dressed in her shroud, entering the room. She tottered across to where her father sat, threw herself upon his lap, and twined her arms around his neck. She nestled down in her stunned parent's arms, but a moment later fell slowly backward. He raised her up, but she sagged limply and lifelessly against him.

The first death had, in fact, been only a coma. The child was pronounced dead for the second time, and her body was buried that same day.

This macabre real-life story went across the ocean to London where it was published in the *Illustrated Police News*.

The 1890 Census of Hallucinations

we that they were really cavalry, that at the next halt one of the Officers took a party of men out to reconnoitre and found no one there." The phantom soldiers were assumed to be English bowmen from the field of Agincourt, where the English had won a great victory over the French in 1415. Interpreted this way, they were symbols of hope to the survivors of Mons.

Soon after the story was published, corroborative reports began to be circulated. In most of these stories, the phantom took the form of battalions of angels coming to the aid of the Allies. Machen confessed that his story was fiction; but by then the need to believe in the angels was too great to be denied. Soon almost every second survivor of Mons was telling his own version of the story; and there are still old men alive today who will swear that they saw the hosts of Heaven marching through gunsmoke toward the German lines.

An ironic postscript to the story was provided by Friedrich Herzenwirth, a former director of espionage for Germany, who claimed in his memoirs, published in 1930, that the angels were motion pictures. German pilots, he said, projected the images onto clouds in an attempt to make the English believe that God was on the side of the Kaiser.

The credulity of the human race, and its readiness to perpetuate colorful and dramatically satisfying ghost stories, has been something of a hindrance to serious psychical research. Hard-headed scientists have been reluctant to devote much attention to a field of research so permeated with old superstitions, literary clichés, and tourist attractions. The conviction persists among these skeptics that any haunting or apparition that can't be dismissed as myth can be ascribed to intoxication or mental instability on the part of the *percipient*—that is, the person who sees it.

Those researchers who have treated the subject seriously and scientifically have discovered plenty of cases that cannot be so easily dismissed. One of the earliest studies was the Census of Hallucinations, conducted by the Society for Psychical Research in 1890. The Census asked 17,000 people in Britain the following question: "Have you ever, when believing yourself to be completely awake, had a vivid impression of seeing or being touched by a living being or inanimate object, or of hearing a voice: which impression, so far as you could discover, was not due to any external physical cause?"

Of the 17,000 people that were polled, 1684, just under 10 percent, answered "Yes." Similar studies were carried out in France, Germany, and the United States, and yielded an overall "Yes" response of 11.96 percent from a total of some 27,000 replies. Those who answered "Yes" in the British survey were then asked to give as detailed an account as possible of their experience. They were carefully questioned and their stories evaluated by the SPR.

The purpose of the Census was to test for telepathy—the hypothesis being that one person could somehow project an image of himself to another person. Many of the apparitions fell into this category; but others were of people known, or later discovered, to be dead.

Among the most interesting cases was that reported by Miss

Opposite: the parish church of Stoke Dry, Rutland, England. A compartment above the door is allegedly haunted by the ghost of a woman imprisoned there and starved to death for practicing witchcraft.

The Ghost Had a Regular Routine

Morton (pseudonym), a medical student. For seven years between 1882 and 1889, her home was haunted by the figure of a tall woman wearing a dark dress. The ghost's routine was to walk down the stairs into the drawing room, stand for a moment beside the bow window, leave the drawing room, and disappear through the door leading to the garden. Miss Morton saw and heard the figure on various occasions, and was able to describe it in some detail. It was, she said, "dressed in black of a soft woollen material, judging from the slight sound in moving. The face was hidden in a handkerchief. I saw the upper part of the left side of the forehead, and a little of the hair above. He left hand was nearly hidden by her sleeve and a fold of her dress. As she held it down, a portion of a widow's cuff was visible. . . . There was no [widow's] cap on the head, but a general effect of blackness suggests a bonnet, with long veil or a hood." For the first two years, the apparition was so solid looking as to be mistaken for a living person. After 1884 it became less distinctive and appeared less often.

Several people beside Miss Morton saw the apparition, and their description of it tallied with her own. Her father, however, was unable to see it. Miss Morton provided the SPR with accounts of the figure's appearances, including this incident:

"The following evening, 12th August, while coming up the garden, I walked toward the orchard, when I saw the figure cross the orchard, go along the carriage drive in front of the house, and in at the open side door, across the hall and into

Right: in a World War I newspaper story by Arthur Machen, angels appeared to British soldiers at the Battle of Mons. The angels were English bowmen, supposedly spirits of those who had fallen in the Battle of Agincourt in 1415. As symbols of a great English victory, the mythical bowmen revived the morale of the defeated and exhausted soldiers at Mons, and soon eyewitness accounts of the ghostly phenomenon were appearing in the British press. They were taken as an omen of divine support for the Allies. Machen's revelation that his story was fiction made little impression on a populace who wanted desperately to believe in the symbolic help of the angels.

the drawing room, I following. She crossed the drawing room and took up her usual position behind the couch in the bow window. My father came in soon after and I told him she was there. He could not see the figure, but went up to where I showed him she was. She then went swiftly around behind him, across the room, out of the door and along the hall, disappearing as usual near the garden door, we both following her. . . ."

Around 8 o'clock that same evening both Miss Morton and her sister saw the figure in the drawing room, where it remained by the window "for ten minutes or a quarter of an hour."

In an effort to understand the nature of the phenomenon, Miss Morton glued a piece of thread across the stairs; the figure passed through the thread without disturbing it. When she tried to touch the apparition, it always managed to be just beyond her reach. When she spoke to it, it would sometimes pause and look as though it were going to speak, but never did.

The description of the figure was found to resemble a Mrs. S. who had lived in the house until her death in 1878, although positive identification was impossible because the specter always partly covered her face with the handkerchief. The widow's weeds were one clue, Mr. S. having died two years before his wife, and the handkerchief held to the face might have been another. The marriage had apparently been an unhappy one. Mr. S. had become a heavy drinker after the death of his first wife, and the second Mrs. S. not only failed in her attempt to reform him, but began to drink heavily herself. According to

Above: this man is not an extra in a ghost-story film, but an employee of the São Paulo, Brazil, traffic department which, in 1971, mounted a safety campaign to "spook" drivers into driving more carefully. Presumably the sight of a phantomlike figure weaving among the cars reminds drivers of their mortality.

Left: this drawing by Cruikshank shows a man who wakes in the middle of the night and gets scared by his own clothes, which he has draped over a chair and hung on the back of a door in such a way that they suggest two phantoms to his sleep-fogged brain. Countless cases of alleged hauntings have been proved to be optical illusions, just as many spectral footsteps turn out to be mice or the contraction of old timbers as a house cools at night.

Ghost Stories

Below: *The Ghost Story* depicts a farmer entertaining his family with a tale of the supernatural. He has obviously just reached a spine-chilling development, and in a moment both he and his enthralled listeners will jump out of their chairs in fright as the jug crashes to the floor. Innumerable supposed hauntings can be traced to cats, whose stealthy movements and glow-in-the-dark eyes produce many ghostly effects.

Right: "It leapt towards him upon the instant," an illustration of the climactic moment of the ghost story "Oh, Whistle, and I'll Come to You, My Lad" by M. R. James. The story tells of the experience of a skeptical professor who, on a trip to the east coast of England, finds an ancient whistle, idly blows upon it, and in so doing apparently conjures up some evil spirit. Or has he conjured up those superstitions that lurk in his own subconscious mind—perhaps an inherited racial memory? The ambiguity in James' narrative reflects the ambiguities underlying the whole question of ghosts as myth or reality.

people who had known Mrs. S., the behavior and general appearance of the ghost seemed reminiscent of the unhappy, often intoxicated widow.

If you're inclined to regard Miss Morton's dark lady as a product of the Victorian death-obsessed culture, consider a simpler case that occurred in 1929. It was reported by Andrew MacKenzie in his book *Apparitions and Ghosts*. Mrs. Deane (pseudonym) was spending a weekend at the home of her daughter's nurse in Cleveland, Ohio. The nurse, called Mrs. Mills in the account, was a widow with a young son whom Mrs. Deane had met. Other than these facts, Mrs. Deane knew little of Mrs. Mills' family.

On the first evening of her visit, Mrs. Deane was undressing for bed when, in her own words, "I heard a sound at the bedroom door as if the knob were being turned, and on opening it saw a good-looking young girl, normally dressed, standing there. I said 'Hello, who are you?' to which she replied, 'I'm Lottie and this is my room,' but when I said 'Won't you come in?' she just smiled and entirely disappeared.

"Strangely, I did not feel at all nervous and slept quite soundly that night. In the morning I said to Mrs. Mills, 'Who's Lottie?' She replied, 'Lottie was my pet name for my daughter Charlotte who died a few years ago, but how did you know about her?'

Have Spirits Been Photographed?

Right: a triumph of Victorian "spirit photography." The ghost of the mother, cut from another negative and suitably pared down to look ethereal, hovers over her sleeping child. Real apparitions cannot fly, any more than living people can, but they have sometimes been seen to walk up non-existent stairs that had existed when the person was alive.

Right: this German photo of the 1880s is one of the more obvious fakes of its kind. The skull is somewhat at variance with the Spiritualist belief that bodies on the other side are versions of our earthly bodies.

"So I told her of the visit to my bedroom the night before. She showed me a photograph of Charlotte, who looked just as I had 'seen' her."

Mrs. Mills was very upset about the incident and reluctant to discuss her daughter. Some 40 years later, after Mrs. Deane reported the incident to him, Andrew MacKenzie tried to locate the record of the girl's death, but in spite of the cooperation of the Registrar in Cleveland, the attempt was unsuccessful. The year of death was not known, and could not be obtained because Mrs. Mills and her son could not be located.

Whether the figure outside the door had any connection with Charlotte Mills, it certainly was real enough, for a few moments, to Mrs. Deane. Perhaps it was only a draft in the hall that caused the noise of the doorknob being turned. Perhaps Mrs. Deane was in an agitated state at the time. Perhaps she only imagined the brief conversation with the girl. It would be hard to deny, however, that Mrs. Deane and all the thousands of other people whose ghost stories have been examined by psychical researchers, have had some contact with phenomena that can't as yet be explained by modern science.

Ghosts—whatever else they may be—are a fact of life.

Below: a ghost photograph that may be genuine. Mrs. Mabel Chinnery of Ipswich, England, took this picture of her husband in their car before they returned from the cemetery where they had been laying flowers on her mother's grave. When she received the prints of the film she found an image of her mother (arrowed) in the back seat. The photographic expert of the *Sunday Pictorial*, the paper that published the picture in 1959, declared that it was genuine, and a psychical researcher, Tom Hardiman Scott, said: "There appears to be no natural explanation for this remarkable photograph."

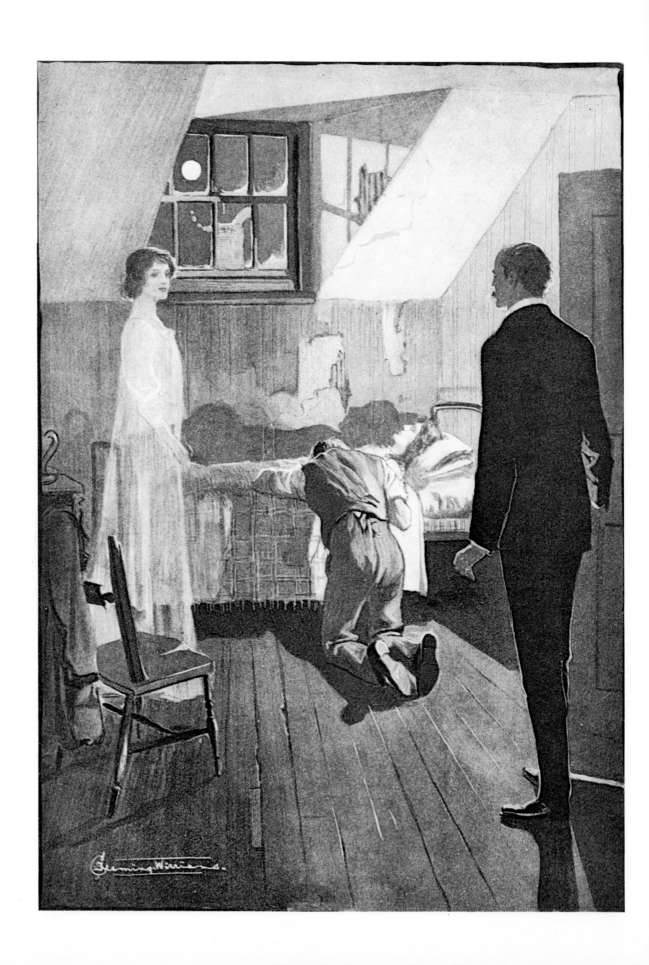

Chapter 2
Alarms and Predictions

Are there ghosts which are messengers from the future as well as lingering witnesses of the past? Some specters have become famous as omens of disaster, their very presence predicting death for the unfortunate percipient. Many ordinary unimaginative people have had visions of loved ones in danger—which they subsequently discover predicted or coincided with identical events, often many miles away. Sometimes an apparition of a person arrives, followed shortly by the actual arrival of the same person. Is there an explanation for these unnerving experiences when time itself appears to have become confused, with the past, the present, and the future unaccountably scrambled together?

One day around the middle of the last century, a little girl of about 10 was walking along a country lane in England not far from her home. Evidently rather advanced for her age, she was reading a book on geometry. Suddenly the scene in front of her faded away, and she saw in its place the bedroom in her house known as the White Room. Her mother was lying on the floor, apparently dead. The vision was complete and vivid, and it remained before her eyes for several minutes. Then gradually it faded away. So convincing was the scene that the child went immediately to the family doctor and persuaded him to accompany her home. When they arrived at the house, they and the girl's father went straight to the White Room. There they found the child's mother lying on the floor. She had suffered a heart attack, and the arrival of the doctor at that moment saved her life. This case, reported in *Phantasms of the Living* by Gurney, Myers, and Podmore, is significant not only because the image was confirmed by reality—even down to a detail such as a lace-edged handkerchief lying beside the woman, but also because the mother had apparently been perfectly well at the time the child left the house. The girl herself was not at all anxious about her mother until she saw the vision, and the father, corroborating the story, stated that he had been surprised to find the doctor at the door and had asked, "Who is ill?" The facts suggest that the vision had somehow been transmitted to the child by her mother at the moment of the crisis.

Opposite: this illustration for "Barbara of the Shining Garments," a Christmas ghost story, shows a crisis apparition of a young woman at the point of death. The fact that so many apparitions are of people who, at the moment they are seen, are undergoing some physical or mental crisis has led psychical researchers to draw the conclusion that the apparition is a kind of message sent telepathically from the person undergoing the crisis to the person who sees the figure.

Crisis Apparitions

Below: this old German engraving shows the apparition of a drowned traveler appearing to his wife. The housekeeper, at left, is just rushing in with news of the tragedy. An unusual feature of this case is that the man is naked; almost all other reported apparitions are clothed.

A vision of a person who, at the time, is undergoing some traumatic experience such as severe illness, injury, or death, is known as a "crisis apparition." Put simply, the theory behind the phenomenon is that the person undergoing the crisis telepathically sends a picture of himself to someone with whom he has a close relationship, and that if that person is sufficiently sensitive he will pick up the picture. The sender, or "agent," is probably unconscious of sending the message, though in the case of a death crisis we have no way of discovering whether or not this is true. Some psychical researchers prefer to include apparitions seen several hours after death in the category of "delayed" crisis apparitions, and to suggest that the agent transmitted the picture while still alive—even if at the point of death.

A typical case of a delayed crisis apparition, discussed by G. N. M. Tyrrell in his book *Apparitions*, was experienced by a Mrs. Paquet whose brother worked on a tugboat in Chicago's harbor. One day Mrs. Paquet awoke feeling unaccountably depressed, and could not shake the mood off. Having gone into the pantry for some tea, she saw her brother Edmund standing a few feet away from her as she turned around. "The apparition stood with back toward me, or rather, partially so, and was in the act of falling forward—away from me—seemingly impelled by two loops or a loop of rope drawing against his legs. The vision lasted but a moment, disappearing over a low railing or bulwark, but was very distinct. I dropped the tea, clasped my hands to my face, and exclaimed, 'My God! Ed is drowned.'" Soon after this experience, she received the news that her brother had fallen overboard and drowned, exactly as she saw it happen, but about six hours before her vision.

If a person can involuntarily project his image at a moment of crisis, it would seem possible that some people might be able to do so voluntarily through a great effort of will and concentration. Various people have tried this, occasionally with success. Around the turn of the century a Mr. Kirk made some attempts at transmitting his own image to a friend referred to as Miss G. These experiments were reported in the *Proceedings* of the SPR.

Over a period of 10 days between the hours of 11 p.m. and 1 a.m. every night, Mr. Kirk concentrated on making himself visible to Miss G.—without, of course, letting her know of his experiment. Several times during this period he saw Miss G., and although she complained of being restless and having trouble sleeping, she reported no apparitions. It was not until some days after Mr. Kirk stopped the experiment that she revealed she had seen him in her room—not at night but during one afternoon.

It had been on June 11 around 3:30 or 4:00 p.m. Mr. Kirk had been at his office doing some auditing work, and had begun to feel rather tired. He leaned back and stretched, and on an impulse decided to try his telepathy experiment. Not knowing where Miss G. might be at the moment, he chose her bedroom. What happened next was reported to the SPR by Miss G.

"In the afternoon (being tired by a morning walk) while sitting in an easy chair near the window of my own room, I fell asleep," she said. "At any time I happened to sleep during the day . . . I invariably awake with tired uncomfortable sensations, which take some little time to pass off; but that afternoon, on the contrary, I was suddenly quite wide awake, seeing Mr. Kirk standing near my chair, dressed in a dark-brown coat, which I had frequently seen him wear. [Mr. Kirk reported that he was wearing that coat at the time, although he seldom wore it in the office.] His back was toward the window, his right hand toward me; he passed across the room toward the door . . . but when he got about four feet from the door, which was closed, he disappeared . . . I then thought, knowing he must be at the office at the time I saw him . . . that in this instance, at least, it must be purely imaginary, and feeling so sure it was only fancy, resolved not to mention it, and did not do so until this week when, almost involuntarily, I told him about it."

Much more difficult to account for is the case of a Mrs. Crone of west London who, one day in 1951, was working in her kitchen when she saw the image of a friend who lived in southeast London. She saw only the head and shoulders of this woman, whom we'll call Miss A., but was struck by the extremely anxious look on her face. Somehow the apparition made Mrs. Crone suspect that her own little boy might be in trouble, and she hurried to the dining room where she had left him in his baby carriage.

The baby, who was strong for his 18 months, had managed to rock the carriage over to a sideboard, had taken several knives including some carving knives from a drawer, and had put them in the carriage. Mrs. Crone quickly rescued him.

Reporting the incident to psychical researcher Andrew MacKenzie, who included it in *Apparitions and Ghosts*, Mrs. Crone expressed her surprise that the warning should come from Miss A., who was not a close friend. In fact, Mrs. Crone never told Miss A. of the event. At the time she saw the apparition, Mrs. Crone was, in her own words, "not thinking of anything in particular," but "when you have a young child he is never far from your mind." She had on other occasions seen images of people, always just of the head and shoulders. In view of her psychic tendency, it would not have been too surprising had she seen an image of her son reaching for the knives. Why, then, did she see a vision of Miss A. instead?

Another kind of apparition is a curious one called the "false-arrival" hallucination. In such a case the percipient sees, or usually just hears, another person arrive—the opening of the gate, footsteps on the path, the opening of the front door— perhaps half an hour or an hour before the person actually arrives. The true arrival is an exact repetition of the false one—except that the person is really there. Apparently this phenomenon is fairly common in Scandinavian countries. A professor of physics at the University of Oslo who has investigated such occurrences has discovered that the false arrival usually is heard at the time the person is deciding to set out on his journey. He speculates that this is a form of communication that has evolved especially among people who live in isolated rural areas.

A sparsely populated part of England, the Norfolk Fen district, was the scene of a visible case of false-arrival, included in *Phantasms of the Living*. The story concerned two brothers who had married two sisters, and who lived with their respective families about a mile and a quarter apart. One day, a friend who was visiting one of the brothers glanced out the window and said,

Below: an apparition called the "enfant brilliant" appearing to Lord Castlereagh while he was visiting a friend in Northern Ireland. The future Foreign Minister awoke in the middle of the night and saw a lovely shining figure of a child by his bed. He approached the child, who gradually disappeared. Castlereagh is also said to have seen the child once in the House of Commons and again on the day he committed suicide.

"Here is your brother coming." The friend's report continues:

"My host advanced to the window and said, 'Oh, yes. Here he is; and see, Robert has got Dobbin out at last.' Dobbin was a horse, which, on account of some accident, had not been used for some weeks. The lady also looked out of the window, and said to me, 'And I am so glad, too, that my sister is with him. They will be delighted to find you here.' I recognized distinctly the vehicle in which they rode . . . also the lady and gentleman."

The visitors turned the corner, and disappeared along the side of the house. Inside the others waited for a knock on the door, but none came. The host expressed astonishment that his brother and sister-in-law had passed by the house without stopping in, "a thing they never did in their lives before." A few minutes later the niece, a young woman of 25, burst into the house, very upset. "Oh, aunt, I have had such a fright," she said. "Father and Mother have passed me on the road without speaking. I looked up at them as they passed by, but they looked straight on and never stopped nor said a word. A quarter of an hour before, when I started to walk here, they were sitting by the fire; and now what can be the matter? They never turned or spoke, and yet I am certain that they must have seen me."

About 10 minutes later, the carriage and its occupants were seen again, heading in the same direction. This time they actually arrived in the flesh. At the time the phantom was seen, the couple were just beginning their journey.

An Englishwoman, Miss J.B., recounts a case of a ghost seen years in advance of its arrival.

"When I was a small child in Yorkshire, just after the First World War, I lived with my parents in a large old farmhouse in the Dales. . . . The kitchen was my favorite place, and on winter days I spent most of my time at the kitchen table drawing and painting while the daily help bustled around preparing meals. I must have been about six when I saw my 'ghost.' She was thin and pale, with long dark hair tied in a bun at the nape of her neck, and she stood by the kitchen range sobbing and muttering in a language which I could not understand.

"Her dress was gray and worn, and her shoes were in need of mending, but she had an air of gentility about her. When I mentioned the 'lady in gray' both my mother and the 'help' seemed surprised, and I think they must have thought that I was daydreaming."

Miss J.B. saw the figure again about a year later, and subsequently came across her, always weeping, about nine or 10 times during the next few years. "For some reason I never spoke to her; I got the impression that she needed sympathy, but that I would be unable to help her. By this time I was certain that she was a ghost, but I felt no fear of her. I used to slip out of the kitchen and leave her to her misery."

Shortly after her 14th birthday, Miss J.B. went to live with an uncle in Ireland, and remained there throughout World War II. She returned to Yorkshire in 1945.

"I was driven to the old house from Leeds by my mother who explained that, as the place was too big for her since my father's death, she had a family of Polish refugees staying—a mother and two young daughters. The father, she said, had vanished during

Their Ghosts Got There First

Opposite: two lovers of the Middle Ages meet their doppelgangers, or ghostly doubles, in this romantic painting by Rossetti. The sight of one's doppelganger was, according to legend, an omen of death. Rossetti's flesh-and-blood lovers react to the sight with terror.

A Glimpse of the Future

At the age of 22 the German poet Johann Wolfgang von Goethe had completed his studies in Strasbourg and was about to return home. While in Strasbourg he had fallen in love with the daughter of a pastor in a nearby village. He loved her but didn't want to be tied in marriage.

He paid one last visit to his Fredericka before leaving the town. "When I reached her my hand from my horse, the tears stood in her eyes and I felt sad at heart," he wrote in his autobiography. Then, as he rode away, he had a strange vision. "I saw, not with the eyes of the body, but with those of the mind, my own figure coming toward me on horseback, and on the same road, attired in a suit which I had never worn—pike gray with gold lace. As soon as I shook myself out of this dream the figure had entirely disappeared . . . eight years afterward, I found myself on the very road, to pay one more visit to Fredericka, in the suit of which I had dreamed."

Although the phenomenon of seeing one's doppelganger is traditionally regarded as a death omen, Goethe did not interpret his experience in that way. "However it may be with matters of this kind generally, this strange illusion in some measure calmed me at the moment of parting."

Ghostly Heralds of Coming Events

Below: an illustration from S. Baring-Gould's short story "Mustapha," which contains a ghostly prediction of death. The young Englishman has tricked Mustapha, an Egyptian, into breaking a vow never to drink anymore. He had made the vow to fulfill his obligations as a Moslem, and so win the girl he loved. After breaking it he feels honor-bound to cut his own throat, but his ghost haunts the guilty young Englishman, who is eventually found dead— his throat cut—in front of the mosque.

the German occupation, and the mother was still grief-stricken over his loss. When we entered the kitchen there—to my astonishment—was the 'lady in gray' of my youth, standing by the kitchen range, weeping.

"Two little girls were standing near her, hanging onto her skirts, but apart from this she was exactly as I remembered her. She dried her eyes as we came into the room, and forced a smile."

When she got to know the woman better, Miss J.B. tried to explain to her about the vision, but as her guest spoke only a little English, she was never able to understand. "What did happen, though, was that because I seemed to know her as an old acquaintance, I think I was better able to comfort her and give her reassurance in her new country."

Miss J.B. thinks that the vision she had as a child was not transmitted by the Polish woman herself, whose grief, after all, was not caused until years after the apparitions occurred, "but from some benign intelligence—Heaven or God if you like— that, with the knowledge of what was to come, wanted to build up sympathy in me in advance."

If the vision was not projected by any intelligence, and if it was not a product of the child's own mind that just happened to resemble the Polish woman, we are left with the idea that there is another kind of time coexisting with the time we know, and that somehow a moment in the future overlapped *visibly* with a moment in the present as experienced by the young girl. The theory of different systems of time is an extremely complex and difficult subject, beyond the scope of this book. But every now and then one encounters a ghost story—like that of the Polish woman—which strongly suggests that the future can be seen.

Wing Commander George Potter looked into the future one evening during World War II, and did not like what he saw. At the time he was a squadron leader stationed at a base called R.A.F. Shallufa in Egypt. From this base, light bombers flew out over the Mediterranean to plant torpedoes and mines in the paths of the German General Rommel's supply ships. Because the squadron operated at night, they usually flew during the "bomber's moon" period when the bright reflection of the full moon on the sea helped them to navigate.

The atmosphere on the base between bombing periods was one of nervous gaiety. Pilots, navigators, gunners, and bombardiers spent their leisure evenings drinking and smoking.

On one such evening, just before the bomber's moon came again, Potter entered the mess with Flying Officer Reg Lamb for a nightcap. He glanced idly around the room, noting who was there. Among those present was a wing commander whom Potter, in telling the story, calls Roy. He was surrounded by friends.

Potter and Lamb finished their drinks, and Potter bought another round. As he did so, he heard a burst of laughter from the group around Roy, and it made him glance their way.

"Then," he says, "I saw it. I turned and saw the head and shoulders of the wing commander moving ever so slowly in a bottomless depths of blue-blackness. His lips were drawn back from his teeth in a dreadful grin; he had eye-sockets but no eyes; the remaining flesh of his face was dully blotched in greenish, purplish shadows, with shreds peeling off near his left ear.

"I gazed. It seemed that my heart had swollen and stopped. I experienced all the storybook sensations of utter horror. The hair on my temples and the back of my neck felt like wire, icy sweat trickled down my spine, and I trembled slightly all over. I was vaguely aware of faces nearby, but the horrible death mask dominated the lot."

Afterward Potter had no recollection of how long the experience lasted, but he gradually became aware of Flying Officer Lamb tugging at his sleeve. "What the hell's the matter?" Lamb asked. "You've gone as white as a sheet . . . as if you've seen a ghost!"

"I *have* seen a ghost," said Potter, pointing a trembling finger. "Roy. Roy has the mark of death on him."

Reg Lamb looked over to where Roy and the others were gathered. He saw nothing unusual; but by his side the normally unshakable Potter was still ashen-faced and unsteady. Both of them knew that Roy would be flying on the following night, and Potter did not know what, if anything, to do.

"I was in a quandary," he says, "but I think I made the right decision. I decided against going to the group captain with my story in the hope that Roy would be withdrawn from the mission, and I am certain that Roy himself would have refused to be kept

Above: *Saul and the Witch of Endor,* a depiction of the scene in I Samuel in which King Saul, whose nation is threatened by the Philistines, asks the witch to conjure up the spirit of the priest Samuel in order to gain his counsel. The ghost of Samuel rebukes Saul for not obeying the voice of the Lord, and predicts that he will be vanquished by the Philistines—a prediction that comes true.

The Phantom Takes a Hand

Below: the Roman leader Brutus is visited in his tent by a specter who is his own evil spirit. According to myth, it visited him again the night before he was defeated and killed at Philippi.

from his crew. I am convinced that the decision not to interfere was . . . part of a preordained sequence of events."

The following night was a tense one for Potter. Toward morning the telephone shrilled, and he snatched the receiver from its cradle. The message: Roy and his crew had been shot down, but their plane had been seen to ditch safely, and a companion aircraft had circled above while they clambered into a life raft.

"I felt an enormous sense of relief and elation," says Potter. "The air-sea rescue boys would soon have them out of it. But my elation was short-lived. They searched and searched, but no one ever saw Roy and his crew again. And then I knew what I had seen; the blue-black nothingness was the Mediterranean Sea at night, and he was floating somewhere in it, dead, with just his head and shoulders held up by his Mae West."

The vivid, accurate details of the terrible vision suggest that Potter had, for a moment, been able to look into the future. Another kind of supernatural prediction of death is that in which an apparition of someone known to be dead warns the percipient of his own approaching death. Such ghostly warnings are common enough in fiction, but they occasionally occur in real life as well. An apparition of this kind—if later fulfilled—suggests not only that it is possible to see into the future but also that the apparition and warning have been projected by a surviving personality, who knows in advance what will happen.

The ghost seen by Mrs. Gertrude Ashimi appeared in a dream, which makes it less startling than a waking hallucination.

Born in a small township in Nigeria of a prosperous family, Mrs. Ashimi was taken to Europe as a child, and educated by Roman Catholic nuns. Later she studied law in London, and in 1968, after qualifying as a lawyer, she returned to Nigeria for a visit with her widowed mother and brothers.

One morning, Mrs. Ashimi told her family that she had had a vivid dream. She had seen an old, smiling woman who, she was certain, was her maternal grandmother—although she had never seen her. In her right hand the old woman held a gold crucifix with a pearl in its center, attached to a fine gold chain. "My grandmother beckoned for me to follow, and walked out into the garden where she pointed to a certain tree. She tapped with her foot on the ground near the base of the tree and said, 'It is here, for you.' Then she vanished."

At her description of the old woman, Mrs. Ashimi's mother became excited. It was certainly her own mother, she said. What was more, the chain and crucifix sounded exactly like the one that the old woman had worn, and that had vanished shortly before her death. The whole family went into the garden and gathered around the tree to which the woman in the dream had pointed, while Gertrude Ashimi began to dig in the hard-baked earth. A few inches down she found the cross and chain.

Mrs. Ashimi returned to London with her husband, also a lawyer, and they set up a legal practice. In 1972, while awaiting the birth of her baby in a London hospital, she told a friend the story of the crucifix which she wore around her neck. She also told the friend that she had "an uneasy feeling" about the baby, for once again her grandmother had appeared to her in a dream and this time the old woman was not smiling but sad-faced. Mrs.

Ashimi was 27 and in robust health, and she gave birth to a fine little boy. A few days after the birth, however, she died suddenly.

Not all spectral predictions involve death. John Aubrey, a 17th-century English gentleman who collected anecdotes about prominent people of his day, recounts a curious story of a spirit who may or may not have been the ghost of Martin Luther.

Back in the 16th century Luther's discourses had been banned by the Pope after he excommunicated the reformer as a heretic. The order was that all copies should be burned, and the penalty for disobedience was death. (The ban, of course, did not apply in those German states that adopted the Lutheran faith.) During the turmoil of the religious wars in Germany in the early 17th century, a Lutheran named Caspar von Sparr discovered a copy of the discourses, and decided that the best way to preserve them was to smuggle them to England where they could be translated into English and republished. He entrusted the task of doing this to an English diplomat named Captain Bell, and Bell accordingly took the book with him to London.

Bell was a busy man, however, and months went by while the book lay unopened and gathering dust in his library. Then one night he awoke with a start to see a gaunt figure standing by his bed; its bones stood out from the transparent flesh, and a long white beard hung down to its waist. To Bell's horror the phantom suddenly shot out a hand and nipped his ear in an amazingly firm grasp between finger and thumb.

"Sirrah!" it roared, "will you not take time to translate that book which is sent you out of Germany? I will provide you both a place and a time to do it!" With that it vanished, leaving Bell wiping the cold sweat from his forehead and nursing a sore ear. The ghost was as good as its word—or perhaps it simply had a gift for prediction. A few days later, after an unforseen disagreement with the Lord Chancellor, Bell was thrown into prison and left there without trial for 10 years. With nothing else to do, he settled down to translating Luther's discourses.

Was the apparition the spirit of Martin Luther? It certainly didn't look like him, and its command of English was somewhat remarkable for a German of that day. Perhaps it was one of Luther's more ardent followers, or simply a projection of Bell's conscience. One wishes the SPR had been there to investigate.

Below: the ghost of the Earl of Strafford, who is supposed to have appeared to several people including King Charles I. Strafford's ghost warned the king not to take on Cromwell's forces at Naseby the next day. The king disregarded the warning and was defeated.

Chapter 3
Haunts and Hauntings

The great house, set in gloomy woods with eerie noises and a splendidly dressed ghost drifting down the main staircase, has been a staple of spine-chilling fiction. But do haunted houses really exist? Are there actual battlefields on which ghostly armies repeat the carnage of war over and over again? Do long-dead queens run shrieking down palace galleries which now more often echo to the clatter and chatter of eager tourists? And what about cemeteries, those silent and gloomy precincts of marble plaques and tombstones: are they truly peopled at night by the unquiet dead? Is there evidence for the whispered tales?

Lieutenant John Scollay was normally an even-tempered man, but at the moment he was losing patience with his sergeant-major. Here, in a little wood outside Dunkirk, Scollay was trying to hold his company together in the face of sporadic but deadly German sniper fire. Too many of the green-kilted Scottish Highlanders had crumpled into the undergrowth that day in June 1940, and now, as night fell, the sergeant-major's absurd notion cracked Scollay's calm.

"What the bloody hell do you mean, *haunted*?" he snapped. "This wood is haunted by Huns, laddie, that's all you need to know and think about at the moment."

The sergeant-major was persistent. "The wood is haunted, sir," he whispered. "I know it and the lads know it. For the love of God, sir, we're no' scared of Germans. If we have to we'll advance, or we'll force a way through the Jerries on our flank—but we canna stay here another night!"

Ridiculous as the idea sounded, Scollay couldn't entirely dismiss it. For the past 48 hours his company had been holed up in this straggling thicket. They were surrounded by fields in which German soldiers were entrenched awaiting the arrival of tanks, which would mean the end for the little band of Scots. During those two days, the Highlanders had fought with their usual cheerful savagery, raking the enemy with Bren gun fire and cracking off rifle shots at any moving shadow. Now they seemed to be losing their morale—an unheard of occurrence

Opposite: a painting of a phantom battle seen by the inhabitants of Verviers, Belgium in June 1815, within weeks of the actual Battle of Waterloo.

Tales of Haunted Battlefields

among the 51st Highlanders. Because of *ghosts*?

"It's just a presence, sir," explained the sergeant-major, "but we've all felt it. It's a kind of force pushing us away. And it's something that none of us can fight sir—something uncanny."

Eventually the 51st dropped back, joining the other British troops in the disastrous retreat from Dunkirk. Once clear of the "haunted wood" Scollay's men regained their determination and high spirits, but against the Panzer tanks and Stuka dive-bombers they could do nothing. Most of them were either slain or taken prisoner on the dunes of Dunkirk.

Scollay himself spent the duration of the war in a German P.O.W. camp, where he occasionally pondered the words of the sergeant-major on that night in June. When the war ended, he went back to the "haunted wood." Some research in a Dunkirk library uncovered a significant fact: in the summer of 1415, a few months before the Battle of Agincourt, English soldiers had fought the French in that same thicket.

Had the spirits of the slain English and French soldiers whose bodies had lain in the underbrush somehow come back to haunt their successors, more than 500 years later? Or was the area permeated with an aura of death, which the Scots began to sense after two days of exposure to it? There was no local tradition of haunting on that spot, but perhaps the psychic force had lain dormant for five centuries to manifest only under the stimulus of fresh violence.

Scollay is not sure what that force was, but he is convinced of its existence. "There could never be any question of the courage of those men in battle," he says. "Their valor is a matter of record. But something more than gunfire frightened the hell out of them that day."

If that little wood in northern France is haunted, it is only one of the battlefields with supernatural reputations. According

Below: *The Heroes of Marathon*, a painting depicting the battle between Greeks and Persians in 490 B.C. According to legend, the battle was reenacted by ghostly combatants every night for several years after the Greek victory there.

to legend, the battlefield of Marathon was such a place. For several years following the Greeks' victory over the Persians there in 492 B.C., the battle was mysteriously repeated every night. Anyone visiting the field after sunset heard the clash of steel upon steel and the screams of the wounded and dying, and smelled the odor of blood. Those who were unfortunate enough actually to see the ghostly warriors reportedly died within the year.

Spectral battles are a dramatic example of the kind of apparition we call a haunting. When most people think of ghosts they think of the kind that appear over and over in the same place. The "single-appearance" apparition, such as a crisis apparition, is less familiar. A ghost that appears to one person—or even a group of people—at one time only is a private kind of ghost. But a ghost that is associated with a particular place and has been seen there more than once is a ghost that might be seen by anyone. Moreover, the haunting ghost usually has a dramatic story behind it—some reason why the person's spirit, or image, seems to be fixed there. The supposed reason for the haunt is usually found to be either great unhappiness experienced by the person in that place, or great emotional attachment to the place, or some form of violence.

Following this line of thought, we can assume that if *any* place is haunted, a battlefield surely would be. The pain and terror once concentrated there, the pride in victory and shame in defeat, not to mention the prodigious energy expended by the men would somehow be impressed on the spot, capable of being sensed or even seen and heard by people with sufficient psychic awareness. If this theory is correct, one would expect all battlefields to be haunted, but relatively few of them have this reputation.

Of such battlefield hauntings, one of the most famous took

Above: the surrender of the 51st Highland Division to Field Marshal Rommel (left) at Saint Valery-en-Caux, France, shortly after the Allied defeat at Dunkirk in June 1940. A peculiar incident in the battle was experienced by a small group of the Highlanders. They became convinced that the thicket in which they were fending off the surrounding Germans was haunted.

Left: the English cavalry in a painting of *The Morning of the Battle of Agincourt*. The supposedly haunted thicket where some Highlanders fought in 1940 had been the scene of an English-French skirmish shortly before Agincourt. Could it have been ghosts of that encounter that the Scots perceived 500 years later?

Right: an engraving of the English Civil
War battle at Edgehill in 1642. For several
months after the battle people reported
seeing a phantom reenactment of it. The
ghostly forces included Prince Rupert,
commander of the Royalist troops (left),
who was still alive at the time that the
apparition was seen.

Below: a painting of the American Civil
War Battle at Shiloh. More than 24,000
soldiers were killed in this battle, a
hard-won Union victory and one of the few
Civil War battles reputed to have left
ghosts of soldiers at the scene.

place in England at Edgehill, Warwickshire. There, on October 23, 1643, Royalist troops commanded by the King's nephew, Prince Rupert, and Parliamentarian troops under Oliver Cromwell fought the first battle of the English Civil War. After the battle, which was indecisive, the bodies of some 5000 men lay on the frozen ground of Edgehill.

A month after the battle some local shepherds saw a strange sight—the soldiers of King and Parliament locked once more in struggle, drums beating, harnesses creaking, cannons belching shot and smoke. This time, however, there were no bodies left on the ground. When the phantom armies were seen again, on Christmas Eve, news of the phenomenon was sent to Charles I. The King ordered several officers, some of whom had fought at Edgehill, to go and investigate.

On their return the officers brought detailed confirmation of the news. Not only had they interviewed the shepherds and recorded their accounts in detail, but they had also on two occasions seen the battle themselves. They recognized some of the men known to have died at Edgehill. They also recognized the figure of Prince Rupert, who was very much alive. Whether or not anyone took notice of it at the time, this particular observation was a strong piece of evidence for the theory that ghosts are not the spirits of the departed, but rather a kind of recording of a scene that is left to be replayed under certain circumstances.

King Charles interpreted the ghostly battle as an omen that the rebellion against him would soon be put down—an interpretation that was proved wrong six years later when Cromwell's party assumed power and had the King beheaded.

The American Civil War was perhaps the greatest tragedy in the history of the United States, and we might expect its battlefields to echo with this terrible conflict that swallowed up the lives of nearly half a million men. Yet the Civil War battlefields remain, for the most part, silent. Occasionally a story surfaces about phantom troops at Gettysburg, but the only Civil War battlefield widely reputed to be haunted is Shiloh. This spot in Tennessee was where General Johnston's Confederates surprised the encamped army of General Grant on April 6, 1862. After two days' fighting, in which more than 24,000 men were killed, the Union Army defeated the Confederates. The river is said to have run deep pink with blood for days afterward. As soon as the terrible debris of battle had been cleared away, rumors began to circulate of phantom armies appearing on the field every now and then—rumors that persist even today.

Whether real or imaginary, the ghosts of Shiloh indirectly aided the founding and early success of the Ku Klux Klan. The legend of the ghosts spread into other Southern states, being elaborated as it was retold. The spirits of Confederate soldiers, according to the story, were riding back to their homelands, where they would terrorize anyone who tried to change the traditional way of life.

The defeat of the South in 1865 put an end to that way of life—the most radical change being the freeing of hundreds of thousands of slaves. The white southerners feared the anger of this unleashed force, but soon some of them accidentally hit

Phantom Battles, Spectral Armies

Above: a 1920 illustration of a Ku Klux Klan gathering. Members of the original Klan often pretended to be the ghosts of dead soldiers of Shiloh.

Britain: the Most Haunted Country

upon a way of frightening the blacks into passivity. A few ex-Confederate officers, who had formed a little club, rode drunkenly one night through the streets of Pulaski, Tennessee, draped in sheets. When they heard that many of the blacks had taken them for the legendary Shiloh dead, the group, who then called themselves the Kuklos Klan (*Kuklos* being the Greek for "circle"), realized the possibilities of their disguise. Throughout the Reconstruction period, the raids of the white-sheeted and hooded "ghosts" kept the black population effectively intimidated.

A real ghost can be seen anywhere—in broad daylight, in the most commonplace surroundings. Many ordinary houses, some of them quite new, are haunted. But the ghost stories that achieve wide fame are the ones connected with great and often gloomy houses, ruined abbeys, and castles. If the ghost is a royal personage, so much the better. There is a rather flimsy legend, for example, that the ghost of Queen Elizabeth I has appeared in the Queen's Library in Windsor Castle. The ghost of Katherine Howard, the fifth wife of Henry VIII, is said to run screaming through the rooms of Hampton Court Palace.

The Tower of London is saturated with pain and suffering endured by the victims of royal displeasure in the bad old days, and it has its share of ghost stories, though few of these are well authenticated. One story concerns the chapel of St. Peter-ad-Vincula, one of two chapels within the Tower, which is supposed to be the burial place of Henry's second wife, Anne Boleyn. Like her successor Katherine Howard, she was charged with infidelity, which was treason, and beheaded. One night a sentry, spotting a light in the chapel, climbed up to investigate along with another officer. Inside the chapel they saw a procession of people in Tudor dress walking up and down the aisles, led by a figure resembling Anne Boleyn. After a while, the figures and the light vanished.

We may hear these picturesque royal ghost stories with a skeptical smile. They are so transparently the products of wishful thinking. Yet they have a certain logic. If a haunting is caused

Right: a portrait believed to be Katherine Howard, fifth wife of Henry VIII. She was beheaded for infidelity.

Far right: a portrait of an unknown lady believed to be Anne Boleyn, by Holbein. Anne, Henry VIII's second wife, was imprisoned in the Tower of London and beheaded on the accusation of infidelity. Her ghosts haunts the Tower as well as other places she lived.

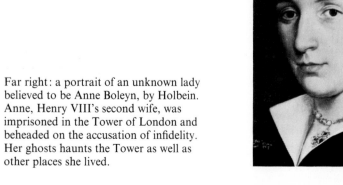

in some way by a concentration of intense emotion in a particular spot, then whose figures would be likelier to appear than those of the people who were caught up in the ruthless intrigues and conflicts of their time? If one believes in ghosts at all, one can easily believe that the ghost of the unhappy Anne Boleyn, awaiting execution for a crime of which she is generally thought to have been innocent, and having indirectly caused the torture and death of several of her friends, might well become imprinted on the atmosphere of the Tower.

Britain is often said to be the most haunted country in the world. Actually, it is probably no more or less haunted than any other country, but as a people who cherish their traditions, the British do more than other nations to keep their ghosts alive so to speak. There is scarcely a country house from one tip of the island to the other without its resident phantom.

The ghosts of Littlecote, a manor in Wiltshire, recall a tragic and gory incident of Elizabethan days. In the 16th century the mansion belonged to "Wicked" Will Darrell. One stormy night in 1575, Darrell sent for the midwife Mrs. Barnes, who lived in a village some distance away. She was offered a large fee to attend a lady in childbirth, but was blindfolded by Darrell's servants so that she would not remember the route to the house.

Arriving at Littlecote, Mrs. Barnes was led upstairs by the master of the house to a richly furnished bedchamber where she found a woman in labor, wearing a mask. Darrell told the midwife that if the woman were delivered safely, she would be handsomely rewarded, but that if the woman died, she herself would lose her life. The terrified midwife did her work, and soon the lady gave birth to a son. When Mrs. Barnes showed the baby to Darrell, he led her to a fireplace on the landing and commanded her to throw the child into the fire. On her knees the distraught woman begged him to let her keep the child herself, but Darrell snatched the baby from her and hurled it into the flames. In the morning Mrs. Barnes was blindfolded

Above: Windsor Castle is said to have several ghosts, including Charles I, George III, and Elizabeth I. She was first see there a few days after her death at Richmond Palace, walking in the library. Some people have reported seeing the ghost of Queen Elizabeth on the castle walls.

The Haunting of Country Houses

Above: Littlecote, a manor house in Wiltshire, is haunted by several ghosts including the figure of a midwife clutching a baby who, according to a ghastly story, was thrown into the fire by his own father, "Wicked Will Darrell," in 1575. Darrell's own ghost reputedly haunts the spot where he was thrown from his horse and killed.

Right: the ruins of old Scotney Castle in Kent. Another branch of the Darrell family (here spelled Darell) owned Scotney for more than 250 years. At the funeral of Arthur Darell in 1720, the coffin was being lowered into the grave when a stranger in a black coat, unknown to the mourners, said, "That is me they think they are burying." The man was never seen again, but a century or more later, the sexton opened an old coffin and found it filled with heavy stones. Arthur Darell's ghost does not haunt Scotney, but villagers say that every now and then the ghost of a drowned excise collector crawls out of the moat.

again and returned to her home.

While she had awaited the baby's birth, however, Mrs. Barnes had stealthily cut a piece of cloth from the bed curtains and sewn them up again. With this scrap of evidence and her description of the house, she went to the local magistrates, who were able to identify the house as Littlecote. Because of his wealth and influence, however, Darrell was able to escape justice by bribing the judge.

Ultimately another kind of justice dealt with Will Darrell, for one day when he was riding to hounds, he was thrown from his horse and his neck was broken. According to legend the place where he fell was haunted by the image of a child enveloped in flames—like the innocent baby he had murdered.

Within the house itself, the bedchamber where the unknown lady gave birth, and the landing where the murder took place have occasionally echoed with the screams of midwife, mother, and baby, and some people claim to have seen the figure of the anguished midwife clutching the child.

Leaving aside the specters who were victims of violence, let's consider a haunting that took place a few years ago in a charming and comfortable rectory in the village of Yattendon in Berkshire, England. Part of the house was built in the 18th century, but extensive alterations were made around 1900. One of the two ghosts that haunted the house—a pleasant-faced elderly lady—was sometimes seen to follow the path of a staircase removed during the alterations. This kind of behavior is

Above: Bosworth Hall in Leicestershire is said to be haunted by Lady Lisgar, a Protestant who married into the Catholic family that has always owned Bosworth. She is supposedly condemned to haunt the place as punishment for not letting a priest enter the house to attend a dying maid-servant. The present owner keeps a record of Lady Lisgar's visits.

Left: a portrait of Lady Lisgar, the ghost of Bosworth Hall.

common to many haunts; a part of a wall through which a ghost habitually disappears, for example, often turns out to be the site of a former doorway.

A detailed account of the haunting at Yattendon Rectory appears in Dennis Bardens' book *Ghosts and Hauntings*. Bardens visited the house some years ago and talked to four people who had seen the ghosts: the Reverend A. B. Farmer, the former Rector; his wife; their daughter; and a Mrs. Barton who had stayed with them for several months. Mrs. Barton saw the younger looking of the two ghosts, and described her as "rather pretty" and dressed in a "silvery gray frock" of 18th-century design. A "light seemed to be shining around her." Both Mrs. Barton and Mrs. Farmer, who had seen the figure on another occasion, noticed that she walked above the level of the floor.

This rather elegant lady was not so frequent a visitor as "Mrs. It," whose appearances, said the rector's wife, were quite a "usual occurrence." The figure varied in its distinctness, sometimes resembling a cloud of dark gray smoke, at other times appearing nearly human. She too was dressed in 18th-century clothing. Her skirt, said Mrs. Farmer, was "of thick, black, watered silk. It has a full round bottom, is very voluminous, and the top part of her is covered by a dark shawl, probably wool, under which she carries a basket or handle— her head is covered by a hat (with cap underneath) which is tied on with ribbon under her chin."

Mrs. It seemed to take an interest in the doings of the family.

Spectral Lights in the Graveyard

Below: portrait of a high-spirited ghost who frolicked around the home of the Murrays of Sandwich, Massachusetts in the 1880s. The couple were often awakened by her nocturnal revels. They attempted to put an end to the nuisance by throwing boots and shoes at her, but the missiles passed through her. Mrs. Murray finally left home; and after Mr. Murray was knocked down by the ghost once, he too abandoned the house.

"During the preparation for my daughter's wedding," said Mrs. Farmer, "she was seen inspecting the wedding presents and the arrangements in the kitchen." Was the ghost really aware of what was going on around her? If so, why did she walk up a stairway that no longer existed? But then, ghosts are obviously not bound by the limitations of our world, and perhaps Mrs. It had had a fondness for the stairway when she lived in the rectory some two centuries ago.

Eventually the Farmers left the house, and a new rector came to live there. The new family was not enthusiastic about spectral visitors, and they asked Mr. Farmer to conduct a service of exorcism. He obliged, and the ladies have not been seen since.

The popular notion that graveyards are apt to be haunted has not been confirmed by psychical research. Traditional stories of picturesquely draped figures, clanking chains, and sepulchral voices issuing from the graves are just that—stories. A phantom is much more likely to appear in the places the person frequented while alive.

There is at least one graveyard, however, that does seem to be haunted—by what exactly no one has yet been able to determine. The cemetery lies on a hill in the Wet Mountain Valley area of Colorado, and its phantoms—whatever they are—appear nearly every night for all to see.

In 1880 the township of Silver Cliff enjoyed a "silver rush." Miners and their families invaded the area, and by the end of the year the town's inhabitants numbered more than 5000. The boom did not last, however, and today Silver Cliff is a ghost town in more ways than one, having a living population of only about 100, slightly less than the town's old graveyard.

The strange phenomena that haunt this graveyard were first seen in 1880, when a group of drunken miners returning to their diggings reported seeing eerie blue lights hovering over each grave. Nor were these lights just a by-product of whiskey—they appeared on other nights to sober observers. Many years later in 1956 the ghost lights were written up in the *Wet Mountain Tribune*, and in 1967 they attracted the attention of the *New York Times*. Hundreds of tourists came to see the uncanny spectacle. Two years later, in an article about Colorado in the *National Geographic*, assistant editor Edward J. Linehan described his first look at the lights.

Linehan drove out to the graveyard accompanied by local resident Bill Kleine. It was dark when they reached the place, and Kleine told Linehan to switch off the headlights. They got out of the car, and Kleine pointed: "There! See them? And over there!"

Linehan saw them—"dim, round spots of blue-white light" glowing above the graves. He stepped forward for a better look at one, but it vanished, then slowly reappeared. He switched on his flashlight and aimed it at one of the lights. The beam of the flashlight revealed only a tombstone. For 15 minutes the men pursued the elusive ghost lights among the graves.

Kleine told Linehan that some people theorized that the lights were caused by the reflections of the town lights of Silver Cliff and nearby Westcliff. Linehan turned to look back at the two small towns in the distance. The tiny clusters of their lights seemed far too faint to produce the effect in the grave-yard. What's more, Kleine remarked that both he and his wife had seen the ghost lights "when the fog was so thick you couldn't see the towns at all."

Other theories have been advanced to explain the phenome-non. One is that the ghost lights are caused by radioactive ore; but a Geiger counter test of the whole area revealed no trace of radioactivity. Another says the ghost lights are luminous paint, daubed on the tombs by hoaxers; but no evidence has ever been found to support this charge. Still another theory is that the ghost lights reflect the mercury vapor of the Westcliff street-lights; but there were no mercury vapor lights until recently, and once when a power failure shut off every light in town, the graveyard lights still shone.

An entirely different approach to the puzzle has been offered by the anthropologist and folklorist Dale Ferguson. He notes that the Cheyenne and other Plains Indians laid their dead to rest on hilltops "sacred to the spirits." Sometimes a particu-larly powerful medicine man would feel his own death approach-ing, walk to the "dead men's hill," and lie down there until his soul was "taken." A number of Indian tales, he says, mention "dancing blue spirits" on such sites.

Among the old-timers of Silver Cliff only one explanation holds good: the blue-white spots are the helmet lamps of long dead miners, still seeking frantically for silver on the hillside.

"No doubt someone, someday, will prove there's nothing at all supernatural in the luminous manifestations of Silver Cliff's cemetery," concludes Linehan. "And I will feel a tinge of disappointment."

Below left: the tomb of a gentleman named Robert Cooke in Digby, England. The churchyard is haunted by a man on a gray pony, but this phenomenon is somewhat banal compared to the whimsical legend surrounding Cooke's grave. It is said that if one runs 12 times backward around the tomb, then listens, one can hear the rattle of cups and saucers in the grave.

Below: an early 19th-century French stage set design showing spirits rising from their graves. The popular notion that ghosts are likely to be seen in a graveyard is not borne out by psychical research. A haunting ghost usually haunts a place that the person lived in or frequented while he was alive. Only a gravedigger's ghost would be likely to haunt a graveyard.

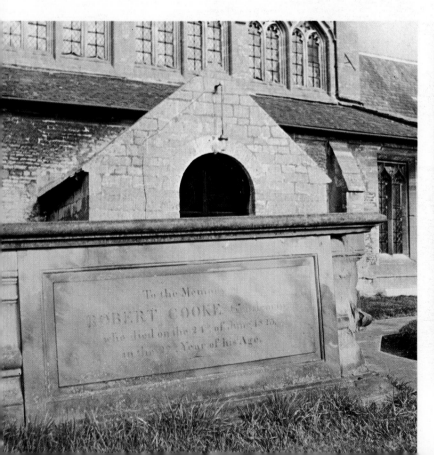

50

A.B.FROST.

Chapter 4
Ghosts Unhuman

Are all apparitions human? The evidence suggests that some are not. The Wild Hunt—demon dogs driven by devilish huntsmen—has raced across the skies of Europe for generations. In the American West the Wild Hunt is paralleled by the phantom stampede. There are ghostly cats, spectral horses, and strange unearthly black dogs. Empty coaches—driven by headless coachmen—are reputed to thunder down country lanes. There was once even a mysterious vanishing London doubledecker bus, tearing through quiet streets in the middle of the night, long after normal services had stopped running. Reported sightings of these eerie animal and mechanical ghosts persist: can they be explained in the cold light of day?

People who assert that ghosts are spirits of the dead—or, as they are sometimes called, "revenants"—are faced with one vexing problem: the supposed revenants almost never appear in the nude. It is conceivable that in the next world we may be clothed in some way, but it seems extremely unlikely that the spirits of people who died in the 18th century, for example, have been provided with knee breeches and wigs. Scientist and writer Lyall Watson puts the problem neatly when he says, "While I am prepared in principle to concede the possibility of an astral body, I cannot bring myself to believe in astral shoes and shirts and hats."

Nor is ghostly clothing the only aspect of the problem. A great many apparitions are not of human beings at all. They include such diverse objects as horse-drawn carriages, ships, motor vehicles, and flitting blue lights. While some people might argue that animals are as likely as humans to have souls, or that the soul might well manifest itself as a blue light, few would credit the motor bus that once haunted a section of London with a spirit of its own.

Many of the most picturesque stories of hauntings concern animals. Few of these are of the domestic pet variety. There is usually something larger than life, and rather sinister, about most spectral beasts. Typical of the breed is England's "Black Shuck," an enormous dog "black as a coal scuttle, big as a donkey, with eyes like saucers." The legend of Shuck appears to

Opposite: this picture is an illustration for Lewis Carroll's whimsical poem entitled "Phantasmagoria." The creature in the cave is a phantom gaining experience in haunting. According to the poem he is a rather unprepossessing humanlike spirit, but the gloom of the cavern and the imaginations of his victims endow this phantom with beastly ferocity.

The Legend of the Wild Hunt

Below: *Diana the Huntress*, a 16th-century
French painting of the Roman goddess
(known as Artemis to the Greeks) who is
sometimes associated in legend with the
Wild Hunt, a ferocious band of hunters and
hounds said to ride across the sky at the
time of the full moon. One of the most
widespread and ancient of European
legends, the Wild Hunt is known in France,
Germany, and England.

have crossed the Atlantic, for the Delaware Valley area of the
United States boasts a similar creature called "Black Shep."

The European Wild Hunt also has an American counterpart.
Once widespread in Europe, the Wild Hunt myth may have
sprung from ancient stories of Diana, goddess of the hunt and
of the moon. According to the legend of the Wild Hunt, savage
packs of demon dogs driven on by devilish huntsmen are seen
riding the sky at full moon. Today the legend remains firmly
entrenched in some parts of Europe; the Breton peasants of
northwestern France are reluctant to leave their homes at
night when the moon is full. An English variation of the legend
concerns Herne the Hunter, said to have been Keeper of the
King's Dear sometime during the Middle Ages. According to
tradition, Herne and his ghostly hounds roam Windsor Forest
on the death of a monarch. The American version of the Wild
Hunt is the story of Stampede Mesa. Like all folklore it has
several variations, one of which was collected and retold by the
cattleman-turned-author J. Frank Dobie. His story is set on the
Loving Trail in the 1870s, when huge herds of longhorns were
driven north from Texas to Kansas. Already the open range
was being fenced in by farmers, contemptuously termed
"nesters" by the free-riding cowhands, and the bouts of violence
that broke out between cattlemen and farmers are part of the
history of the West.

On one drive north, a trail boss came across a group of
nesters who had begun building fences and stockades right
across the trail. They were prepared to fight. When the cattle-
man drew his pistol, the nesters leveled rifles and shotguns at
him. The infuriated cattle boss wheeled his horse and rode to
the rear of the herd.

"Move 'em!" he shouted to his men, firing his Colt into the
air. Within seconds the cattle were panicked into a stampede,
thundering wildly toward the farm settlement. Fences were
smashed, wagons overturned, crops trampled. The nesters
were crushed to death under the thundering hooves.

When the herd arrived in Abilene, the cattle boss reported
the stampede as an accident, and after a brief inquiry the
incident was closed. But the truth spread among Texas cowboys,
and the place where the massacre occurred on the edge of a
mesa, or flat-topped hill, became known as Stampede Mesa.
Soon campfire tales included a ghostly sequel to the story. On
moonlit nights, it was said, a phantom herd could be seen
crashing over the ground, the dying screams of the farmers
mingling with the rumble of hooves and the crack of gunfire.

Shortly after Dobie's written account of Stampede Mesa
appeared in print, a popular song, "Ghost Riders in the Sky"
further immortalized the story in the words:

". . . . and all at once a mighty herd of red-eyed cows he saw,
A-ploughin' through the rugged sky, and up a cloudy
draw . . ."

While many stories of animal apparitions conform to some
such standard folklore pattern, there are some striking exceptions. There is something terrifyingly individual, for
instance, about the black cat of Killakee. From 1968 until the
early 70s, intense poltergeist activity (the movement of objects

by an unseen force) occurred in Killakee House in County
Dublin, Ireland. Despite exorcism and the investigations of
psychical researchers these phenomena continue sporadically
today. Killakee is now an Arts Center, where Irish artists paint,
sculpt, and display their work. It is owned by Mrs. Margaret
O'Brien, who bought the house in the late 1960s and had some
alterations made on it.

For years stories had circulated locally of a large cat, the
size of an Airedale dog, that haunted the overgrown gardens of
the house—"haunted" because the tales covered a period of 40
or 50 years, much longer than the life span of a normal animal.
Early in 1968 Mrs. O'Brien herself caught fleeting glimpses of a
big black animal that would disappear into the shrubbery.

At the time two local men and Tom McAssey, an artist friend
of Mrs. O'Brien's, were at work in the house, redecorating the
ballroom and the stone-flagged hall. One dark night in March,
they were just finishing the day's work in the hall when something peculiar happened. McAssey's account follows: "I had
just locked the heavy front door, pushing a six-inch bolt into its
socket. Suddenly one of the two men with me said that the door
had opened again. We turned, startled. The lock was good and
the bolt was strong . . . and both fastened on the inside.

Above: Herne the Hunter, the phantom
believed to ride through Windsor Forest
where the original Herne once served as a
keeper. A malignant spirit, formerly
blamed for many misfortunes including
cattle diseases, he now foretells the death of
the British monarch.

"A Monstrous Black Cat"

Above: La Grande Bête, a phantom bull of French folklore, may be related to the spectral and mythical bulls venerated by the Celts.

Above right: Tom McAssey's painting of the Black Cat of Killakee, done shortly after he saw the beast crouching in the hallway of the house. Several other residents of the area also got close looks at the cat, which has haunted the vicinity for some hundred years. Various old effigies of a cat have been discovered on the premises of Killakee House—tangible evidence that some kind of feline legend or cult has existed there for some time.

"We peered into the shadowed hallway, and then I walked forward, and sure enough the door stood wide open, letting in a cold breeze. Outside in the darkness I could just discern a black-draped figure, but could not see its face. I thought someone was playing a trick and said 'Come in. I see you.' A low guttural voice answered: 'You can't see me. Leave this door open.'

"The men standing directly behind me both heard the voice, but thought it spoke in a foreign language. They ran. A long drawn snore came from the shadow, and in panic I slammed the heavy door and ran too. Halfway across the gallery I turned and looked back. The door was again open and a monstrous black cat crouched in the hall, its red-flecked amber eyes fixed on me."

Val McGann, the former Irish pole-vault champion who also paints and shows his work at Killakee, was not in the least surprised by McAssey's story. He lives in a cottage in the woods nearby, and on several occasions has seen a similar cat. "The first time it frightened me stiff, but on subsequent occasions I have been more amazed at the sight of it. It is about the size of a biggish dog, with terrible eyes. I've even stalked it with my shotgun, but have never been able to corner it."

Behind Killakee House looms Montpellier Hill, a steep bare mount surmounted by the ruin of what was once a hunting lodge. This is known locally as the Hell Fire Club, and there is some evidence that in the 18th century it was used by the young rakes of Dublin for orgies. Tradition holds that the Devil burned it down—rather ungratefully—during a Black Mass. Another story connected with the place says that a huge black cat was enthroned there during orgies to symbolize Satan when

Left: the tomb of Lord Byron's dog Boatswain at Newstead Abbey, the Byrons' ancestral home. The poet buried his dog on the site where the high altar had stood in the days when Newstead was a real abbey. A phantom hound is said to haunt the place —as does the Goblin Friar.

Below: Fred Archer, a famous British jockey who died in 1886 at the age of 29, is reputed to haunt the track at Newmarket in Suffolk. The sight of his ghost on a phantom horse is supposed to have occasionally caused live horses to shy or stumble during a race.

Above: *The Student Recognizing His Mother* is a melodramatic Victorian engraving of a potential hazard of the practice of robbing graves to obtain bodies for dissection. The medical student, supervising two grave robbers, is horrified to discover the body of his own mother.
Right: a "resurrectionist" is interrupted by an outraged ghost.

he did not turn up in person. The specter of this cat, say the locals, is the thing that haunts Killakee Arts Center.

Not far from Killakee lies the township of Rathfarnham, the haunt, it is said, of another unhuman ghost: a black coach driven by a headless coachman. This is a variation on a theme which, like black dogs and wild hunts, recurs in both Britain and the United States. A similar coach was said to hurtle over Boston's Beacon Hill in the 19th century, and the famous Deadwood stage was reported rumbling along its old route in North Dakota decades after it had made its last run.

Unfortunately for the romantics, historians have a plausible explanation for these phantom coaches. In both America and Britain, fresh corpses for dissection in the medical schools were hard to come by until the early 19th century. At that time various "anatomy laws" were passed permitting doctors to experiment on the bodies of dead paupers and vagrants. Until then graverobbers, variously known as "ghouls" and "resurrection men," did a brisk trade in newly buried corpses. To transport a body was obviously difficult without being spotted, and the penalties for grave robbing were high. So the ghouls transported their grisly wares in black coaches after first spreading frightening tales of ghostly conveyances throughout the neighborhood.

No such simple explanation was forthcoming when, in the mid-1930s, a modern version of the phantom coach began to plague London's Kensington area. The junction of St. Mark's Road and Cambridge Gardens had long been considered dangerous because of the sharp corner, and to add to the danger the big red buses on the Number 7 route turned into Cambridge Gardens at that point. Hundreds of minor accidents—and several fatal ones—took place there before the local authority finally straightened out the bend.

The decision to do so was partly influenced by a spate of reports from late night motorists. They said they had crashed at the spot after swerving to avoid a careering double-deck bus that traveled silently down St. Mark's Road in the middle of the night—when no buses were in service.

One report read: "I was turning the corner and saw a bus tearing toward me. The lights of the top and bottom deck, and the headlights, were full on but I could see no sign of crew or passengers. I yanked my steering wheel hard over, and mounted the pavement [sidewalk], scraping the roadside wall. The bus just vanished."

This report was typical. The local coroner discovered more evidence while conducting an inquest on a driver who had hit the wall head on, rather than merely scraping it. An eye witness said that the phantom bus had suddenly appeared, speeding toward the car the second before the driver made his fatal swerve. When the coroner expressed doubt, dozens of residents offered to testify that they had seen the apparition. Among the volunteer witnesses was an official from a nearby bus depot who said he had seen the vehicle draw silently up outside the depot in the small hours, and then disappear.

The mystery was never solved, but it may be significant that after the road alterations were made the bus was not seen

The Coach that Wasn't There

One night in August 1878 Major W. went to the front door of his house in an isolated part of Scotland for a breath of air before going to bed. As he stood looking out, he saw a coach and pair coming up his drive. Two men were sitting on the coachman's box. They drove swiftly up the drive and over the lawn toward a stream, oblivious of the Major's warning shout about the water beyond. Then they wheeled sharply and drove back.

By this time Major W.'s son had joined him with a lantern, and the boy was able to catch a glimpse of the carriage's occupant. It was a stiff-looking figure, probably a woman, draped in white from head to toe. This person gave no sign of recognition, nor did the coachman and his companion. The Major did not recognize his visitors or their carriage, which he found odd because he knew the neighborhood well. The coach left as it had come.

The following day Major W. made inquiries, but no one had heard of or seen the mysterious coach—no one except the Major, his son, and his wife and daughter who had been drawn to the window by his shout. They examined the ground over which the coach had driven. It was soft and damp, but bore no trace of wheels or hooves.

The Case of the Phantom House

again. Had it somehow been projected onto the scene to dramatize the danger inherent in the intersection? If so, it was a rather drastic measure—and on the part of whom? A more likely explanation is that it was a visible form of the apprehensions of the motorists themselves, who expected danger at that point. This theory, however, doesn't account for the visions of the bus depot official and other bystanders. The phantom bus will probably remain an unsolved puzzle.

It is also extremely difficult to account for what a Miss Wynne saw one gray afternoon in autumn 1926 while out for a walk. At that time, Miss Wynne had recently moved to a village near Bury St. Edmonds in Suffolk, England, and she often took walks in the afternoon to explore the countryside. On this particular day she and a companion, Miss Allington, set out through the fields to see the church of the neighboring village, Bradfield St. George. Here is her account of the experience, given in Sir Ernest Bennett's *Apparitions and Haunted Houses*:

"In order to reach the church, which we could see plainly ahead of us to the right, we had to pass through a farmyard, whence we came out onto a road. We had never previously taken this particular walk, nor did we know anything about the topography of the hamlet of Bradfield St. George. Exactly opposite us on the further side of the road and flanking it, we saw a high wall of greenish-yellow bricks. The road ran past us for a few yards, then curved away from us to the left. We walked along the road, following the brick wall round the bend, where we came upon tall, wrought-iron gates set in the wall. I think the gates were shut, or one side may have been open. The wall continued on from the gates and disappeared round the curve of the road. Behind the wall, and towering above it, was a cluster of tall trees. From the gates a drive led away among these trees to what was evidently a large house. We could just

Right: Okehampton Castle in Devonshire. One of the most sinister of England's many phantom coaches is said to follow the old road between Tavistock and Okehampton. It is constructed of human bones—those of the four husbands of the wicked Lady Howard, whose pale and sheeted specter rides inside it. A skeleton hound runs before her, and according to the legend, his task is to pluck each night a blade of grass from Okehampton Park to take back to Fitzford, the lady's family home. This penance for her supposed murder of her husbands is to continue until every blade of grass is plucked—that is, until the end of the world itself.

see a corner of the roof above a stucco front, in which I remember noticing some windows of Georgian design. The rest of the house was hidden by the branches of the trees. We stood by the gates for a moment, speculating as to who lived [there]."

It was not until four or five months later that Miss Wynne and Miss Allington took that walk again. "We walked up through the farmyard as before, and out onto the road, where, suddenly, we both stopped dead of one accord and gasped. 'Where's the wall?' we queried simultaneously. It was not there. The road was flanked by nothing but a ditch, and beyond the ditch lay a wilderness of tumbled earth, weeds, mounds, all overgrown with the trees which we had seen on our first visit. We followed the road round the bend, but there were no gates, no drive, no corner of a house to be seen. We were both very puzzled. At first we thought that our house and wall had been pulled down since our last visit, but closer inspection showed a pond and other small pools amongst the mounds where the house had been visible. It was obvious that they had been there a long time."

Inquiries revealed that no one in the area had ever heard of the house. Only the two women seem to have seen it (Miss Allington corroborated Miss Wynne's report). If it was an hallucination it is certainly an hallucination on a grand scale. What psychic force brought it into existence? Did some buried memory of such a house in such a situation exist in the mind of Miss Wynne or Miss Allington—a memory that one of them subconsciously wanted to visualize, and was able not only to visualize but also to project so that her companion saw it too? Or, to consider an even more fantastic idea, were they somehow transported back or forward in time so that their own lives for a few moments coincided with the actual existence of the house?

Clearly, an apparition such as this, observed by two people in broad daylight raises some intriguing questions about the nature of humans and about the nature of the world we see.

Above: a Spitfire, most famous aircraft of the Royal Air Force in World War II. People who live near Biggin Hill Airfield claim that one of these planes, piloted by a flier who never returned from his mission, has been heard screaming in to land. Some report seeing the plane, and say that the pilot signals his return with a low victory roll, a sideways flip, announcing a successful mission.

Chapter 5
Family Ghosts

Are there families pursued by spirits who seem to haunt them down through the generations? The legendary banshee is well-known to the Irish and their descendants around the world—what prompts the unearthly keening that strikes terror into so many? Is it possible for a person's spirit to become so attached to a house that its skull will scream if it is removed from the building? And what about the legendary curses that pass down through a family, like the secret of Glamis Castle, known only to the Earl of Strathmore and his heirs—can these strange stories be true?

"It started low at first like, then it mounted up into a crescendo; there was definitely some human element in the voice . . . the door to the bakery where I worked was open too, and the men stopped to listen. Well, it rose as I told you to a crescendo, and you could almost make out one or two Gaelic words in it; then gradually it went away slowly. Well, we talked about it for a few minutes and at last, coming on to morning, about five o'clock, one of the bread servers came in and he says to me, 'I'm afraid they'll need you to take out the cart, for I just got word of the death of an aunt of mine.' It was at his cart that the bansidhe had keened."

More commonly spelled "banshee," as it is pronounced, "bansidhe" is the Gaelic word for "fairy woman," a creature whose mournful cry is said to foretell death. The above quotation was taken from a British Broadcasting Corporation program that Irish psychical researcher Sheila St. Clair conducted with several people who claimed to have themselves experienced the hideous wail of the banshee. In the same program an elderly man from County Down described the fairy death wail in more detail. "It was a mournful sound" he said; "it would have put ye in mind of them ould yard cats on the wall, but it wasn't cats, I know it meself; I thought it was a bird in torment or something . . . a mournful cry it was, and then it was going a wee bit further back, and further until it died away altogether . . . "

The banshee cried for ancient Irish heroes. It wailed for King Connor McNessa, Finn MacCool, and the great Brian Boru,

Opposite: the Screaming Skull of Bettiscombe Manor, long supposed to be that of a West Indian slave taken to England in the 18th century, is shown here beneath a portrait of John Pinney, the landowner who brought the slave to Bettiscombe. The skull is alleged to scream if it is removed from its home, a characteristic shared by other family skulls found both in Britain and in the United States.

Above: a banshee warns a man of approaching death in his family. Normally heard rather than seen, the banshee wails whenever a member of the family she watches over is about to die. Many Irish and Scottish Highland families claim to have such guardian spirits.

whose victory over the Danes in 1014 ended their sovereignty over Ireland. More recently its eerie voice is said to have echoed in the Cork village of Sam's Cross when General Michael Collins, commander-in-chief of the Irish Free State Army, was killed in an ambush near there in 1922. A few months later when Commandant Sean Dalton was shot in Tralee, a song recalls: "When Dalton died sure the bansidhe cried, in the Valley of Knockanure."

Although its name translates as "fairy woman," most authorities define the banshee as a spirit rather·than a fairy. In some families—the O'Briens, for example—the banshee is considered to be almost a guardian angel, silently watching over the fortunes of the family and guiding its members along safe and profitable paths. When an O'Brien dies this guardian performs her last service, keening for the departing soul.

A County Antrim man gave his interpretation of the banshee to Sheila St. Clair. He claimed that the Irish, as a reward for their piety, had been blessed with guardian spirits to take care of their individual clans. Because these celestial beings were not normally able to express themselves in human terms and yet became involved with the family under their care, God allowed them to show their deep feeling only when one of their charges died. Then the banshee was permitted to howl out its sorrow.

James O'Barry was the pseudonym used by a Boston business-man who wrote to the author on the subject, and if O'Barry's testimony is to be believed the banshee, like some other creatures of European folklore, has crossed the Atlantic.

Like many of Boston's Irish Catholics, O'Barry is descended from a family that arrived in Massachusetts in 1848, fleeing the great famine that decimated Ireland's population in the 19th century. His great-great grandfather started a small grocery business, and today O'Barry and his two brothers run a super-market chain which has branches throughout New England.

"When I was a very small boy," O'Barry recalls, "I was lying in bed one morning when I heard a weird noise, like a demented woman crying. It was spring, and outside the window the birds were singing, the sun was shining, and the sky was blue. I thought for a moment or two that a wind had sprung up, but a glance at the barely stirring trees told me that this was not so.

"I got up, dressed, and went downstairs, and there was my father sitting at the kitchen table with tears in his eyes. I had never seen him weep before. My mother told me that they had just heard, by telephone, that my grandfather had died in New York. Although he was an old man, he was fit as a fiddle, and his death was unexpected."

It was some years before O'Barry learned the legend of the banshee, and he then recalled the wailing noise he had heard on the death of his grandfather. In 1946 he was to hear it for the second time. In May of that year he was an administrative officer serving with the U.S. Air Force in the Far East. One morning at six o'clock he was awakened by a low howl.

"That time," he said, "I was instantly aware of what it was. I sat bolt upright in my bed, and the hair on the back of my neck

"Like a Demented Woman Crying"

Left: the body of the Irish revolutionary leader Michael Collins lying in state in Dublin in 1922. The voice of the banshee is said to have keened in the village of Sam's Cross, County Cork, when Collins died there in an ambush.

Spirit Harbingers of Death

Right: England's Brown Lady of Raynham Hall is one of the few specters ever to be caught by the camera—or partially caught, anyway. The photographer, who had come to Raynham to photograph its staircase one day in September 1936, saw only this transparent figure. Earlier manifestations of the Brown Lady were better defined. She was said to wear a coif and a brocade gown, and to have empty eye sockets. According to one legend, the appearance of the lady heralds a death among the family owning the house.

prickled. The noise got louder, rising and falling like an air-raid siren. Then it died away, and I realized that I was terribly depressed. I knew my father was dead. A few days later I had notification that this was so."

Seventeen years later, O'Barry heard the hair-stiffening voice of the banshee a third time. He was in Toronto, Canada, by himself, enjoying a combined holiday and business trip.

"Again I was in bed, reading the morning papers," he said, "when the dreadful noise was suddenly filling my ears. I thought of my wife, my young son, my two brothers, and I thought 'Good God, don't let it be one of them.' But for some reason I knew it wasn't."

The date was November 22, 1963, the time shortly after noon, and the Irish banshee was bewailing the death of an acquaintance of O'Barry's—John F. Kennedy, President of the United States.

The banshee is rarely seen as an apparition, but when she does appear she takes the form of a red-haired, green-eyed woman. The Welsh have their own harbinger of death, a revolting old woman known as "The Dribbling Hag." In Scotland, "death women" can sometimes be seen on the banks of westward-running streams, washing the clothing of those about to die. One Scottish family, the Ewens of the Isle of Mull, Argyllshire, preserve a curious legend concerning their own death spirit. In the early 16th century Eoghan a' Chin Bhig—Ewen of the Little Head—lived at Loch Sguabain Castle, Isle of Mull, as clan chief. His wife was the daughter of another chief, The MacLaine, and Ewen and his father-in-law were forever quarreling. In 1538 matters reached serious proportions, and both sides collected followers for a showdown.

The evening before the battle, Ewen was walking near Loch Sguabain when he came across an old woman washing a bundle of blood-stained shirts in a stream. She was dressed from head to foot in green and Ewen knew that she was a death woman, and that the shirts were those of the men who would die in the morning. He asked if his own shirt was among them, and she said that it was. "But," she added, "if your wife offers you bread and cheese with her own hand, without you asking for it, you will be victorious."

As dawn broke and Ewen buckled on his sword he waited anxiously for his wife to offer him the food. She failed to do so. Demoralized, Ewen led his followers to defeat at the hands of the MacLaines. At the height of the battle a swinging ax cut off his head clean from his shoulders. His black horse galloped away, its headless rider still sitting upright in the saddle. From that day onward, the dead chief himself became his clan's death warning, for when a Ewen was to die the phantom horse and headless rider were seen and heard thundering down Glen More on the shores of Loch Sguabain.

Three members of the Ewen family within living memory have reported seeing the phantom. At Lochbuie, home of the present clan chief, the vision is said to herald serious illness in the family as well as death itself.

Sheila St. Clair offers a theory to account for the banshee. In her book *Psychic Phenomena in Ireland* she says: "I would suggest that just as we inherit physical characteristics—for instance red hair, blue eyes—we also inherit memory cells, and that those of us with strong tribal lineages riddled with intermarriage have the 'bansidhe' as part of an inherited memory. The symbolic form of a weeping woman may well be stamped on our racial consciousness. Ireland's women are experts at weeping over their slain sons and daughters. And just as our other levels of consciousness are not answerable to the limitations of time in our conscious mind, so a particular part of the mind throws up a symbolic hereditary pattern that has in the past been associated with tragedy in the tribe, be it woman, hare, or bird, as a kind of subliminal 'four-minute warning' so that we may prepare ourselves for that tragedy."

Essentially this theory agrees with psychiatrist C. G. Jung's theory of the "collective unconscious," an inherited storehouse of memories of mankind's early experiences.

Above: Cortachy Castle in Aberdeenshire, Scotland, the home of the Ogilvys, Earls of Airlie since 1641. An approaching death among the Ogilvys is signalled by the sound of ghostly drumming outside the castle walls. According to legend, a handsome young drummer was once caught in a compromising position with a Lady Airlie. As punishment, he was sealed in his own drum and hurled from the highest tower of the castle.

Ghostly Horrors of Glamis Castle

The inherited memory theory—which might be applied to other family death warnings as well—is a fairly comfortable one compared to the belief, held by many of these families, that the warning represents a curse on their lives.

Mrs. Mary Balfour, an octagenarian who has outlived most of her noble Scottish family, believes her clan spirit, a phantom piper, to be the result of a curse.

"According to tradition the curse was laid by a dying man, fatally wounded by one of my forebears in a clan feud. He said that from then onward our family should know of a death in their ranks two or three days before it took place. As the death would be inevitable, it was a kind of torture. Over the years it has been a torture to me; I've heard the piper, who plays a lament on the Great Pipes, in Edinburgh, on the Isle of Skye, on trains, and in my own flat in Berkeley Square, London.

Right: Glamis Castle in Scotland, the ancestral home of the Bowes-Lyon family, is as likely a place for a ghost as can be imagined. A specter of a 16th-century Lady Glamis is said to haunt the clock tower, but she is quite eclipsed by the legendary "horror" of Glamis, a secret known only to the head of the family. This has not stopped outsiders from speculating as to its nature. One theory is that a secret room in the castle contains skeletons of members of another clan who, centuries ago, were locked in the room by the earl and left to starve to death.

Below: Duncan's Hall, one of the castle's 100-odd rooms, is named for the king murdered in Shakespeare's *Macbeth*, but the real Duncan never visited the castle.

Left: this portrait of the Third Earl of Strathmore and his family hangs in the drawing room at Glamis. The small, slightly distorted boy in the picture feeds the legend that the secret of Glamis is a "monster child" born to the Bowes-Lyons and hidden in the castle.

Above: Sawston Hall, Cambridgeshire, is reputedly haunted by the Queen nicknamed "Bloody Mary" for her persecution of the Protestants in the 16th century. But if Mary does visit Sawston, it is as a friend, for its owner gave her shelter when, before becoming queen, she was in danger of her life.

Right: the Tapestry Room at Sawston, where Mary spent the night and supposedly still appears.

"So far I have never seen him. On occasion I have been relieved to turn around when the music sounded and see a street piper, such as used to be common in Edinburgh and Glasgow years ago. At such times I knew that no warning was intended. I first heard the lament as a girl of two or three in Inverness, and I know that when I last hear it, it will be calling me."

Other eminent families are afflicted with different kinds of ghosts. Perhaps the most haunted family in Britain is that of the Bowes-Lyons, Earls of Strathmore, the family of the present queen's mother. Their ancestral home, Glamis Castle in County Angus, was the setting of Shakespeare's *Macbeth*—although King Duncan may not have even visited the castle, let alone been murdered there. Glamis (pronounced "Glahms") was, however, the place where King Malcolm II was stabbed to death in the 11th century. A stain said to have been caused by his blood still marks the floor in one of the castle's myriad rooms. Several ghosts haunt Glamis—a little black boy, a lady in gray, a former earl who supposedly played cards with the Devil and lost. But the most celebrated—and chilling—of all the castle's legends is the "Horror" of Glamis.

No one outside the Strathmore family knows what form the Horror takes, but evidence suggests that it is not merely an old wives' tale, and that some terrible mystery does lurk within the grim stone walls. The most frequent story is that a monster child was born to the Strathmores, so hideous that to look upon it was to invite madness. The thing lived to an unnaturally old age—and some say that it still lives locked away in a hidden room.

The possible existence of a hidden room in which the monster could be kept intrigued a party of house guests at Glamis some years ago, and they organized a search for it. Methodically the guests hung a piece of linen from every window they could find. When they went outside, they discovered that over a dozen windows were unaccounted for. The then-Lord Strathmore, who had been away during the experiment, returned unexpectedly and, realizing what his guests had been up to, flew into an uncharacteristically furious temper.

It was he who some years later told a friend who asked about the Horror: "If you could know of it, you would thank God you were not me."

Another theory about the Glamis Horror is presented by Eric Maple in his book *The Realm of Ghosts*. According to Maple, centuries ago during a clan feud some members of the Ogilvie Clan fleeing from the Lindsays, sought refuge at Glamis. The Earl of Strathmore was bound by the laws of hospitality to admit them, but not wishing to appear partisan he took them to a remote room of the castle, locked them in, and left them to starve. Many years after they had died, their screams continued to echo occasionally in that part of the castle. Eventually one earl decided to investigate, and he made his way to the room from which the noises seemed to come. On opening the door and glimpsing the scene within, he fell backward in a faint into the arms of his companion. The earl refused to tell anyone what he had seen, but he had the door to the room bricked up. "There is a tradition,"

Haunted Rooms and Passageways

Below: this passageway at Longleat is haunted by Lady Louisa Carteret. According to legend, Lady Louisa's husband and her lover fought a duel, ending in the lover's death. The apparition of the lady has been seen, and feelings of terror experienced here.

Skulls Kept as Family Heirlooms

writes Maple, "that the spectacle within the haunted room was unbelievably horrible, for some of the starving men had actually died in the act of gnawing the flesh from their arms."

Both this story and the monster child story may be mere speculation. The truth of the matter is known only to the Earl of Strathmore. Tradition has it that each Strathmore heir is told the secret by his father on his 21st birthday. Lady Granville, a member of the Bowes-Lyon family, told ghost hunter J. Wentworth Day that female members of the family are never let in on the mystery. "We were never allowed to talk about it when we were children," she said. "My father and grandfather refused absolutely to discuss it."

There, as far as outsiders are concerned, the matter rests.

Some less prominent families have a more tangible form of ancestral Horror. Skulls kept as guardians and treated with a mixture of awe and affection were almost a fashion at one time, according to Celtic folklore—and again the custom seems to have crossed the Atlantic to America. The late A. J. Pew, a journalist from California, told the author of his family's own skull.

Pew's family was French, and arrived in the Louisiana Territory during the late 17th century. Family records from the earliest days of their settlement told of a skull, supposedly that of an ancestor who had been burned as a heretic in the Middle Ages, which was kept in a carved wooden box.

Like other such cranial family heirlooms, the skull—affectionately called "Ferdinand" by the Pews—showed an apparent sensitivity to its surroundings. "It had to be kept in the family house," wrote Pew, "and if it was taken off the premises it screamed. If it screamed *indoors*, it meant a death among us."

Below: a kind of "still life with death" including the Screaming Skull of Bettiscombe Manor. Here serving as an ornament of sorts, the skull was also at one time used as a toy by the children of a tenant of Bettiscombe; and local villagers even maintain that unidentified persons or phantoms bowled with it.

Above: Burton Agnes Hall in Yorkshire houses the skull of Anne Griffith, who lived there. Shortly after it was finished, Anne was attacked by robbers while out walking, and mortally wounded. On her deathbed she asked her sisters to keep her head within the Hall, but they failed to keep the promise. Frightful noises broke out in the house—stamping footsteps, crashing doors— and a few weeks later the intimidated sisters had Anne's skull restored to her home.

Apparently, however, Pew's father suspected the story to be a
myth. He had the skull examined by a surgeon, who stated that
in his opinion it had all the characteristics of an Indian skull,
possibly one from the Florida area.

"I've rather lost touch with the relic and the branch of the
family who owned it," Pew said, "but from that evidence I would
guess that it came into the hands of the Pew family after their
arrival in America, not before. Possibly some ancestor wanted to
establish himself in this country, and cooked up the skull story to
add an air of mystery to himself. Certainly my father never found
concrete evidence of the skull actually screaming—only people
who remembered people who had heard it scream."

The Pew family skull is not the only one of its kind. Several
English families have possessed—sometimes reluctantly—bony
relics that resist any attempts to give them a decent burial.

Burton Agnes Hall, a beautifully restored Elizabethan house,
was for many years haunted by the apparition of Anne Griffith,
the daughter of Sir Henry Griffith who had built the house
around 1590. Anne particularly loved Burton Agnes, and on her

Above: Wardley Hall in Leicestershire
houses the skull of Father Ambrose, a
Catholic priest who was executed for
treason in 1641.

Left: another skull that refuses to be buried
is this one at Chilton Cantelo, Somerset. It
once belonged to one Theophilus Broome
who, on his death in 1670, asked that it be
kept in the farmhouse where it can be seen
today. In the past, attempts to bury it have
been followed by "horrid noises, portentive
of sad displeasure," according to the
inscription on Theophilus Broome's
tombstone.

Skulls that Won't Stay Buried

Below: the mummified remains of Jeremy Bentham, founder of the philosophy of Utilitarianism, preserved in a case at the entrance to University College of the University of London. The head is a wax replacement, the original being sufficiently decayed to make it an unsuitable object for display. Something of an eccentric, Bentham wanted his body to be preserved, partly so that it could attend meetings of his followers when they might wish to honor him. His ghost haunts the College.

deathbed, according to the story, she asked that her head be cut off after she died and kept inside the house. Several subsequent owners of the house apparently disobeyed her request and removed the skull for burial, whereupon it would begin to scream. The fact that "Awd Nance"—as she was known to the Yorkshire locals—was frequently seen walking through the house was taken as an indication of her sense of insecurity about the resting place of her skull. Around 1900, the occupant of Burton Agnes Hall had the skull sealed into one of the walls to prevent its being removed. Since then Awd Nance has appeared infrequently.

At Wardley Hall, near Manchester, the resident skull is supposed to be that of a Catholic priest executed for treason in 1641. After being displayed on a Manchester church tower as a sinister warning to sympathizers, the priest's head was secretly removed and taken to Wardley Hall, the home of a Catholic family. For many years the skull was kept on view at the head of the staircase. Occasional attempts to remove it for burial brought repercussions in the form of violent storms and other disturbances. Once it was thrown into a pond but, in the words of ghost hunter Eric Maple, "managed to find its way back to the Hall again."

The folklore surrounding family skulls is full of such bizarre images. The best-known of them all, the Bettiscombe Manor Skull, was once buried nine feet deep in the earth by an owner who wanted to be rid of it. The owner was appalled on the following day to discover that the skull had worked its way to the surface, and was lying there apparently waiting to return home.

The Bettiscombe skull case is a classic example of the confusion and distortion that go into making a ghost legend. One version says that the skull is that of a black slave brought to Bettiscombe, Dorset, in the 18th century. In 1685 the owner of the manor, Azariah Pinney, had been exiled for political reasons and sent to the West Indies. The Pinneys prospered in the New World, and Azariah's grandson, John Frederick, eventually returned to Bettiscombe, bringing with him a black slave as his manservant. Pinney seems to have treated his slave well, and when the man asked that on his death his body be returned to Africa for burial, the master gave his promise.

After the black man's death, however, Pinney broke his promise, and had the man buried in the village churchyard not far from the manor house. During the course of the following weeks neither Pinney nor his family were able to sleep because of mysterious groans, shrieks, and bumps in the night. Finally the master disinterred the body and brought it back to his own loft. This seemed to satisfy it, for no more noises occurred.

The body remained in the loft for years until at some point— no one seems to know when or how—it disappeared. Except for the skull. That remained, minus its jawbone, and has been kept in the house almost continuously ever since. In 1847 a visitor at the house was shown the relic by a housekeeper, who told him: "While this skull is kept, no ghost will invade the premises." This was the first recorded mention of its supernatural qualities.

While investigating the Bettiscombe story in the mid-1960s, Maple found that the local people had plenty of tales to tell about the skull. He learned that on several occasions it had been removed from the Hall, only to bring various disasters on the area: thunderstorms that destroyed crops at harvest time, for example, and the wholesale death of cattle and other livestock. It was even asserted that several owners of Bettiscombe who had removed the skull had died within a year.

One man remembered as a youth hearing the skull "screaming like a trapped rat" in the attic—which somewhat contradicts the idea that it objects only to being removed from the house. Others mentioned peculiar rattling noises coming from the attic, believed to be "them" playing ninepins with the skull. Exactly who "they" were was left to the imagination.

The black slave has lingered in the folk-memory of the villagers 200 years after his death. Tales are told of a screaming black man "kept prisoner in a secret room and fed through a grating." And yet, other versions of the story say that John Pinney treated his slave kindly. Who can say what was the truth? A completely different legend says that the skull is that of a white girl who "long ago"—a favorite phrase of the legend-spinners— was kept prisoner in the house and then murdered.

Neither of these stories is likely to be true, for when the skull was examined by Professor Gilbert Causey of the Royal College of Surgeons, he pronounced it to be much older than anyone had suspected. It was, he said, the skull of a prehistoric woman.

The present owner of Bettiscombe Manor, Michael Pinney, believes it to be the relic of some foundation sacrifice which was placed in the building originally constructed on the site in order to propitiate the gods and bring good fortune. The later story of the black man was somehow grafted onto the original story of this sacrifice.

Although Pinney and his wife claim to regard their strange heirloom merely as a conversation piece, he has so far refused to allow it to be taken out of doors. Both he and his wife were slightly shaken when a visitor who stayed with them during World War II, and who knew the history of the skull, inquired: "Did it sweat blood in 1939, as it did in 1914?"

African or Caucasian, curse or good luck charm, the yellowing relic continues to keep a firm grasp on the imaginations of the Dorset farmers of the neighborhood. If it is, in fact, a reminder of ancient sacrifice, its continuing hold on people's minds for more than 2000 years is scarcely less remarkable than that of the wailing banshee, that "symbolic form . . . stamped on our racial consciousness."

Below: the rather grisly head of a body that used to stand in a glass-fronted coffin in the vestibule of St. James's Church in the City of London. Familiarly called Old Jimmy, he may have been one of the City's early Lord Mayors. During World War II's Blitz, a bomb fell through the roof, struck the edge of the coffin, and landed, unexploded, in the vaults. After that unsettling event, Old Jimmy's ghost became active. It was occasionally seen in the nave, and it was believed to be responsible for the movement of objects and peculiar noises.

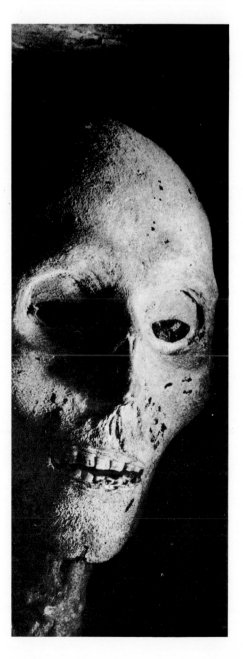

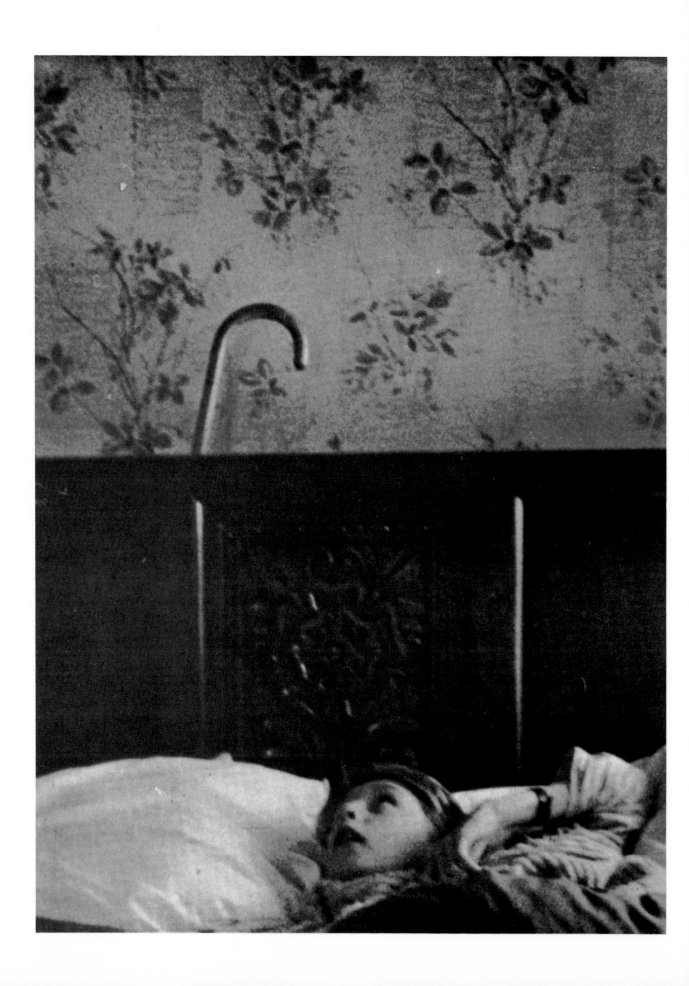

Chapter 6
The Poltergeist

Of all the mysterious happenings associated with ghosts and spirits, surely the ones easiest to verify scientifically are the workings of the poltergeist, whose strange noises can be heard by anyone present, or when objects—visible to all—fly through the air. What is the evidence for the existence of these psychic events? Is it a modern phenomenon or has it been known to history? Is there a possible scientific explanation for the disturbing behavior of these "noisy spirits," banging and crashing around what seemed to be normal, everyday households? The evidence suggests that some poltergeists may even have a mocking sense of humor . . .

To all appearances Shirley Hitchins was an ordinary teenager. She lived with her parents, Mr. and Mrs. Walter Hitchins in one of a row of identical houses that lined Wycliffe Road, a thoroughfare in a working class area of London. Like many of her friends she had left secondary school early to go to work, and she seemed happy enough with the position she found as a salesgirl in a London department store. Then in 1956, a few months after her 15th birthday, Shirley ceased to be ordinary.

Her troubles started one morning when she woke up to find a shiny new key lying on her bedspread. She had never seen it before, her parents knew nothing about it, and it did not fit any of the doors in her home. During the following nights her bedclothes were brusquely yanked from her as she lay asleep, and thunderous knockings sounded on her bedroom walls. During the day such knockings were accompanied by tappings and scratchings in other parts of the house, and heavy pieces of furniture moved mysteriously around the rooms.

Within a few days the girl was haggard through lack of sleep, and arranged to stay a night with neighbor Mrs. Lily Love in an attempt to get some rest, away from it all. "It" followed her. An alarm clock and some china ornaments were shuffled around a shelf in Mrs. Love's house by an invisible agency, a poker was hurled across a room, and Shirley's wristwatch was pulled from her arm and thrown to the floor.

After this her father, a London Transport motorman, decided

Opposite: one of the few photographs of a poltergeist in action. A stick "jumps" over 14-year-old Yorkshire schoolboy Michael Collindridge, in a Barnsley hotel in 1965.

An Unseen Force Pushed the Girl

to sit up one night to see exactly what went on. He was accompanied by his brother. Shirley went to bed in her mother's room. All was quiet for a while, and then a resonant tapping began to shake the bed in which she lay. She was still wide awake, lying with her hands outside the covers. After a while she called to her father and uncle to say that the bedclothes were moving. The two men grabbed the bedclothes and found they were being tugged with considerable force toward the foot of the bed. As they struggled with the invisible force, they and Shirley's mother saw the girl suddenly go rigid. To their astonishment her stiff body rose six inches into the air without any support whatever.

Fighting back their fear, the Hitchins brothers lifted the floating body clear of the bed. Shirley, who had seemed dazed at the time, later said that she had felt a tremendous pressure in the small of her back, lifting her up. The levitation occurred only once and seemed to mark the peak of the strange events, for the following day the disturbances reverted to the form of rapping noises. These went with the girl everywhere, even onto the bus that took her to work. At the store her co-workers persuaded her to see the store doctor. Skeptical at first, the doctor was finally persuaded that "something was going on" when the knockings began in his own consulting room. He was still puzzling over the mystery when, almost a month to the day after the first mysterious appearance of the key, all the phenomena abated, and then ceased for good.

Today, some 20 years later, it is impossible to judge the happenings in Wycliffe Road with total objectivity, for we have only the contemporary newspaper stories and reporters' inter-

Below: one of the various attempts to free Shirley Hitchins from the poltergeist that plagued her for a month was an exorcism held by a medium, Harry Hanks, a friend of her family. After going into trance, Mr. Hanks made contact with a spirit, and eventually received the assurance that the poltergeist would trouble Shirley (right of fireplace) no longer.

Below right: Shirley holds a boot that was the focus of some poltergeist activity during the seance.

views with witnesses as evidence. From these, however, we can infer that Shirley Hitchins, her parents, Mrs. Love and her family, and the doctor who examined the girl were all rational down-to-earth people, none of whom had ever previously experienced any form of psychic phenomena.

It seems probable that the Shirley Hitchins case was a genuine example of poltergeist phenomena. The German word poltergeist, meaning a "noisy spirit," is today commonly used by psychic investigators to describe certain apparently supernormal physical effects—whether or not the investigator believes that they are caused by a spirit.

In his book *Can We Explain the Poltergeist?*, Dr. A. R. G. Owen clearly defines the term. It is, he says, the occurrence of one or both of the following taking place in an apparently spontaneous, often sporadic way: (a) production of noises, such as tappings, sawings, bumpings; (b) movement of objects by no known physical means.

These two kinds of phenomena include a host of distinct effects. The noises, for example, may be impersonal in character, such as the rappings that followed Shirley Hitchins around, or they may suggest a human or superhuman agent. The movement of objects may take many forms: pictures may fall from the wall, vases fly across the room, heavy pieces of furniture be moved. On rare occasions, poltergeist activity may involve levitation, like that experienced by Shirley Hitchins.

The poltergeist has a long history. One of the earliest recorded cases took place in the German town of Bingen-am-Rhein in A.D. 355. Stones whizzed through the air, apparently of their own volition; sleepers were tossed out of their beds; and banging and crashing noises echoed in the streets. Since then many other cases have been reported in other parts of the world.

In a book entitled *The Story of the Poltergeist*, the late psychical researcher Hereward Carrington listed 375 cases of alleged poltergeist activity, from the Bingen-am-Rhein case to one in 1949, a few years before the book was published. After analyzing the cases Carrington concluded that 26 were undoubtedly fraudulent, and 19 were "doubtful." Assuming that all the doubtful cases were fraudulent as well, 330 cases remained "unexplained." In other words, they were apparently caused by some supernatural force.

Carrington admitted that the standard of evidence varied greatly, and that in many cases it was not high. In fact, such substandard evidence, coupled with the proven frauds, has always strengthened the arguments of the skeptics. As early as 1584 Reginald Scot in his *Discoverie of Witchcraft* was writing: "I could recite a great Number of Tales, how Men have even forsaken their Houses, because of apparitions and Noises; and all has been by meer and rank Knavery; and wheresoever you shall hear that there are such rumbling and fearful Noises, be you assured, that it is flat Knavery, performed by some that seem most to complain, and are least suspected . . ."

Scot was a remarkable man who, in an age of superstition, hit out with considerable force against those who believed in witchcraft; but his strong skepticism on the subject of the occult in general seems to have led him to throw the baby out with the

The Drummer of Tedworth

The magistrate of Tedworth in Wiltshire, England, could not have imagined the consequences when he confiscated the drum belonging to William Drury—an itinerant magician caught in some shady dealings—and told him to leave the district.

That was in March 1662. Hardly had the culprit left Tedworth when the drum began to produce drumming noises itself. It also flew around Magistrate Mompesson's house, seen by several people besides the magistrate. After several sleepless nights, he had the drum broken into pieces. Still the drumming continued. Nor was that all. Shoes flew through the air, and chamber pots were emptied onto beds. Children were levitated. A horse's rear leg was forced into its mouth.

The possibility that the exiled drummer had sneaked back and was causing the trouble was fairly well ruled out when it was discovered that he had been arrested for theft in the city of Gloucester and sent to the colonies. The Reverend Joseph Glanville, chaplain to King Charles II, came to Tedworth to investigate the phenomena. He heard the drumming himself, and collected eyewitness reports from the residents. No natural cause was found for the effects, which stopped exactly one year after they had started.

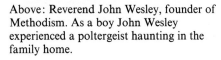

Above: Reverend John Wesley, founder of
Methodism. As a boy John Wesley
experienced a poltergeist haunting in the
family home.

Above right: Epworth Rectory, the Wesley
home in Lincolnshire. The poltergeist
produced a variety of noises—knockings,
groanings, footsteps, and a curious sound
like the winding up of a jack were among its
effects. Several members of the Wesley
household claimed to have seen a
phantom during the two-month haunting.
On two occasions they saw what looked like
a badger; and a servant once saw
something like a white rabbit. Emily
Wesley, one of the sisters, believed
witchcraft was at the bottom of the
Epworth haunting.

bath water. Today most psychic investigators would agree that
there have been many instances of genuine poltergeist effects.

One characteristic that most poltergeists have in common is
that they generally occur in a household containing an adolescent. It seems possible that the onset of puberty may in some way
generate the forces that produce the poltergeist effects.

This factor was certainly present in the case of the Wesley
poltergeist. John Wesley, the founder of the Methodist Church,
was a boy of 13 when in 1715 strange knocking noises began to
be heard in the family's house, Epworth Rectory, in Lincolnshire,
England. The Wesleys were a large family. Besides John there
were 18 other children including Molly, aged 20; Hetty, 19;
Nancy, 15; Patty, 10; and Kezzy, 7. In a letter to her eldest son
Samuel, Mrs. Wesley described the beginning of the events:
"On the first of December our maid heard, at the door of the
dining room, several dismal groans, like a person in extremes,
at the point of death." When the maid looked behind the door
she found no one there.

The following day various raps were heard, and on the third
day Molly heard the rustle of a silken gown passing quite close
to her. The same evening something began to knock on the dining
table, and footsteps were heard on the stairs. As the days passed
other noises were added: the sound of a cradle rocking; another
like the turning of a windmill; another like a carpenter planing
wood. The poltergeist frequently interrupted family prayers.

Gradually the Wesleys became accustomed to the disturbances,
and even jocularly nicknamed the unseen presence "Old
Jeffrey." In the record he kept of the events, John Wesley wrote:
"Kezzy desired no better diversion than to pursue Old Jeffrey
from room to room."

Suddenly, after a visit of two months, Old Jeffrey left the

Wesleys, and the Rectory at Epworth has been quiet ever since.

The Wesley poltergeist attracted the attention of no less a scientist than Joseph Priestley, a Fellow of the Royal Society for the Advancement of Science, and the discoverer of oxygen. Priestley mulled over the facts of the Wesley case, and in 1784 reported his findings in the *Arminian Magazine*. His article showed that he suspected Hetty Wesley of some unconscious part in the phenomena. It was significant, said Priestley, that "the disturbances were centered around Hetty's bed, and were marked by Hetty's trembling in her sleep."

The Wesley case was typical of most poltergeists in that it harmed no one. The Wesleys were also fortunate in that Old Jeffrey confined itself to noises. Many poltergeists have a destructive streak, and hurl crockery about with reckless abandon. Oddly, though, these flying objects rarely strike anyone, and when they do their impact is slight—even when they appear to travel at great speed. Occasionally poltergeist activity takes the form of showers of stones—or even coins, or shoes.

Although poltergeists rarely hurt anyone, there is one striking exception to the rule. This was the notorious "Bell Witch," a malevolent force that tormented the Bell family of Robertson County, Tennessee, for nearly four years. It apparently caused the death of the father, John Bell. The word "poltergeist" was not widely known in the United States in 1817 when the phenomena first occurred. Neither the family nor their neighbors knew what to call the thing that plagued them. The birth of Spiritualism was 30 years in the future, and in any case, once the thing began to talk, it asserted that it was not the spirit of someone who had died, but "a spirit from everywhere." Once it called itself a witch, and that was the term that stuck.

John Bell was a prosperous farmer, well-liked and respected

John Wesley and the Poltergeist

Left: an illustration from a Victorian story about a family troubled by a poltergeist. Poltergeists seldom cause physical harm, but they can certainly turn a house upside down. The late psychical researcher Harry Price believed that poltergeists are spirits of some kind, but many modern researchers would tend to attribute the effects to some force emanating from living persons on the premises.

Above: Nandor Fodor, modern psycho-analyst who made a deep study of psychic phenomena, including poltergeists. Among his work is a detailed analysis of the "Bell Witch"—a poltergeist that tormented a Tennessee family in the early part of the 19th century.

Right: the curé of the village of Cideville and his housekeeper, beset with flying furniture and levitating pets—an illustration for a famous 19th-century poltergeist case. The curé had annoyed a local white witch. According to local opinion, the witch got his revenge through a stooge, a peasant named Thorel. The poltergeist activity—which Thorel took the credit, or blame, for—centered on two teenage pupils in the curé's house. When the boys were finally sent to their homes, the activity continued briefly in the home of the younger boy.

by his neighbors, who lived with his wife Luce and his nine children in a large farmhouse surrounded by outbuildings and slave quarters. At the time of the first outbreak Bell's daughter Betsy, who figured prominently in the case, was a robust, apparently contented girl of 12. Richard Williams Bell, who later wrote an account of the disturbances entitled *Our Family Trouble*, was a boy of six.

The disturbances began with knockings and scrapings that seemed to come from the outside of the walls and windows of the house. Later the sounds entered the house, taking the form of gnawing noises on bedposts, scratchings on the floorboards, and flappings on the ceiling. Gradually the noise increased until at times it seemed to shake the house. The Witch continually added new sounds to its repertoire: chairs being overturned, stones raining on the roof, heavy chains being dragged across the floor. According to Richard Williams' book the noises bothered Betsy more than the other members of the family.

It began to show physical strength. Richard Williams Bell was awakened one night by something pulling at his hair. "Immediately Joel [one of the children] yelled out in great fright, and next Elizabeth [Betsy] was screaming in her room, and after that something was continually pulling at her hair after she retired to bed."

Up to this point the family had kept their curious troubles to themselves, but now they decided to ask the advice of a friend

and neighbor, James Johnson. Johnson listened attentively to the noises, and concluded that some intelligence lay behind them. He performed a simple exorcism, which helped for a while.

When the Witch returned it did so with renewed vigor, and concentrated on Betsy to such an extent that her parents became seriously worried. It slapped her face, leaving crimson patches on her cheeks, and it pulled her hair with such force that she screamed in agony.

By this time Johnson was convinced that whatever the thing was, it could understand human language and ought to be capable of communication. He advised John Bell to call in more neighbors to form an investigating committee. Unfortunately, the committee seems to have done more harm than good. The members, fascinated by the effects and presumably safe enough themselves, invited it to "rap on the wall, smack its mouth, etc., and in this way," wrote Richard Williams, "the phenomena were gradually developed."

The Witch began to throw sticks and stones at the Bell children as they went to and from school. Apparently the children soon became accustomed to this and they developed a game with it. When a stick was thrown at them, they would mark it and throw it back. "Invariably," wrote Richard Williams, "the same sticks would be hurled back at us."

This sort of thing was harmless enough, but the Witch was now becoming more violent. Occasionally it struck people in

Malignancy of the Bell Witch

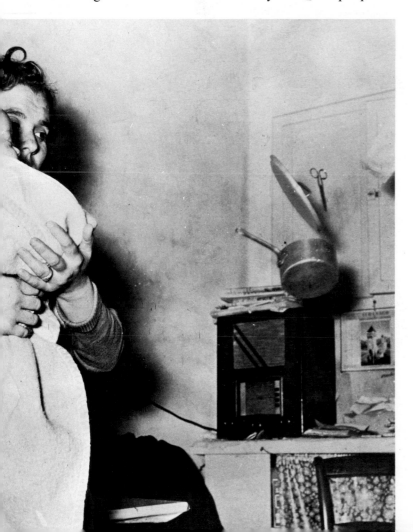

Left: this French picture is of a poltergeist. The newspaper *Samedi Soir* sent a photographer to the home of a family named Costa near the French-Italian frontier, which was the scene of poltergeist activity. The photographer set up his camera in the kitchen, and after an hour-and-a-half wait he snapped these objects in flight.

An Increase of Spirit Attacks

Right: a re-creation of an event in the bewildering, electrically charged life of Adolphine Benoit, a French servant girl. She had been rocking a child in a cradle when suddenly the locked wardrobe doors opened, linen was thrown around the room, and a cloak lying on a bed wrapped itself around the cradle so tightly that it was difficult to remove. After this incident, the girl found herself the target for all sorts of objects. Baskets of bread fell onto her head; bits of meat and her mistress' earrings mysteriously found their way into her pockets; a large sack fell over her, covering her completely. Once when she went into the stables, the horses' harness jumped on her, and she had to be rescued. A priest who tried to exorcise her was shaken, and his glasses broken by the unseen force. When her employers finally sent the girl home she ceased to be troubled; but the phenomena recurred in the employers' house, centering on an infant son. Another exorcism banished the spirit.

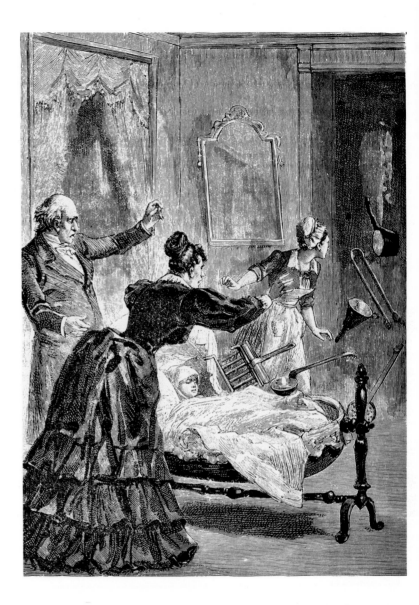

the face with what felt like a clenched fist. Meanwhile Betsy, who had always been robust, began to suffer fainting fits and shortness of breath, each spell lasting for about half an hour. During these attacks the Witch remained silent, but as soon as the girl had recovered her composure it began to whistle and talk again. Its voice, which had been faint and inarticulate at first, gradually developed to a low but distinct whisper. Because the talking never occurred while Betsy was suffering a seizure, someone suggested that she might be producing the voice herself, by ventriloquism. A doctor "placed his hand over Betsy's mouth and soon satisfied himself that she was in no way connected with these sounds."

The Witch's first utterances tended to be of a pious nature. It showed an astonishing ability to reproduce, word for word, the Sunday sermons of the two local parsons, even imitating their voices. In a commentary on the case, included in *The Story of the Poltergeist*, psychoanalyst Nandor Fodor observes that the Witch "would have made a grand 'spirit communicator' if it had been imbued with mediumistic ideas." After its pious phase, however, the Witch began uttering obscenities—very distressing to a Bible Belt family. It also declared its hatred for "old Jack Bell" and said it would torment him for all his life.

From that time onward the farmer began to decline. He complained of stiffness in his mouth and of something punching either side of his jaw. His tongue became so swollen that he could neither eat nor speak. These attacks sometimes lasted as long as 15 hours. Then he developed a nervous tic in his cheek. It seemed to spread to the rest of his body so that eventually he was permanently bedridden, twitching in a kind of constant delirium.

The Witch seemed to have mixed feelings toward the rest of the family. The mother, whom Betsy adored, was showered with presents of fruit and nuts which appeared from nowhere. Joel, Richard, and Drewry were frequently thrashed by the Witch, but never seriously hurt. As for Betsy herself, after her fainting spells ceased she seemed to be left in peace—at least physically. But the Witch began persecuting the girl emotionally. She had already become engaged in her early teens to a neighbor, Joshua Gardner. The Witch relentlessly sought to break up the engagement, whispering into the girl's ear, "Please, Betsy Bell, don't have Joshua Gardner, please, Betsy Bell, don't marry Joshua Gardner," and adding that if she married the boy she would never know a moment's peace. Eventually it succeeded in breaking up the relationship.

In the autumn of 1820 John Bell managed to rouse himself from his bed and go about the farm business. But the Witch was not about to allow this. Richard Williams recalled how his father staggered suddenly, as if stunned by a heavy blow to the head, and slumped pathetically onto a log by the side of the road while "his face commenced jerking with fearful contortions." The father's shoes would fly off as fast as the boy could put them on. All the while "the reviling sound of derisive songs" and "demoniac shrieks" rang around them. Finally the shrieks faded away, the contortions ceased, and the boy saw tears running

Above: Angelique Cottin, a French girl who, at the age of 14, developed a kind of electrical force. It first manifested one evening while she was weaving. The loom began to jerk. The movement would cease when she backed off, and resume when she approached. People standing near her would feel shocks; anything touching her apron would fly off. The effects diminished if she stood on a carpet, and stopped in three months.

Left: servants in a house in St. Quentin, France, recoiling from one of the poltergeist effects that troubled the house in 1849. The windows were struck by invisible projectiles that left holes but did not crack the glass. When one of the servants was fired, the poltergeist phenomena ceased.

Right: Mrs. Katinka Parker of Denver, Colorado, standing in front of her house, which she claims is haunted. Not only does something go bump in the night; something twice pushed her downstairs.

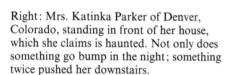

Above: Mrs. Betty Sargent, photographed in 1950 after she and her husband and baby were driven out of their apartment by a poltergeist. The force dragged her out of bed one night, and another time it tried to strangle her. In a less violent mood, it tore her stockings.

down his father's quivering cheeks.

Defeated, John Bell returned to his bed. On December 19, 1820, he was discovered in a deep stupor and could not be roused. His son John Jr. went to the medicine cabinet, but instead of Bell's prescribed medicine found a "smoky looking vial, which was about one-third full of dark colored liquid."

The doctor was sent for, but when he arrived the Witch was heard crowing: "It's useless for you to try and relieve old Jack— I have got him this time; he will never get up from that bed again." Bell died the next morning. As his coffin was lowered into the grave, the Witch had a final gloat: its voice could be heard singing a raucous song, "Row me up some brandy, O."

The family doctor tested the potion found in the medicine bottle on a cat, and the cat immediately went into convulsions and died. Instead of analyzing the liquid, the doctor threw it into the fire. No satisfactory medical explanation of John Bell's death was ever given.

After his death the phenomena gradually faded. As his family was sitting down to supper one evening, a kind of smoke bomb burst in the room and a voice announced that it was going but would return in seven years. The return took place as promised, after Betsy had left to marry another man and only Mrs. Bell, Joel, and Richard Williams remained in the house—but consisted only of a brief scuffling and twitching of bedclothes. After that the Witch vanished forever.

Although some of the peripheral aspects of the Bell Witch case may have become distorted with the passing of the years, it seems certain that the principal phenomena did take place. The case is still regarded as worthy of serious study, and it has been explored at length in several works on parapsychology.

The most interesting psychological aspect of the Bell Witch mystery lies in the relationship between Betsy Bell and her father. First of all, let's consider the symptoms experienced by the girl. Dr. Fodor points out that Betsy's fainting fits and dizzy spells—

The Pranks of Poltergeists

Left: Mrs. Vera Stringer of London sweeps up the charred remains of a wastebasket after the annual Eastertide visit of "Larry," a poltergeist, while her son Steven, age 4, watches. The Stringers' poltergeist has a visible form: it manifests as a fluorescent column of vibrating light, and is about the size of a grown man.

immediately followed by the voice of the Witch—are very similar to the symptoms exhibited by a medium while going into trance. He also notes that the girl was healthy and sexually precocious.

Her father, on the other hand, showed all signs of what a modern psychiatrist would recognize as acute guilt expressed in physical ways: the nervous tic, the inability to eat or speak, and the general withdrawal from the world. Despite some evidence that an unknown person might have administered the poison that finally killed him, the strong possibility remains that he killed himself—goaded beyond endurance by the phantom.

Describing the Bell Witch, Dr. Fodor notes that the entity could not account for itself or its strange powers when asked by the committee of neighbors. It was singularly human in its emotional behavior, playing pranks, imitating people, occasionally showing great solicitude for Luce Bell.

It also loathed John Bell with the most profound loathing.

Dr. Fodor concluded that Betsy Bell suffered from a split personality—that in some mysterious way part of her subconscious mind had taken on a life of its own. This renegade part of Betsy's psyche methodically plagued her father to death.

Modern Theories and Research

Right: the home of Mr. and Mrs. James Herrmann in Seaford, Long Island, the setting of one of the most thoroughly investigated poltergeist cases of modern times.

Below: Mrs. Herrmann points to the cabinet under the kitchen sink where the poltergeist caused some bottles containing ammonia and liquid starch to "blow their tops." Flying glassware and moving furniture—typical poltergeist pranks—were some of the effects that made life rather tempestuous for the Herrmann family back in 1958.

The psychology of such a split is still a mystery. Only very rarely do cases of multiple personality appear, but when they do, some powerful emotional shock is usually the triggering factor. Drawing on cases of neurosis and psychosis with which he was familiar, Dr. Fodor made a "purely speculative guess" at the origin of the Bell Witch. Noting that the onset of puberty and budding sexuality would tend to be traumatic in the puritanical surroundings in which Betsy grew up, he speculated that in her case the shock might have been aggravated by the awakening of long-suppressed memories. What were these memories? Dr. Fodor's theory was, as he put it, "not for the grim and prudish." He thought that in childhood Betsy may have been molested by her father.

The theory may sound far-fetched, but incest is not as uncommon as we tend to assume—particularly in rural communities. Dr. Fodor points to the fact that the first appearance of Bell's severe guilt symptoms coincided with Betsy's puberty. Perhaps Bell's guilt was so extreme that to some extent he cooperated with the Witch in causing his own illness.

As to why the Witch persecuted Betsy, this is comprehensible if we accept the premise that it was part of the girl's own subconscious. If part of Betsy's psyche was determined to kill John Bell, it would at the same time have terrible guilt feelings about this, and would exact some penance from her conscious self. This took the form of blighting her youthful romance. "The sacrifice [of her engagement] came first," says Fodor, "but the murder, mentally, had been envisioned long before."

Had the Bell Witch case occurred in the first part of the 20th century instead of 100 years earlier, we would be in a better position to evaluate it, both psychologically and psychically. Today psychical research is becoming more and more sophisticated. The Parapsychology Laboratory at Duke University, founded by Dr. J. B. Rhine, is perhaps the best equipped psychical research unit in the world. The staff members go to painstaking lengths in examining many paranormal phenomena, including cases of poltergeist activity. Dr. Rhine's assistant, J. Gaither Pratt, described some of the laboratory's methods in his book *Parapsychology*. In one chapter he tells of the Seaford Poltergeist, which troubled a middle-class Long Island family and was investigated by Dr. Pratt and William G. Roll, another psychical researcher, during February and March 1958.

Mr. and Mrs. James M. Herrmann lived with their two children James, age 12, and Lucille, 13, at their home in Seaford, Nassau County, New York. Over a period of two months, 67 recorded disturbances were investigated not only by the Duke University team but also by the Nassau County Police. The phenomena fell into two categories: the unscrewing of bottle caps followed by the spilling of the bottles' contents; and the moving of furniture and small objects.

Although Dr. Pratt states that no firm conclusion could be reached as to the cause of the Seaford poltergeist, he observes that nothing ever happened when all the family were out of the house, when they were fast asleep, or when the children were both at school. He also notes that the disturbances usually took place nearer to James than to any other member of the family.

Dr. Pratt's account is of interest mainly in showing to what lengths a psychical researcher must go before concluding that an alleged poltergeist is genuine. Between them Dr. Pratt, Roll, and Detective Joseph Tozzi first ruled out the possibility of hoax by one or more members of the family. Observing the tangible evidence of the force—the smashed objects and spilled liquids— they could quickly rule out collective hallucination. Next, they checked the possibility that the disturbances could be caused by high frequency radio waves, vibrations, chemical interference (in the case of the spilled liquids), faulty electrical wiring, drafts, water level alteration in a well near the house, possible underground streams, radio frequencies outside the house, and subsidence of the land under the house. They held a conference at nearby Adelphi College with members of the science departments, and they called in structural, civil, and electrical engineers from the Nassau Society of Engineers. They examined the possibility that takeoffs and landings at nearby Mitchell Air Field might be causing the events, and they checked the house's plumbing installations from top to bottom.

All of their findings were negative. After almost two months on the spot, Dr. Pratt tentatively gave his opinion that they were not dealing with the "kind of impersonal psychical force which perhaps sometime in the future will fall within the scope of physics . . . If the Seaford disturbances were not fraudulent—and no evidence of fraud was found—they clearly make a proper claim upon the interests of parapsychologists." In other words, in his opinion some intelligence lay behind the disturbance.

Dr. Pratt did not overlook the fact that in the Seaford case, as in most poltergeist cases, adolescent children were on the scene. So far as he could tell during his short visit, neither of the Herrmann children had psychological problems. Perhaps no

Pyromaniac Poltergeist

Father Karl Pazelt, a Jesuit priest, came to the aid of a California couple in 1974 when they were troubled by a poltergeist. The couple, who reported their story to the *San Francisco Examiner* anonymously, believed that it was a devil.

The poltergeist pulled the standard prank of throwing shoes, but also plagued them by setting fires. At one point a plastic wastebasket (in the house) caught fire and melted. Frightened for the safety of their two-year-old son as well as for themselves, they asked Father Pazelt to exorcise the malevolent force. In his opinion this was a case of "demonic obsession"— that is, the "devil is not *in* the people, but *around* the people." According to the couple, the devilish spirit made its presence strongly felt during the exorcism rite "by knocking both of us down."

The Flying Bicarbonate

The manager and staff of the Co-operative Stores in the English village of Long Wittenham, Berkshire, were not amused in late 1962 when jam jars, cereal boxes, and other normally stationery objects began flying off the shelves and circling overhead. In fact, one salesgirl fainted. To add to the confusion, the invisible prankster switched the lights on and off. For some mysterious reason, the poltergeist concentrated on the bicarbonate of soda, transferring boxes of the substance from the shelf to the window ledge.

After a week of chaos, the local vicar offered his services and exorcised the shop. The ritual proved effective, and groceries stayed put at last. The exhausted manager and staff set about restoring the stock to order. Despite the apparent success of the exorcising ceremony, however, they decided to take precautions with the bicarbonate of soda. They put it under lock and key.

This case is one of many in which possible natural causes, such as earth tremors or an underground river, fail to provide a satisfactory explanation for flying objects. If such natural vibrations were responsible, for example, the bicarbonate of soda would hardly have been given such special attention.

such problem is required; perhaps puberty itself can trigger off poltergeist phenomena as its energies react with other forces.

The existence of other forces can't be completely dismissed, for there have been some poltergeist cases in which no adolescents were involved. This was true in the case of the poltergeist phenomena at Killakee Arts Center in Ireland, which was also haunted by a phantom black cat. Margaret O'Brien, the only person who lived on the premises throughout the entire disturbance period—from the late 1960s to the end of 1970—is a mature and intelligent woman. Furthermore, she was absent from the house on several occasions when phenomena occurred. It's impossible, therefore, to link the trouble with any one person.

It does seem possible, though, that the Killakee poltergeist may have been goaded into activity—perhaps even created—by some amateur psychic investigators. It's worth remembering that the Bell Witch investigating committee helped to develop the phenomena by urging the presence to "smack its mouth" and make other noises. Old Jeffrey, the Wesley poltergeist, was encouraged to some extent by Kezzy following it from room to room, teasing it. A poltergeist may be an unhuman force, but it often seems capable of reacting to human interference.

After the appearance of a monstrous black cat during the renovation of Killakee House, several other apparitions were reported, though none of them was as vivid as the cat.

Following reports of these strange events in the Irish press, a group of show business personalities from Dublin persuaded Margaret O'Brien to let them try a seance at the house. They arranged letters of the alphabet in a circle on a table and used a glass turned upside down as a pointer that could be controlled by any psychic forces present. The results of the seance were inconclusive—although the lights failed, apparently without cause, at one point during the evening. Within a couple of days of the seance, however, serious disturbances began.

They began sporadically at first with bumps and rappings in the night, and lights being switched on and off. Then some of the artists living in the Center began to suffer sleepless nights, kept awake by the chiming of bells, although there were no bells in the neighborhood. The next stage of activity was more vigorous. Heavy pieces of furniture in locked rooms were found overturned, a stout oak chair was pulled apart joint from joint, and another solid chair was smashed to slivers.

For a few weeks after the chair smashing, peace descended. Then the disturbances began again. This time crockery was flung about and shattered, wide areas of the walls were smeared with glue, and several of the paintings were ripped to shreds.

Toward the end of 1970 the most peculiar of all the incidents occurred. They followed an attempt at exorcism by a Dublin priest.

At this time Mr. and Mrs. O'Brien were still making improvements to the premises, and had not yet installed a refrigerator. Consequently the milkman made use of a natural "icebox" in the form of a cool stream that runs through the grounds. He left the milk bottles standing in its shallow water. One morning when Mrs. O'Brien went to the stream to get a bottle, she found that the foil caps of all the bottles had been removed, though the milk

Psychic Antics at Killakee Center

Left: the House of Bewlay, a tobacco shop in Chester, England, the scene of poltergeist activity for several years from 1968 on. Wailing and stamping sounds broke out in the shop, terrifying the staff. Doors opened and shut themselves. A secure picture crashed to the floor, and the screw on which it had hung was found cut in two. Bolts popped out of an oak door. The poltergeist activity would reach its peak in August.

Left: an **SPR** researcher fixed a mechanical vibrator to the wall of a house due to be demolished, to test the theory that poltergeist effects are caused by tremors in the earth, underground tidal movements, or other natural phenomena. The device produced violent vibrations, bringing the house to the verge of collapse, but it did not produce any typical poltergeist effects such as flying furniture.

Below: the psychical researcher Harry Price, a clergyman, Mrs. Rhodes (right), and others await developments in a room of Mrs. Rhodes' home near Crawley, England, which was the scene of heavy poltergeist activity around the end of World War II. At the invitation of Mrs. Rhodes, who lived with her 12-year-old grandson Alan, Price conducted an investigation of the phenomena along with a reporter and a photographer.

inside was undisturbed. This continued for several days.

At first the O'Briens assumed that birds were pecking off the tops, although no trace of foil was ever found. To stop the nuisance Mr. O'Brien built a four-sided box of heavy stone on the stream bed, covered it with a massive slab of slate, and instructed the milkman to place the bottles in the box and replace the slate lid. Still the caps disappeared.

As if in compensation, though, other kinds of caps began to appear inside the house. In view of the various disturbances, the O'Briens naturally enough made a practice of locking all doors and windows before retiring for the night. Despite this, caps and hats began to appear all over the house. There were Derby hats

and opera hats, children's knitted hats with woolly pom poms on top, and men's and women's straw sun hats. The pride of the collection was a lady's linen cap with drawstrings which was identified as 19th-century in style, although it appeared new.

This peculiar activity ceased suddenly at the end of 1970, and although occasional knockings and footsteps are still reported, Killakee Arts Center has settled down to a relatively quiet life. It was investigated at the height of its activity, but only in a limited way in the course of preparing a television program on the strange occurrences. It seems a pity that no thorough scientific investigation was conducted at Killakee, for it certainly ranks among the most fascinating poltergeist mysteries.

An Investigation by Harry Price

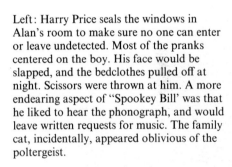

Left: Harry Price seals the windows in Alan's room to make sure no one can enter or leave undetected. Most of the pranks centered on the boy. His face would be slapped, and the bedclothes pulled off at night. Scissors were thrown at him. A more endearing aspect of "Spookey Bill" was that he liked to hear the phonograph, and would leave written requests for music. The family cat, incidentally, appeared oblivious of the poltergeist.

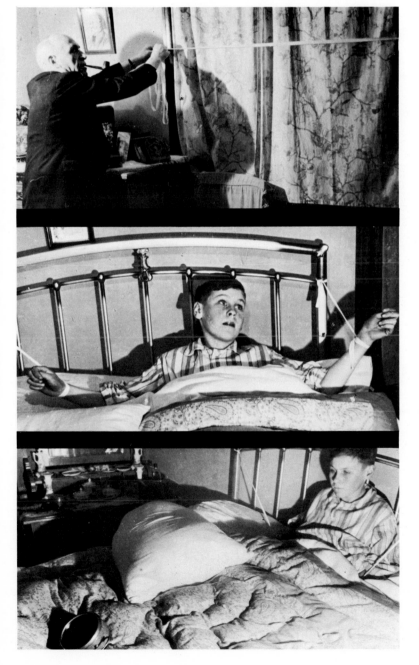

Left: Alan lies in bed with his wrists tied to the bed rails with lengths of tape. He can move each hand about 18 inches, and the bed is near the door so that he can knock to alert those waiting outside as soon as anything happens. Poltergeists, according to Price, tend not to perform when people— other than the victim—are watching, but are not reluctant to give proof of their presence.

Left: an alarm clock lies on the bed— apparently thrown there by the poltergeist. This is one of several effects produced on the night of the investigation. Shortly after this happened, a trinket case from the dressing table was discovered on the bed. The case was not locked, and would have been difficult for the boy to move onto the bed using his feet, assuming that this were possible, without spilling its contents.

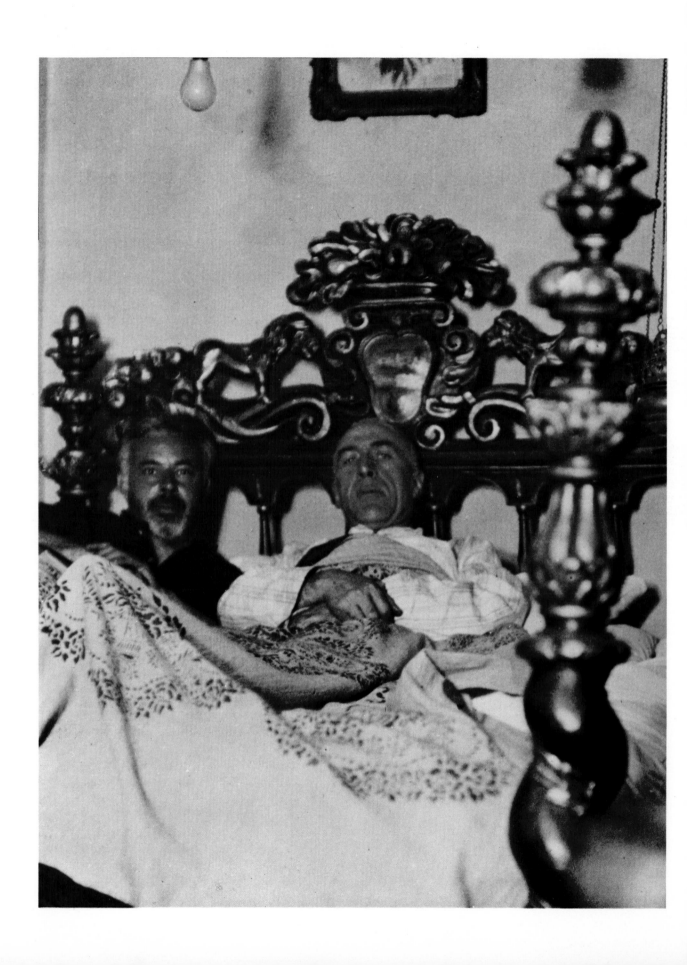

Chapter 7
Enter the Ghost-hunters

Ghost stories have been told around fires for hundreds of years, and skeptics have listened to the tales and determined to investigate the truth for themselves. Is it possible to study ghosts scientifically? How do the ghost hunters do their work, and what is their standard of evidence? What sort of phenomena are they trying to record? As well as the scientific investigators, there are those who are willing to try to expel the troublesome spirits, to exorcise them—to bring peace to the unfortunate people who are haunted, and presumably to the unquiet spirit as well. Are they successful? How do they challenge the mysterious presences?

Just before Christmas in 1323, strange stories began to circulate in and around the town of Alais in southern France. A merchant named Guy de Torno had recently died, and had returned to haunt his widow in the form of a disembodied voice. News of the haunting spread quickly, and within a few days it reached the ears of Pope John XXII in Avignon, 40 miles away. (This was during the Great Schism, when there were two popes, one in Rome and one in Avignon.) The Pope decided to investigate. Fortunately he was able to call on the services of Brother John Goby, Prior of the Benedictine Abbey in that part of France, and reputed to be able to deal with psychic phenomena. Brother John was summoned to Avignon and directed by the Pope to conduct an investigation and submit a report. His report, which was later printed in the official *Annales ecclesiastici*, even today remains an impressive document in the history of psychical research.

Brother John lost no time in setting about his task. On Christmas Day, accompanied by three fellow Benedictines and about a hundred of the town's most respected citizens, he called upon the widow and began his investigation. First he made a thorough search of the house and gardens. Then he deployed his volunteer forces to stand guard around the premises to watch for unauthorized persons. Brother John, the three other Benedictines, and a "worthy and elderly woman" posted themselves in the bedroom. This was the room most frequented by the spirit, and

Opposite: an allegedly haunted 16th-century bed in a museum in West London is tested for supernatural effects by Harry Price (right) and Dr. C. E. M. Joad, formerly head of the Department of Philosophy and Psychology, Birkbeck College, University of London. The test took place on the night of September 15, 1932, and according to Dr. Joad, the only activity was an altercation among three newspaper photographers as to who had exclusive rights to take pictures. This picture was taken automatically, with no one else in the room. Toward morning, the ghost hunters noticed that the bell-cord above the bed was swinging—much to Price's gratification after an uneventful night—but they soon discovered that a railway line ran under the museum, and every time a train passed the cord moved.

Above: a 6th-century Roman pyx—a vessel in which the Sacrament is carried. One of these was carried by Brother John Goby in his investigation of the ghost of Alais, and the ghost detected its presence under the Prior's robes. In an age when the Church suspected all supernormal entities of being sent by the Devil, Brother John approached the case with remarkable cool-headedness. His report to Pope John XXII is a classic in the history of psychical research.

the bed was the usual focus of the attention. The widow lay down on the bed, and the elderly woman lay beside her to watch for possible trickery. Apparently with a view to protecting the ladies against malice from the spirit world, the four Benedictines sat on the edge of this ample bed.

Then the watch began. The monks recited the Office for the Dead in the hushed room, and soon they became aware of a sweeping sound overhead like the brushing of a stiff broom. As the noise approached the bed, the wife cried out in terror. A monk asked her to ask the ghost if it really was that of her husband. A thin voice assured them: "Yes, I am he."

At this point some of the men posted outside the bedchamber were overcome with curiosity and excitedly rushed into the room. Eventually Brother John restored order and arranged the men in a circle around the bed. Then he resumed the questioning.

Addressed by each monk in turn, the spirit assured them that it was not an emissary of the Devil, the usual assumption in those days, but that it was the earth-bound ghost of Guy de Torno, condemned to haunt its former home because of the sins it had committed there. The spirit said that it had every hope of getting to Heaven once its period of purgatory was over. It added that the sin for which it was being punished was adultery. This last confession was triggered by the spirit's realization that Brother John had concealed in his robes a *pyx*—a silver box in which the Sacrament is carried. Adultery was considered a grave sin in medieval times, and those guilty of it were forbidden to attend Mass. The presence of the Host in the room—a fact known only to Brother John—presumably stung the spirit's conscience. After disclosing this information, the spirit emitted a long-drawn-out sigh and departed. Shortly afterward Brother John and his retinue left, and soon his report was dispatched to Avignon.

This investigation retains its interest because of the efficiency with which it was conducted. Unlike many early investigators of alleged psychic activity, particularly the hunters of the witch, werewolf, and vampire, Brother John apparently did not set out with the assumption that the thing was necessarily supernatural. His search of the premises and posting of guards shows that he considered the possibility of the voice being that of a living person. He covered himself against possible accusations of trickery by involving a large number of the town's most worthy citizens, some of whom were in the room during most of the time. Fortunately Brother John was under no orders to do anything about the ghost, so he could approach the phenomenon with a relatively objective attitude.

A significant aspect of the case was the spirit's discovery of the pyx carried by Brother John. Although the presence of the Host was almost obligatory at such investigations as a protection against any evil spirits that might be present, he had told no one that he was carrying it. Conceivably one of the other monks might have had it. Yet the ghost knew instantly where it was.

Of course the investigation left several questions unanswered. The sighing noises seem less remarkable when one remembers that during the winter that part of France is almost continually swept by the mournful wind called the Mistral. The possibility that the widow could have created the voice by ventriloquism, consciously or unconsciously, is a reasonable theory—especially if she suspected her husband's infidelity and wanted revenge. Conscious trickery seems unlikely, however, for in those days to communicate with spirits was to invite suspicion of witchcraft and death at the stake. This potential risk, and the fact that the widow cooperated willingly with the investigation, suggests that she was innocent of any deliberate fraud. Yet the annals of modern psychical research are full of cases in which the apparent victims of poltergeists and other psychic disturbances have themselves unconsciously caused the phenomena. In 1323, however, such a possibility was inconceivable, whereas spirits of the dead were not only conceivable but also accepted as real.

Brother John Against the Voice

Left: amateur ghost hunters flock to the Ferry Boat Inn in England's Fen Country on March 17, the night when the ghost of a girl who hanged herself for unrequited love some 900 years ago is supposed to rise from her gravestone, embedded in the pub's floor, and drift down toward the river. The tradition endures, despite the fact that no one living has ever seen the ghost of the unfortunate girl.

Ghost Hunters Become Scientific

Right: a Spiritualist seance as depicted in a turn-of-the-century lithograph. The medium shown at left, is in a trance, and the materialized spirit looms up beside him. While most present-day ghost hunters regard neither apparitions nor poltergeists as spirits of the dead, some do believe spirits are behind these effects, and try to make contact with them. They may employ a medium to discover the reason for the haunting and help to set the spirit free of its haunt.

A weak point of the investigation is that it was concluded quickly. There seems to have been no follow-up to the first encounter with the alleged spirit, nor any private interviews with the servants to get independent verification of the haunting or of the events in the household while the master was alive.

Even so, Brother John's report is remarkable for its lucid and unbiased presentation of the events as experienced by his team of investigators. Certainly many years were to pass before psychic research would surpass the methods of Brother John.

Probably the best-known of all ghost hunters was Harry Price. During his 40 years of psychical research up to his death in 1948, this tireless investigator laid many ghost stories to rest, and brought others to front-page prominence. Using ingenious apparatus, some of his own design, he exposed many a fraudulent medium. But he also discovered and publicized the apparently genuine talents of others. He founded the National Laboratory of Psychical Research, now part of the University of London, and he wrote extensively on his ventures into the world of psychic phenomena.

He was a skilled engineer and devised various pieces of apparatus and methods of ruling out natural causes in an investigation. An account of how such techniques are used today is given by Peter Underwood, President and Chairman of the British Ghost Club, in his book *Haunted London*.

He recounts that Reverend and Mrs. R. W. Hardy, a Canadian couple on vacation in London during 1966, had paid a visit to the historic Queen's House at Greenwich, built for the wife of King Charles I. While there, Reverend Hardy had taken a photograph of the elegant Tulip staircase. On his return to Canada he had the film developed, and to his amazement saw a shrouded but distinct figure standing on the staircase, its hands clutching the railing.

When the Ghost Club heard of the affair they immediately began a thorough investigation of the story and photograph. The picture was submitted to Kodak, whose experts testified that no manipulation of the actual film could have occurred. Officials at the Queen's House corroborated the Hardys' statement that no one could have been on the staircase, which is closed to the public and roped off from the hall.

Arrangements were then made for members of the Society to spend a night in the hall of the Queen's House, joined by the senior museum photographer and two attendants. The official photographer took photographs at intervals throughout the night, all of which had no ghostly figure when developed. At the same time, a movie camera equipped with special filters and infrared film ran continuously, as did a tape recorder. Thermometers were watched to detect any unusual temperature change. Delicate instruments were set to show drafts and vibrations, and the stair rail was coated with petroleum jelly and later checked for fingerprints. Investigators were stationed on the staircase.

Despite all this scientific procedure—plus attempted seances— nothing much came of the night's work, although members of the team reported hearing some sounds that were "never satisfactorily explained." The time factor might be significant, for some haunting apparitions occur only at certain times. The figure in the Hardys' photo may have appeared only in the daytime.

This case is an excellent illustration of a major problem facing any ghost hunter: the ghost often fails to appear. More often than not, the investigator's contribution will consist of discovering a natural cause for the phenomenon. In his book *Ghost Hunting*, Andrew Green describes a case of a mysterious "whistling moan" in a forest clearing which campers attributed to a ghost. Near the camp site was a small dip in the ground filled with junk, and just beyond this point the land sloped down into a valley. A professional ghost hunter arriving on the scene first checked the times at which the sound was heard, then determined the wind strength and direction at a local meteorological office. He soon was able to establish that the moaning sound was created by wind blowing up from the valley into the rubbish pit

Above: Harry Price, British psychical researcher, died in 1948. A controversial figure who loved publicity, Price conducted the most famous ghost hunt of modern times, the investigation of Borley Rectory in Suffolk, England.

"Must Work as a Detective Does"

Right: Harry Price's ghost-hunting kit. Among the items included in the kit were: movie and still cameras, steel measuring tape, drawing materials, a flashlight, a portable telephone for communicating with an assistant, and first-aid supplies including a flask of brandy in case anyone fainted.

Above: British ghost hunter L. Sewell explores a tunnel which he and his team discovered in 1955 at Borley Rectory. This house, described by Price as "the most haunted house in England," was the subject of several intensive investigations. The tunnel, built of 16-century bricks, was believed to have been the escape route used by a nun and her lover, according to legend, to elope. It was the nun whose ghost was said to haunt the Rectory. The discovery of the tunnel, however, only indicated that the Rectory stood on the site of an earlier building, which might possibly have been a convent.

and through a couple of old metal cylinders—the same principle that operates a pipe organ. When the cylinders were turned sideways, across the direction of the wind, the moaning stopped.

Ghostlike noises in old houses often turn out to be no more than creaking timbers, a draft in a closed-off passage, or simply mice. The serious ghost hunter must make a thorough search of the premises, measuring the thickness of walls and tapping them to see if they are hollow, taping doors shut and stringing thread across a passage to determine whether a phantom that walks there might be a living person, and keeping his eyes open for optical illusions and any other peculiar visual or aural effects that might create an impression of ghostly activity.

He must also be a clever and tactful interviewer, collecting various people's accounts of the phenomena and comparing these accounts to see where they agree and differ. In short, he must work as a detective does. Then he must face the possibility that even after he has eliminated all conceivable natural causes, the phantom, or voice, or poltergeist may refuse to come forward.

Left: an independent psychical researcher, Benson Herbert, in his laboratory. He has made machines to detect psychic energy, the stuff of which ghosts may be made.

At this point, the investigator must have plenty of patience, returning to the scene or remaining there until the phenomena do occur, or until it seems likely that they have ceased.

Some ghost hunters use a more active approach. Operating on the assumption that if a haunting is genuine it may be caused by a surviving spirit, they attempt to make contact with the spirit. One ghost hunter uses a medium and a tape recorder. The medium, who is not told in advance the history of the haunting, is taken to the site, goes into a trance, and contacts the supposed ghost. The medium attempts to find out from it the circumstances that cause it to haunt the place. Sometimes this requires a number of seances. Apparently the process of communicating with sympathetic humans often serves to free the spirit from its haunt.

Occasionally, a ghost has apparently been driven from its haunt by the rite of exorcism. The main purpose of exorcism has traditionally been to cast out evil, although churchmen today recognize the fact that people who claim to be possessed by a demon are usually mentally ill and in need of psychiatry rather than exorcism. A ritual to exorcise a place troubled by poltergeist activity was provided in the 17th century by Pope Urban VIII, and some clergymen today will perform an exorcism to free a place from a haunting ghost. They admit the possibility—denied by most psychical researchers—that an apparition of a dead person in some way contains or represents the surviving spirit of that person and thus can be dealt with by spiritual force.

One English clergyman who has performed hundreds of exorcisms is the Reverend J. C. Neil-Smith of Hampstead, a fashionable part of London. Among his more bizarre cases was that of the haunted *au pair* girls (young girls, usually foreign, who live with a family as both nursemaid and housemaid). A family living in a large 19th-century mansion had had a run of bad luck with au pair girls. Three girls in succession had taken on the job, only to leave within a few days muttering unintelligible excuses. Finally one of them explained that a ghost had attacked her in the night, and in a mood of mingled amusement and exasperation, the householder called in Reverend Neil-Smith.

"I went up there about midnight one night," said Reverend

Ghost Hunter as Ghost

One night in early spring 1948, a young Swedish man awoke to find a white-haired gentleman standing at his bedside. For some reason the young man, whom we'll call Erson—wasn't frightened. The stranger began to talk in a language Erson couldn't understand, but thought must be English. He managed to convey the information that his name was Price.

The mysterious Price began to appear fairly frequently, at times in the morning, and he was seen not only by Erson but also by his wife and daughter. The figure appeared solid and lifelike, but when Erson tried to photograph it, he only got a few shadows on the prints. Price seemed amused by these efforts to photograph him.

Finally Erson acquired enough English to understand that his visitor had studied ghosts and related subjects when alive. It was "Price" who urged Erson to go to a particular hospital in Lund to take treatment for a health problem. While there, Erson told a psychiatrist of his ghostly visitor. The doctor, having heard of the famous English psychical researcher Harry Price, decided to find out from the SPR when he had died. It was March 29, 1948—just about the time that Erson's spectral friend had made his first appearance.

The Haunting of the Toby Jug

The Toby Jug restaurant in the Yorkshire village of Haworth can boast of a specter of some distinction: poet and novelist Emily Bronte (above in a portrait by her brother), a native of the village. According to the restaurant's owner Keith Ackroyd, Emily Bronte's ghost appears every year on December 19, the day she died. He once described for a reporter his first glimpse of the phantom in 1966 after taking over the Toby Jug. "I turned and saw this figure smiling and giggling," he said. "She walked across the room to where the stairs used to be and started to climb up to the bedroom." She was small, wore a crinoline and carried a wicker basket.

The ghost of such a famous writer might be considered an asset, but Ackroyd wanted to have it exorcized. He planned to sell the restaurant and feared that a specter might be regarded as a liability. A curate from Leeds agreed to perform the rite, but was prevented by the Rector of Haworth who wasn't sure it was necessary. Perhaps, like many churchmen today, he takes a wary view of highly publicized exorcisms.

Neil-Smith, "and entered the bedsitter [combined livingroom-bedroom] in the basement of the house which was used by the au pairs and had always been servants' quarters. After saying a few opening prayers, I saw the figure of a young girl in Victorian costume—three people with me also either saw or felt her presence. I asked her what she wanted, and it turned out that she had been a lesbian and was attacking the au pairs in the night. I prayed that she would find rest, and then exorcised the building. There was no further trouble after that."

Mrs. Mary Sharman of Leeds, Yorkshire, did not find it so easy to get rid of the ghostly phenomena that tormented her and her family for nearly 12 years. The family's ordeal, reported in the *Yorkshire Evening Post* in June 1974, began in 1962 about a year after they had moved into a house in a public housing development. Mary Sharman, who had six young children, was separated from her first husband.

One night she saw the door of the toilet open. A moment later, she said, "a head poked out from the toilet door. Then an elderly woman came out and stood in front of me. She had white hair with tight curls, her head was on one side, one eye was opened and she was giving me a funny sort of smile. Then she shook her stick at me—a white stick."

The following morning Mrs. Sharman told some of the neighbors what she had seen. "That's old Mrs. Napier," they said. Mrs. Napier, who had been totally blind, had lived in the house on her own before the family moved in. She had been found dead in the lavatory.

After the first manifestation of Mrs. Napier came the poltergeist activity. Mary Sharman and her children watched in awe as ornaments moved back and forth on the mantelpiece, and doors opened and shut by themselves. Sometimes they would hear the sound of dragging footsteps on the stairs. The specter of Mrs. Napier would appear occasionally.

"The children's mattresses were lifted up in the night and the blankets thrown in a heap on the floor," Mary Sharman told the *Evening Post*. "I thought I was going insane . . . The children and myself would not go upstairs at night and slept in a front downstairs room together. Every night we barricaded the room door with a sideboard and chairs."

Finally Mrs. Sharman, a Catholic, went to her local church and told the parish priest. The priest performed a "blessing" ceremony—a shortened form of exorcism. He went into each room blessing it and sprinkling holy water.

Despite the blessing ceremony, the disturbances continued. Most of them were typical poltergeist pranks: coats were thrown around the entrance hall during the night; a roll of linoleum was found unrolled in the morning. But one night something frightening happened.

The children, who were now sleeping upstairs in one room, had formed the habit of singing themselves to sleep. On this particular evening, Mary Sharman suddenly heard the singing stop abruptly. She and her brothers, who were visiting her, rushed upstairs and into the room. They found her son Michael, aged 12, floating about six feet above his bed while the other children stared at him terrified. Michael's eyes were open, but he was in a

Family under Psychic Attack

Left: photograph of the staircase at the Queen's House, Greenwich, taken by Reverend R. W. Hardy, showing a shrouded phantom.

state of deep shock. One of Mrs. Sharman's brothers pulled the boy down and tried to comfort him.

Mary Sharman called the police and an ambulance, and Michael was taken to the hospital. The police stayed a while to restore calm, but one of them left after a short time, saying that he couldn't stand the eerie atmosphere any longer.

After being treated for shock, Michael was sent home from the hospital the following morning. Apparently, however, the levitation had left a permanent mark on him. Ever since that night he has spoken with a stammer.

When Mrs. Sharman consulted the family doctor about the disturbances, he contacted some people he knew who had experience in psychical research. The three investigators spent three nights in the house. Their conclusions are not on record, but by the third morning they had apparently decided that the best course was to move the family elsewhere.

Not surprisingly—considering that poltergeists tend to be associated with people rather than places—the family's troubles went with them. Footsteps continued to be heard and mattresses lifted off the beds. After a while the family began to be haunted by another phantom, that of Mary Sharman's mother, who had recently died. This apparition did not disturb the family, but the poltergeist activity, continuing for years, had its effect on their nerves. At one point Mrs. Sharman called in

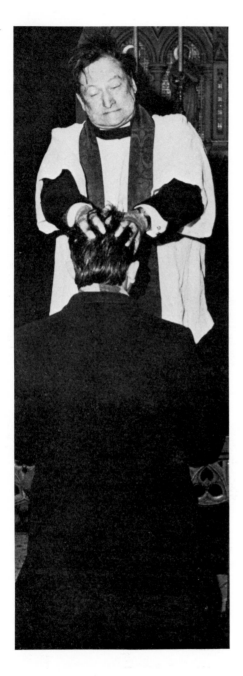

another priest. He stayed only a few minutes and then left, saying, "This is evil."

Whatever this "evil" thing was, it apparently relinquished its hold on the family after they moved to another home early in 1974. Mrs. Sharman, now remarried, told the *Evening Post* reporter that there had been "no happenings" of a poltergeist type in the new house.

The variety of phenomena experienced by Mary Sharman and her family, and the various approaches they used in trying to deal with those phenomena illustrate the complexity of the ghost problem. If the case had been thoroughly investigated, it is possible that several distinct explanations would have been required to account for its different aspects. The family assumed that the poltergeist activity was caused by the spirit of Mrs.

Exorcism, an ancient rite for casting out devils, is frequently used today on disturbed persons who believe they have been possessed by an evil force. It is also occasionally used to free a house or other building of a haunting ghost.
Above: Reverend J. C. Neil-Smith of London performing an exorcism.

Right: the English clairvoyant and exorcist Donald Page frees a woman from the spirit believed to be possessing her. His contorted face reflects the struggle that is taking place.

Exorcism: to Cast Devils Out

Left: Page comforts a woman after freeing her house of a ghost that haunted it for 18 years. The apparition, called "Joe," apparently produced poltergeist phenomena as well as appearing from time to time. Page performed the exorcism with Canon John Pearie-Higgins of Southwark Cathedral, London.

Napier, but few psychical researchers would find this plausible. The presence in the house of several pubescent children would seem a more likely cause for the poltergeist. The fact that the poltergeist followed them to another home, unconnected with Mrs. Napier, further supports this assumption. The other phenomena—the apparitions of Mrs. Napier and of the grandmother—may have been generated in some way by the family themselves. However, it is also possible that the phantom of Mrs. Napier had some objective reality, for she was readily identified by the neighbors from Mary Sharman's description. The terror of the second priest in the presence of something he experienced as "evil" suggests, on the face of it, that some supernatural being had attached itself to the family. Alternatively, it might suggest that suppressed conflicts within the family had generated some negative force to which the priest was hypersensitive. There is also the possibility that the priest's reaction was entirely subjective, created by his own fears.

The ghost hunter must bear many such possibilities in mind when investigating a haunting. If he is skeptical, he will find plenty of evidence to support the assumption that apparitions are all "in the mind," or even that poltergeist effects are caused by earth tremors. Sometimes, however, he may discover a case in which other factors appear to be involved. Similarly, the investigator who is inclined to believe in surviving spirits will find evidence indicating that people occasionally create their own phantoms and poltergeists. Any haunting is a complex phenomenon. Taken together, all the hauntings and apparitions on record constitute one of the most baffling mysteries science has ever attempted to solve.

Chapter 8
Toward an Explanation

Is there a rational explanation for the ghosts and apparitions whose strange behavior has been persistently reported over the centuries? Can there be a simple, wholly natural cause which can account for this range of phenomena? Is it possible that spirits from beyond the grave can return to avenge wrongs or to remain close to places significant in their earthly existence—or are these presences solely the result of human imagination? And if, as skeptics claim, gullibility accounts for ghosts, how can we explain the strange behavior of animals, frightened by the unseen? Can we explain away ghosts, or do they remain a tantalizing spine-prickling mystery?

What is really going on when a person sees an apparition? When several people at the same time see the same apparition? When the same apparition is seen again and again in the same place by different people? When an apparition is reflected in a mirror? When photographic film registers an apparition not seen by the person who took the picture? When a person is touched by a hand he cannot touch himself?

These and numerous other questions have been raised again and again in the hundred years or so since serious psychical research got underway, and we are still far from having a satisfactory answer that will cover all of them. Instead we have several answers, each with certain limitations. We are a lot nearer to understanding the nature of apparitions than we were a century ago, but we are still a long way from understanding them completely.

Before picking up the thorny question of ghosts as possible evidence of life after death, let's consider what happens when we see an apparition of a living person. Evidence gathered in the Census of Hallucinations, taken by the SPR in 1889, indicated that in most cases the person whose apparition appeared was at that time undergoing some crisis, such as a severe illness, an accident, or death. The correlation between the crisis and the apparition in so many cases led the researchers to conclude that the apparition was telepathic. That is, the person undergoing the crisis was thinking about the percipient in such a way as to

Opposite: travelers who climbed to the top of the Brocken, highest peak in the Harz Mountains of central Germany, often returned with tales of gigantic specters haunting its peak. The mountain has for centuries been linked with magical rites and villagers believed it was guarded by the ghostly "King of the Brocken." Around the end of the 18th century a climber discovered the true identity of the specter: his own shadow, projected onto the low-hanging clouds by the sun. Atmospheric conditions so provided what people expected to see.

Perceiving in Different Ways

generate a kind of telepathic message that took the form of a picture of himself.

How telepathic information is communicated is still a mystery, and a telepathic picture is certainly the most mysterious of such communications, particularly when the image appears as a solid, living person. Those of us who have never seen an apparition tend to assume that no one can see anything that is not actually physically present in space. But seeing is much more complex than we normally suppose. We often see things vividly in our dreams, even though we're receiving no visual information through our eyes. While awake, most people can readily see in their mind's eye anything they choose to see, mentally superimposed on what their eyes are looking at at that moment.

The peculiarities of perception are well illustrated in the case of

Right: another impression of the "specter" of the Brocken created by the man standing at lower left with his arms raised. In order for it to appear the sun must be low in the sky and on the opposite side to the clouds. Similar ghostly illusions have been seen on other mountaintops, including those in the north of England.

hypnosis. Experiments have shown that if a highly suggestible person in a hypnotic trance is told that on awakening he will see only the hypnotist—even though there are other people in the room—he will, on awakening, be unable to see those other people until the hypnotist removes the suggestion.

The hypnotist can tell a subject what he will see and what he won't see. Astonishing as such cases may be, they are not quite as remarkable as the case of a person *spontaneously* seeing the image of someone else, as lifelike as if he were there in the flesh. It seems incredible that the agent, or person sending the telepathic hallucination, should be able to achieve at a distance—and in many cases while he is unconscious—what the hypnotist achieves by giving his subject explicit instructions.

The evidence suggests, however, that the agent's mind plays a smaller part in creating the apparition than does the mind of the percipient. This conclusion becomes obvious when we look at details of reported crisis apparitions. Rarely does the figure manifest itself in the agent's form as it is at the moment of crisis— lying on his or her deathbed, for example, or mangled in an auto accident, or falling into a river. Almost always the apparition appears detached from its surroundings at that time. Instead it enters the percipient's surroundings—with which the agent may not even be familiar—and relates to these surroundings just as the agent would if there in the flesh.

In his book *Apparitions*, G. N. M. Tyrrell devotes considerable attention to the ways in which apparitions behave like material persons. For example, he cites cases in which an apparition standing in front of a lamp has cast a shadow. An apparition may also enter a room by apparently opening a door which is later found to be locked. In some cases an apparition has been reflected in a mirror. Apparitions, says Tyrrell, "adapt themselves almost miraculously to the physical conditions of the percipient's surroundings, of which the agent as a rule can know little or nothing. These facts reveal the apparition to be a piece of stage-

Below left: Pepper's Ghost, an ingenious theatrical stunt devised by Professor John Henry Pepper in England in 1863. The white phantom onstage at left is not there at all, but appears to be standing in that spot from the point of view of the audience, at right. The actor stands under the stage out of sight of the audience, and his brightly lit reflection, projected onto the angled glass, creates the illusion of a figure standing some distance behind it.

Below: a French playbill of the 19th century advertising the play *The Specters and the Devil's Manor House*, and illustrating some of the theatrical tricks used to produce phantoms in that day.

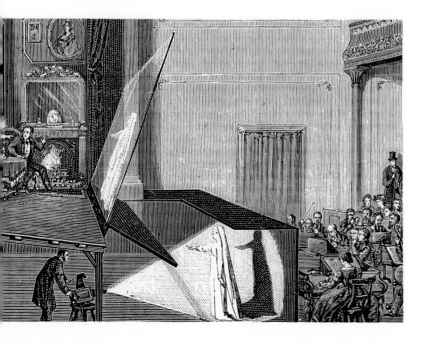

machinery which the percipient must have a large hand in creating and some of the details for which he must supply—that is to say, an apparition cannot be merely a direct expression of the agent's *idea*; it must be a drama worked out with that idea as its *motif*."

In other words, some part of the agent's mind telepathically transmits an idea of himself to the percipient, and some level of the percipient's mind is then stimulated to produce not merely a recognizable image of the agent, but an image that behaves in a lifelike natural way. It is natural for a real human to be reflected in a mirror; consequently that part of the percipient's mind that helps to create the apparition—Tyrrell calls this the "stage carpenter"—produces a figure that is reflected in a mirror.

Such fidelity to natural laws is not a feature of all apparitions. Tyrrell mentions a case in which an apparition close to a mirror did not have a reflection. Another case collected by the SPR illustrates the unrealistic features of some of these apparitional dramas. One day about a hundred years ago, an English clergyman, Canon Bourne, went out fox hunting with his two daughters. After a time the daughters decided to return home with their coachman while their father continued hunting, but they were delayed for several minutes when a friend rode up to talk to them. "As we were turning to go home," reported Louisa Bourne in an account confirmed by her sister, "we distinctly saw my father, waving his hat to us and signing us to follow him. He was on the side of a small hill, and there was a dip between him and us. My sister, the coachman, and myself all recognized my father, and also the horse [the only white horse in the field that day]. The horse looked so dirty and shaken that the coachman remarked he thought there had been a nasty accident. As my father waved his hat I clearly saw the Lincoln and Bennett [hatter's] mark inside, though from the distance we were apart it ought to have been utterly impossible for me to have seen it . . ."

The girls and the coachman quickly rode toward Canon Bourne, losing sight of him as they rode into the dip in the terrain. When they emerged from the dip and approached the place where he had been, he was nowhere to be seen. After riding around looking for him, they finally went home. Later Canon Bourne—who arrived home shortly after them—told them that he had not even been near the place they had seen him.

One peculiarity of this case, apart from the odd feature of the clarity of the hatter's mark, is that no crisis occurred. Canon Bourne suffered no accident, as his daughters and the coachman feared, nor, apparently, did he even narrowly escape having one —which might have triggered an unconscious telepathic call for help. There is a slim possibility that the hallucination was a subjective one, created by the percipients themselves, who may have had some fear that he might have met with an accident.

The trouble with this hypothesis is that the apparition of Canon Bourne was *collective*—that is, it was seen by more than one person at the same time. According to Tyrrell, "those hallucinations which we have best reason to regard as purely subjective are never collective; so that collectivity would seem to be a sign that the case is in one way or another telepathic."

Collective apparitions present problems. A great many have

Above: the apparition of a murdered man appears at the trial of the man accused of his murder. None of the live witnesses in this trial, held in London in 1738, had produced sufficient evidence to convict the accused. Suddenly he cried out that he could see the dead man ready to give evidence against him, and he confessed to the crime. On the face of it, this would seem a subjective hallucination caused by guilt, but it could have been telepathic.

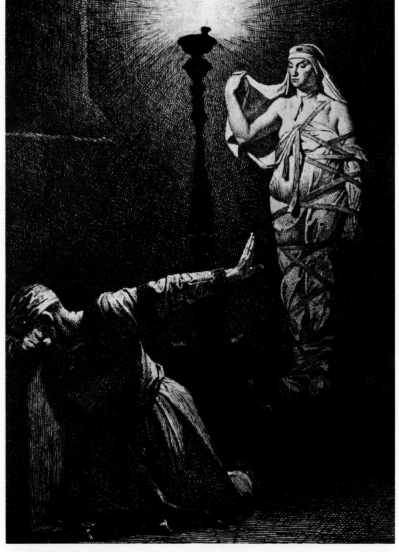

A Phantom Seen Collectively

Left: the apparition of Mariamne, one of King Herod's wives, confronts the king, who in a jealous rage over her supposed infidelity had her put to death along with several members of her family. When an apparition is of a person who has been dead for some time and is seen by only one person, psychical researchers tend to regard it as a subjective hallucination—particularly when the percipient has a strong reason—guilt in King Herod's case—for seeing it.

been reported; 130 had been collected by the SPR by 1943 when Tyrrell published *Apparitions*. It's unlikely that all of these can be dismissed as cases of one percipient verbally persuading others that they see what he sees. On the other hand it also seems unlikely that the agent could convey exactly the same image of himself to several people at the same time. (We are still assuming that the apparition is wholly mental, that it does not exist in the space where it appears to exist.) Tyrrell believes that in collective cases there is a principal percipient who receives the apparition telepathically from the agent, and at the same time telepathically and involuntarily conveys this visual information to the other people present. Of course, not all people are capable of perceiving apparitions, and so in some cases an apparition may be seen by several people at once while someone else nearby sees nothing.

One of the best-known cases of collective apparitions in the history of psychical research is that of Captain Towns of Sydney, Australia. The incident occurred in the Towns' residence in the late 19th century, about six weeks after Captain Towns died, and was reported to the SPR by Charles Lett, the son-in-law of the

"Post-Mortem" Apparition

deceased man. One evening about nine o'clock, Mrs. Lett entered one of the rooms, along with a Miss Berthon. The gaslight was burning. "They were amazed to see, reflected as it were on the polished surface of the wardrobe, the image of Captain Towns. It was . . . like an ordinary medallion portrait, but life-size. The face appeared wan and pale . . . and he wore a kind of gray flannel jacket, in which he had been accustomed to sleep. Surprised and half alarmed at what they saw, their first idea was that a portrait had been hung in the room, and that what they saw was its reflection—but there was no picture of the kind. Whilst they were looking and wondering, my wife's sister, Miss Towns, came into the room and before any of the others had time to speak she exclaimed, 'Good gracious! Do you see papa!'"

One of the housemaids passing by was called into the room. Immediately she cried, "Oh Miss! The master!" The Captain's own servant, the butler, and the nurse were also called in and also immediately recognized him. "Finally Mrs. Towns was sent for, and, seeing the apparition, she advanced toward it with her arm extended as if to touch it, and as she passed her hand over the panel of the wardrobe the figure gradually faded away, and never again appeared." Lett adds that he was in the house at the time, but did not hear when he was called and so did not see the

Right: Edmund Gurney, an SPR founder, authority on hypnotism, and one of the co-authors of *Phantasms of the Living*, published in 1886 two years before he died.

apparition himself.

We can account for the collectivity of this apparition with the theory that a principal percipient—either Mrs. Lett or Miss Berthon—passed it along to the others. But the question then remains: Who was the original source of the apparition?

Here we arrive at a central problem facing the skeptical psychical researcher: many apparitions are of people who have been dead for some time. These are called "post-mortem" apparitions. A scientifically inclined researcher, reluctant to assume the existence of life after death, finds it difficult to account for such cases. Myers, Gurney, and Podmore, the authors of *Phantasms of the Living*, came to the conclusion after studying hundreds of cases that an apparition seen up to 12 hours after the person's death could be counted a crisis apparition sent by a living but moribund person. They reasoned that the percipient might not see the apparition at the moment it was transmitted. He might be busy or preoccupied at the exact time the agent sent the message, so that its visualization was delayed until a moment when the percipient's mind was relaxed and more receptive.

In addition, as Lyall Watson has shown in his book *The Romeo Error*, death is not as clear-cut as we commonly assume. If by "death" we mean the complete cessation of biologic activity in the whole body, its exact moment of occurrence is impossible to pinpoint, for many bodily processes continue after the heart has stopped. Conceivably, that part of the brain that sends telepathic impulses might continue to function for some time after a person is pronounced clinically dead.

Thus we do not have to believe in life after death in order to account for an apparition of a person who has been dead for several hours. Deferred telepathy might explain it—or temporarily continuing brain activity. Still we are left with a great many apparitions of people who have been dead for days, weeks—as in the case of Captain Towns—and even years. Some of these can be explained as subjective hallucinations. In other cases, however, the person seen is not known to the percipient but is later identified as an actual person. In such cases it is virtually impossible to claim that the percipient created the image all by himself with no external stimulus. The following case is a dramatic example of a post-mortem apparition of a person unknown to the percipient.

In 1964 in a Detroit automobile factory a motor fitter suddenly lurched out of the path of a giant body press, which had been accidentally activated during the lunch hour. Shaken but uninjured, the man told his co-workers that he had been thrust out of the way by a tall black man with a scarred face, dressed in grease-stained denims. He had never seen the man before, but some of the older workers recognized the description. In 1944 a tall black man with a scarred left cheek had been decapitated while working in the same area of the shop floor. He had been pressing out parts for bombers. A subsequent inquiry had revealed that although the dead man was skilled at his job and totally familiar with his machine, long periods of overtime had made him sleepy and incautious.

Telling of his miraculous escape, the motor fitter commented: "The colored guy was real enough to me. He had enormous

Above: F. W. H. Myers, one of the founders of the SPR and author of the book *Human Personality and its Survival of Bodily Death*. He suggested that a ghost may be "a manifestation of persistent personal energy" that may continue to appear after the person has died.

The Identifying Mark

Mr. F. G., a traveling salesman from Boston, had returned to his hotel room one afternoon. As he sat working he suddenly became aware of someone in the room. Glancing up he was astounded to see his sister, who had died nine years before. "I sprang forward in delight, calling her by name," he said, "and as I did so, the apparition instantly vanished . . . I was near enough to touch her, had it been a physical possibility . . . She appeared as if alive". Yet there was one noticeable change in her appearance: her right cheek bore a bright red scratch.

Disturbed by this experience, F.G. went to see his parents with the story. When he mentioned the scratch, his mother was overcome with emotion. She revealed that she had made the scratch accidentally while tending to her daughter's body. Two weeks after this, his mother died peacefully.

Psychical researcher F. W. H. Myers pointed out that the figure was not "the corpse with the dull mark on which the mother's regretful thoughts might dwell, but . . . the girl in health and happiness, with the symbolic *red* mark worn simply as a test of identity." He suggested that the vision was sent by the spirit of the girl to induce her brother to go home and see his mother.

Poltergeists or Psychokinesis?

Above: a portrait of Dame Elizabeth Hoby, who is said to haunt Bisham Priory, a Tudor manor. According to local legend, Dame Hoby caused the death of her son. One story says that in a fury over his inability to do his lessons, she boxed his ears so hard that it killed him; another version says that she locked him in a tiny room to finish the work, was called to London by Queen Elizabeth, and returned several days later to find him dead. Her ghost has been seen walking through the house, washing her hands in a bowl of water that floats in front of her. This symbolic act is a bit too picturesque for credibility and suggests that the image may be one of those projected by the percipient.

strength, and just pushed me out of the way like I was a featherweight. I never believed in spooks before, but if this was a spook I take my hat off to him."

One possible explanation is that one of the fitter's older coworkers, seeing him in danger, but perhaps too far away to pull him to safety or even to shout a warning, suddenly had a powerful subconscious image of the dead man which he telepathically transmitted to the endangered man. It is possible to convey the image of another person, although such cases are rare.

We must also consider the physical impact of the push. Hallucinations of touch occasionally accompany a visual hallucination. *Phantasms of the Living* and the *Proceedings* of the SPR include many such cases. For example, one account of an apparition written by the percipient to the person she had seen includes these words: ". . . someone touched my shoulder with such force that I immediately turned. You were there as plainly to be seen as if in the body . . ." Oddly, however, there are no cases of the percipient being able to touch the apparition (if we exclude the supposed materializations of Spiritualist seances). Either the figure moves just out of reach, or the percipient's hand passes right through it.

Following Tyrrell's theory that apparitions duplicate reality, short of becoming substantial, we can accept the possibility that a spectral hand placed on the percipient's shoulder will be felt by the percipient. This is simply the percipient's subconscious effort to create a realistic apparition.

In the case of the dead man pushing the auto worker out of danger we can't easily use this explanation. What the worker felt was not a mere touch but a strong push. Someone—either the man who died 20 years earlier or a living bystander—exerted psychokinetic force.

Psychokinesis, or PK as it is often called, is the movement of objects by mental energy. The existence of such a force has been tested and proven in laboratory experiments—notably at Dr. J. B. Rhine's Parapsychology Laboratory. Some gamblers have demonstrated the ability to will dice to fall in a certain way. Other tests have shown that some people can mentally influence the growth of plants or the behavior of single-celled organisms. Even animals have demonstrated powers of PK. Unconscious PK exerted by humans would seem to account for many cases of poltergeist activity. The fact that such disturbances usually, though not always, occur in the vicinity of an adolescent girl or boy suggests that there may be a connection between awakening sexual energy and PK.

The PK activity encountered in most poltergeist cases is capricious and sometimes destructive in character. A gentler kind of PK apparently caused some peculiar events in a bakery in England, described by Andrew Green in *Ghost Hunting*.

The bakery was purchased from a local family who had operated it for several generations. "Shortly after moving in, the wife of the new owner reported that she could 'feel the presence of someone in the bakery.' This phenomenon developed to a stage where doors were seen to open, baking equipment moved and the woman felt 'the entity push past her on numerous occasions.' Both her husband and son began to

Above: Bisham Priory, the haunted Tudor manor on the Thames River in Berkshire.

experience the haunting. Disturbed, they visited the former owners in an attempt to find out more about the ghost, but were assured that the premises were not haunted and never had been during the entire occupation of the original family.

"It was noticed, during the visit, that 'the old man' [one of the family that had formerly run the bakery] had said little during the conversation and 'seemed half asleep most of the time.'"

Green reports that the phenomena continued to disturb the new owners for about two years. "Suddenly, one Tuesday, 'the place seemed different.'" From that time onward there were no more incidents. On that particular Tuesday, the old man had died. The inference seems clear: having retired from the business, the old man had nothing to occupy his mind except thoughts of his former work. He would sit half-dozing, recollecting the activities that he had once performed every day: kneading the dough, cutting and shaping it, putting the loaves onto the trays, and sliding them into the oven. While yet alive, he was a haunting ghost.

Haunting ghosts often seem to be different in kind from apparitions that appear only once, and they are generally considered to be different by psychical researchers. An apparition may be seen in a place unknown to the agent, and almost

Apparition versus Haunting Ghost

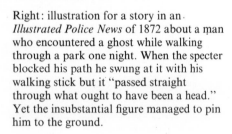

Right: illustration for a story in an *Illustrated Police News* of 1872 about a man who encountered a ghost while walking through a park one night. When the specter blocked his path he swung at it with his walking stick but it "passed straight through what ought to have been a head." Yet the insubstantial figure managed to pin him to the ground.

always appears to a person with whom the agent has some relationship. Often the apparition will seem to communicate with the percipient in some way—by a look, a touch, even speech. By contrast, a haunting ghost almost always seems unaware of the people around it. The place itself—and not any particular human—seems to attract the ghost.

Various theories have been advanced to explain the haunting type of ghost. One of these is the psychometric theory first proposed by Eleanor Sidgwick, an early member of the SPR and the wife of another well-known researcher, Henry Sidgwick. *Psychometry* is the ability shown by certain sensitive persons to receive psychic impressions of a person by touching or holding an object connected in some way with that person. It may be that people who are sensitive in this way can inadvertently psychometrize a building or locality simply by coming into contact with it, so that they will see, hear, or merely sense someone who has been closely associated with it in the past. The apparition would thus be an entirely subjective experience.

One argument against this theory is that almost all dwellings have been inhabited by several, and in some cases, hundreds of people. If a haunting depends on the psychometric abilities of the observer, and not on any action past or present of the persons seen, the observer should be able to see most or all of the people who lived in that place for any length of time. Instead of only seeing the unfortunate Lady L. who committed suicide in 1784, the person would see Lord L., their children, their servants, and scores of people who had lived in the house since that time. Occasionally groups of phantoms are seen—processions of chanting monks, spectral armies—but these are the exception to the rule. Most haunting ghosts haunt alone.

The evidence suggests that one's ability to see a phantom or sense a presence depends partly on some lingering aspect of the person seen or sensed. This possibility is supported by the reactions of animals in cases of haunting. Dr. Robert Morris, a psychologist, has reported various investigations of hauntings using animals. One investigator known to Dr. Morris examined a house in Kentucky containing an allegedly haunted room in which a tragedy had occurred. Instead of the usual team of human investigators, he used a dog, cat, rat, and rattlesnake.

The animals were brought into one of the haunted rooms one at a time. "The dog upon being taken about two or three feet into the room immediately snarled at its owner and backed out the door. No amount of cajoling could prevent the dog from struggling to get out and it refused to reenter. The cat was brought into the room carried in the owner's arms. When the cat got a similar distance into the room, it immediately leaped upon the owner's shoulders, dug in, then leaped to the ground, orienting itself toward a chair. It spent several minutes hissing

Below: a cartoon satirizing the credulity of Hammersmith residents. The ghost of Hammersmith, London, was actually a shoemaker who wanted to frighten his skeptical apprentices into believing in the afterlife. His graveyard appearances caused panic in the area. One woman died of a heart attack, and a bricklayer in a white smock was fatally shot by an overzealous ghost hunter with a shotgun.

Trapped Soul or Psychic Energy?

Below: a typical fabricated ghost of the kind seen in the movies.

and spitting and staring at the unoccupied chair in a corner of the room until it was finally removed . . ."

The rat showed no reaction to whatever had disturbed the dog and cat, but the rattlesnake "immediately assumed an attack posture focusing on the same chair that had been of interest to the cat. After a couple of minutes it slowly moved its head toward a window, then moved back and receded into its alert posture about five minutes later . . ."

The four animals were tested separately in a control room in which no tragedy had occurred. In this room they behaved normally. Apparently, the animals were reacting to some invisible presence in the first room.

What exactly is the lingering aspect of a person capable of being perceived by certain humans and animals? According to Reverend Neil-Smith, it represents the soul of that person. "For the most part," he says, "I believe that the soul of a person who dies a 'natural' death leaves the body for another place. The soul, or spirit, of one who dies violently may not immediately do so; it is bewildered by the sudden transition, and remains earthbound. If you examine cases of haunting which are well authenticated, you generally find that a sudden or unnatural death lies behind the events."

Reverend Neil-Smith thinks that these baffled ghosts tend to develop either a "place reference" or a "person reference." In the first case they haunt a house; in the second case they either possess or consistently appear to a particular person. Reverend Neil-Smith claims to have used exorcism to release many people from possession by a haunting spirit. Most psychical researchers, however, would reserve judgment in such cases on the grounds that there is usually a possible psychiatric explanation for the

Below left: an amateur photographer who took a picture of the altar of St. Nicholas Church in Arundel, England, discovered a priest's figure on it when the film was developed.

Below right: two other priestly ghosts appear in this photo taken in the Basilica in Domremy, France, dedicated to Joan of Arc. This shows Lady Palmer who visited the church in 1929, and was photographed by her companion Miss Townsend. In the developed picture the previously unseen priests appeared.

behavior of the supposedly possessed person. But they would certainly agree with Reverend Neil-Smith's comments on haunting apparitions: ". . . you get the distinct impression that the apparitions are pointless, rather stupid. They wander around, don't say anything in particular, and for the most part don't really frighten anyone. In these cases, I believe, the ghosts are merely trying to call attention to their trapped plight . . ."

Without going so far as to attribute "mind" to the lingering aspect of a person seen, heard, or felt in a haunting, many researchers believe that it consists of some kind of psychic energy generated by the person while still alive. The Oxford philosopher H. H. Price suggested the existence of a "psychic ether" permeating all matter and space. This ether could be impressed with certain mental images. Such an impression would be most likely to occur in traumatic circumstances—violent death, or great emotional suffering. Thus the correlation often noted between unnatural death and subsequent haunting need not be attributed to a trapped soul. The thing trapped in the haunted place would be a kind of recording made on the medium of psychic ether, capable of being perceived in the form of an image, sound, or touch by a sensitive person.

Such a theory has the advantage of bringing the haunting apparition under the same umbrella with the telepathic apparition. If a person is capable of sending a psychic impulse telepathically to a particular person, it seems equally possible that he could project a psychic impulse with no particular receiver in mind, and that that impulse might remain free-floating in the area where the person is at the time he projects the impulse.

Certain cases of hauntings suggest that the generating force behind this impulse may not necessarily be a traumatic incident. Some phantoms have been identified as images of people who lived apparently happy lives and died natural deaths. In such cases, repetition of their presence over a long period of time may suffice to imprint their image on the psychic ether.

The concept of a psychic ether carrying psychic impressions left by various people alive and dead could lead to a plausible and coherent theory of haunting. If psychic impressions can be left in a place, we would have an explanation for those rare cases in which photographic film picked up an image that people present at the time did not see. In such a case the observers were presumably undersensitive compared to the film. In other cases, in which the phantom is seen but does not show up on film, the observers are presumably hypersensitive.

If we continue on the assumption that a haunting apparition was originally imprinted on the scene by some human agent, we encounter yet another problem: what about those cases in which the haunting includes coach and horses or other nonhuman phantoms? We may without too much trouble imagine the agent unconsciously projecting a picture of himself wearing certain clothes, but it strains credulity to imagine his projecting an image of himself borne in a horse-drawn coach.

At this point one of Tyrrell's suggestions may provide an answer. Tyrrell raises the possibility that the latent images— what he calls the "idea-pattern"—may sometimes have a collective origin. He cites the case of persistent legends such as the

Below: this photo of Isabella Houg of Newark, N.J., taken in 1922, includes an image of her long-dead uncle, unseen when the photograph was taken. Only rarely is a photographed ghost visible to the photographer or to other people present at the time. Apparently, the psychic energy of which phantoms are made varies in degree, and is sometimes capable of being picked up on film, sometimes visible to the eye of a sensitive person, and most often incapable of being perceived at all.

Some Phantoms Just Fade Away

ancient belief in the god Pan, "half human and half goat-like, haunting certain places in the woods and uplands and playing his pipe. The widely spread idea that this happened might conceivably sink into the mid-levels [Tyrrell's term for the parts of the mind that govern perception] of the personalities of a whole community, and there form a telepathic idea-pattern, having a multiple agency. Anyone (suitably sensitive) going to the places which, according to the idea-pattern, Pan was especially supposed to inhabit would then see and hear Pan with the same reality that a person going into a haunted house sees and hears a ghost."

One might extend this idea to suggest that unhuman phantoms such as coaches may have been generated and perpetuated in this way by the percipients themselves.

While some phantoms may be in a sense renewed by the unconscious efforts of the percipients, other phantoms seemingly

Right: this illustration from William Gordon Davis' "The Interrupted Ghost Story" is an amusing comment on the effect of state-of-mind on perception. The storyteller has just reached the point where the hero, "transfixed with terror" in a slimy dungeon awaiting some horrible doom, hears an "unearthly yell [ring] through the stilly clearness of the winter's night." At this moment a donkey brays outside the house, causing pandemonium inside it. Such readiness to believe in a ghost will often account for extremely lifelike hallucinations. Yet many apparitions are seen by people in a calm state of mind, totally unprepared to see a ghost; and they often appear so solid and lifelike that they are assumed to be alive.

fade away over a period of time. Andrew Green in *Ghost Hunting* refers to the "ghost of a woman in red shoes, a red gown and a black headdress" which was seen during the 18th century in a remote corridor of an English mansion. "Many years passed before the apparition was seen again, and by then . . . it appeared as a female in a pink dress, pink shoes, and a gray headdress. She was not witnessed again until the mid-19th century, when the figure had dwindled down to 'a lady in a white gown and with gray hair.' Just before the last war all that was reported was 'the sound of a woman walking along the corridor and the swish of her dress.' In 1971, shortly before the demolition of the property involved, workmen 'felt a presence in one of the old corridors.' "

Whether an apparition fades away or remains vivid for centuries, we can usually account for its activities without supposing that they are governed by the surviving spirit of the person it represents. F. W. H. Myers, who devoted considerable effort to

Well-Mannered Specter

During the time of the Napoleonic Wars, a German named Wesermann had been trying experimentally to send his apparition to various people. One night he decided to try instead to transmit the image of someone else. A lady who had died five years before was to appear to a Lieutenant N. in a dream at about 10:30 p.m.

As it happened, Lieutenant N. had not yet gone to bed but was visiting a friend, Lieutenant S. The two were chatting, and N. was just about to go to his room when the kitchen door opened and, in the words of S., "a lady entered, very pale . . . about five feet four inches in height, strong and broad in figure, dressed in white, but with a large black kerchief which reached to below the waist. She . . . greeted me with the hand three times in complimentary fashion, turned round to the left toward Herr N., and waved her hand to him three times; after which the figure quietly, and again without any creaking of the door went out."

The case is interesting because the behavior of the apparition was suited to the circumstances, which were not foreseen by the agent. He had expected N. to be asleep. The apparition behaved like a real person in greeting both men.

Is There a Return From the Grave?

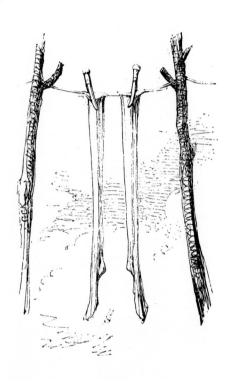

Above: *Ghosts of Stockings* by Cruikshank illustrates the artist's belief that, since spirits always wear clothes, and since theology does not allow for the existence of ghosts of clothes, spirits themselves do not exist. Of course his reasoning was based on a misconception of a ghost's nature.

Opposite: *Apparition*, a painting by Clairin, conveys the mystery that has always surrounded spectral figures, although few of those reported wear the classic white shroud. Many serious researchers regard apparitions—or ghosts in the more common term—as proved beyond reasonable doubt. Yet much mystery remains as to their exact material and spiritual nature.

the study of the survival question, was careful not to let his wish to believe in survival affect his conclusion. In his book *Human Personality and its Survival of Bodily Death*, he defines a ghost as "*a manifestation of persistent personal energy*, or . . . an indication that some kind of force is being exercised after death in some way connected with a person previously known on earth." He goes on to add that "this force or influence, which after a man's death creates a phantasmal impression of him, may indicate no continuing action on his part, but may be some residue of the force or energy which he generated while yet alive." Myers' hypothesis agrees fundamentally with H. H. Price's concept of mental images being impressed upon a psychic ether.

Yet Myers and other serious psychical researchers have occasionally come across cases that strongly suggest that a post-mortem apparition may be more than a remnant of an extinct consciousness. To quote Lyall Watson, "behind every ghost there may be a conscious projector." Watson is not entirely convinced of the likelihood of survival, but in *The Romeo Error* he includes this interesting case relevant to the question:

"In 1921, James Chaffin of North Carolina died, leaving all his property to one of his four sons who himself died intestate a year later. In 1925, the second son was visited by his dead father dressed in a black overcoat, who said 'You will find my will in my overcoat pocket.' When the real coat was examined, a roll of paper was found sewn into the lining with instructions to read the 27th chapter of Genesis in the family Bible. Folded into the relevant pages was a later will than the first one, dividing the property equally between all four sons."

The case of the factory worker saved by the apparent intervention of a person 20 years dead is another piece of evidence in favor of the survival theory. The possibility that in the moment of his own tragic death the first man left a psychic impression of himself in that place does not explain how this lingering psychic impression could act physically when circumstances demanded it. If we suppose that the endangered man happened to pick up the latent image of the dead man, and that at the same time he subliminally became aware of some danger to himself, without realizing what it was, and that he then converted his subliminal fear into a purely subjective hallucination of an arm pushing him out of the way, we are constructing a rather cumbersome and unlikely explanation. Some people would consider it a more unlikely explanation than the idea of the dead man's spirit manifesting itself in the form of an image and a psychokinetic force. The possibility remains, of course, that both the image and the force were transmitted by a living worker. Here, as so often, the case is not airtight.

Chapter 9
The Hydesville Rappings

Is it possible that there are spirits of the dead who are trying to communicate with the living? What caused the strange rappings in the Fox cottage that led to the birth of modern Spiritualism? Can we believe the later confessions of one of the Fox sisters? How can we account for the feats performed by the medium D. D. Home, who was never discovered in fraud? Is it possible for human beings when controlled by spirits to move independently of natural laws? Is it true that the spirits try to convey specific messages to the living—and that they can succeed in this?

John Fox was determined to discover the cause of the strange noises that had kept his family awake for several nights. He rattled a window in the tiny cottage, expecting to find the sashes loose. As if in reply, an echoing rattle sounded in the room.

"Do as I do," said his seven-year-old daughter Kate, as she clapped her hands playfully. The same number of raps was heard as if tapped out by invisible hands.

"No, do just as I do. Count one, two, three, four," chimed in Margaret aged 10. When exactly four raps were heard, Margaret was too frightened to go on with the game the children had started.

The mysterious rappings in the little house in Hydesville, New York in 1848 not only disrupted the Fox family, but also heralded the birth of Spiritualism. The years following the experience of the Fox family with the rappings saw the beginning and growth of this controversial new movement—called a religion by some—as people on both sides of the Atlantic tried to make contact with departed spirits.

The Fox family devised a simple method of communicating with the unseen presence in the cottage. They asked it questions that could be answered simply "yes" (one rap) or "no" (two raps). Using this code, the presence identified itself as the spirit of a murdered peddler whose body had been buried beneath the cottage. News of the rappings spread rapidly in the small town, and soon the Foxes invited their neighbors into the house to hear

Modern Spiritualism—the belief that it is possible to communicate with the spirits of the dead—started with the experiments of the Fox family in Hydesville, New York, after a disturbing series of raps and noises in their home.
Opposite: the three Fox sisters, Kate in the middle, Margaret on the right, and Leah on he left.

conversations with the dead peddler's spirit. When John Fox suggested digging in the cellar to search for the peddler's body, there were plenty of volunteers. However, the dig had to be abandoned when water was struck.

A few months later, however, digging in the cellar was resumed. At a depth of five feet the diggers found a plank, and below the plank, buried in charcoal and quicklime, fragments of hair and bones believed to be part of a human skeleton.

The rest of the skeleton was found 56 years later according to a story in the *Boston Journal* of November 23, 1904. The paper reported that part of a rough wall a yard from the cellar had fallen down. During excavations to repair it, workmen unearthed an almost complete human skeleton. There was a peddler's tin box near the bones. This discovery led to the theory that the murderer—if there was one—first buried the body in the cellar of the house and then, fearing discovery, dug it up and buried it between the two walls.

Spiritualists believe the peddler caused the rappings in order to bring his murderer to justice. If so, the attempt was a failure. The Foxes made his name out as Charles B. Rosma, but such a

Below. a drawing of the dramatic moment in the Fox house when the girls, Kate and Margaret, first playfully challenged the strange rattling and rapping noises to repeat their own patterns of raps. To the family's surprise, the exact patterns were repeated.

person was never traced. A maid, Lucretia Pulver, who four years before had worked for tenants of the house in which the Foxes lived, came forward at the time of the rapping sensation. She told of a peddler's visit to the house when it was rented by her employers, a Mr. and Mrs. Bell. The peddler stayed the night, said Miss Pulver, and she was sent home to her parents. On her return, she was told that the peddler had left.

Even before the Foxes moved in the cottage had had an uncanny reputation, and the previous tenant had left because of the mysterious noises. But there was nothing new about such rappings. History and legend are full of stories of similar disturbances. The Fox family made history by being the first to establish a dialogue with the noises. March 31, 1848, the day on which the first communication occurred, is now regarded as the birth date of Spiritualism.

However, the ground had been prepared for the Spiritualist movement. The most illustrious of its forerunners was Emanuel Swedenborg. This Swedish philosopher and scientist, born in 1688, was a man of wide-ranging abilities. He was an authority on metallurgy, an astronomer, a zoologist, anatomist, physicist, financier, and a profound biblical scholar. In middle age, he developed psychic powers, often in the form of visions.

Swedenborg began to write seriously about the spiritual world in 1744. In dreams during sleep and in visions during wakefulness he wandered in the next world where he was instructed, so he claimed, by the spirits of kings, popes, saints, and biblical personages. His accounts aroused considerable interest in the afterlife, and introduced a new concept of its nature. The established Christian belief was that on a person's death, his soul went to Heaven or Hell—or, as Catholics believe, to Purgatory. In any case, the soul's afterlife was believed to be totally different from its earthly life, and totally separated from this world. By contrast, Swedenborg described afterlife as being very similar to this life, and his talks with the dead indicated—to those who believed him—that communication between the two worlds was possible.

About 75 years after his death, Swedenborg's own spirit

First Dialogue with Spirit Raps

Left: a 1930s postcard of the original Fox cottage in which the mysterious rappings were first heard. The cottage has since burned down, and an exact replica stands as a replacement.

SPIRITUALISM ORIGINATED MARCH 31 1848 IN THIS HOUSE, NEWARK, N. Y.

featured in the mystical experience of another man who was also prone to visions. Andrew Jackson Davis, known as the Poughkeepsie Seer, was an 18-year-old apprentice shoemaker. One day in 1844 he went into a state of semitrance and wandered from his home in Poughkeepsie, New York. The next morning he found himself 40 miles away in the mountains where, he later claimed, he met the spirits of Swedenborg and of the 2nd-century Greek physician Claudius Galen. During that encounter he experienced a state of mental illumination. Although Davis had had no education, he began teaching and writing on the body's supernormal powers. These he referred to as human magnetism and electricity. In 1845 he began to dictate while in trance an impressive work entitled *The Principles of Nature, Her Divine Revelations, and a Voice to Mankind.* In the book, which took 15 months to produce and which was taken down by a minister, Davis made this prediction:

"It is a truth that spirits commune with one another while one

Above: Emanuel Swedenborg (1688–1772) was considered a forerunner of Spiritualism. Although he had some psychic powers in his youth, his more profound knowledge of the spiritual world began in middle age when, while still awake and conscious, he wandered in the spirit world.

is in the body and the other in the higher spheres—and this, too, when the person in the body is unconscious of the influx, and hence cannot be convinced of the fact; and this truth will ere long present itself in the form of a living demonstration. And the world will hail with delight the ushering in of that era when the interiors of men will be opened, and the spiritual communion will be established. . . ."

In his notes dated March 31, 1848, are the following words: "About daylight this morning a warm breathing passed over my face and I heard a voice, tender and strong, saying: 'Brother, the good work has begun—behold a living demonstration is born.' I was left wondering what could be meant by such a message." It soon became clear what the voice may have meant, for it was on that very day that the Fox family for the first time established a form of communication with the unseen. The remarkable coincidence of Davis' revelation and the Hydesville rappings helped establish his reputation as the prophet of Spiritualism.

A Trance Vision of Spiritualism

Left: a seance in 1871 when spirit communication became a vogue in fashionable society.

The Birthplace of Spiritualism

Right: the cornerstone of a shrine to Spiritualism started in 1955 and left uncompleted. The stone is located at the rear of the replica Fox cottage.

Below: the replica of the Fox family's house in Hydesville, New York. It was built during the 1950s by John Drummond, who is shown in this picture.

The presence in the Hydesville cottage soon began to manifest itself in various other ways besides rappings. Gurgling sounds as from the throat, a death struggle, the heavy dragging of a body across the room are all reported to have been heard, night after night. The Foxes, unable to stand it any longer, finally left the house to live with other members of the family. But, according to Nandor Fodor's *Encyclopaedia of Psychic Science*, "the raps continued in the house even after they had left."

The noises also seem to have followed the Fox family. Kate went to her brother David's house in Auburn, and Margaret to her older sister Leah's in Rochester. The raps broke out in both houses, but were particularly violent in Leah's home. One of the tenants became the center of psychic attention in the form of poltergeist activity. Objects were thrown at him, but without ever causing him any injury. Recalling these events, Leah Fox later wrote in her book *The Missing Link* that the family appeared to be the victims of an intelligent but spiteful manifestation. They became convinced that no earthly power could relieve them.

"While on our knees pins would be stuck into different parts of our persons. Mother's cap would be removed from her head, her comb jerked out of her hair, and every conceivable thing done to annoy us." Once a loud noise came from high up on the roof, Leah reported. "It sounded like the frequent discharge of heavy artillery. It was stated to us the next day that the sounds were heard a mile away. We feared that the roof would fall in upon us."

They decided, again, to try to communicate with the invisible noisy force that was causing such havoc. They would recite the alphabet and the raps would respond at a certain letter. In this way a message was slowly spelled out. The first message Leah and her household received was: "Dear friends, you must proclaim this truth in the world. This is the dawning of a new era; you must not try to conceal it any longer. When you do your duty God will protect you and good spirits will watch over you."

From that moment on, as the Foxes received more communications, the spirits became more orderly. The family held seances during which a table rocked, objects moved, a guitar seemingly played itself, and sitters felt the touch of invisible hands.

The first meeting of a small band of people calling themselves Spiritualists was held on November 14, 1849, in the Corinthian Hall, Rochester. Public reaction to the demonstrations given by the Fox sisters at this meeting was mixed, and some of it was hostile. A group of citizens formed a committee to investigate the Spiritualists' claims. When this committee did not dismiss the phenomena as fraud, indignant skeptics appointed another committee. Its members, too, found no evidence of fraud. They reported that when the Fox sisters were standing on pillows "with a handkerchief tied around the bottom of their dresses, tight to the ankles, we all heard rapping on the wall and floor distinctly."

Many people still found the claims of the sisters outrageous, and some responded to them with violence. On one occasion, the sisters narrowly escaped being lynched. Attention was soon partly diverted from them as others began to demonstrate similar powers. Throughout the country, various people found they could produce raps and table tappings in their own homes.

In the growing enthusiasm for the new belief, the Fox sisters

Margaret Fox's Confession

Margaret Fox was a little girl of 10 when the first strange rappings were heard in the house she lived in. Her sister Kate was three years younger, and her married sister Leah was considerably older. After the interest and belief in the rappings had led to the establishment of Spiritualism, it was Leah who became the first professional medium. She took command over her sisters.

In later years the relationship between Leah and the other two became strained. It blew up when Margaret was left in poverty and illness by widowhood. In an attempt to hurt the successful Leah—and perhaps to profit from the publicity—Margaret publicly confessed to fraud in 1888.

Her published confession said that the raps had been made at first by bumping or dropping an apple on the floor. Later she and Kate developed such perfect control of their muscles that they could snap the joints of their fingers and toes without detection. Margaret demonstrated her technique of producing raps before an audience at a New York theater.

Was it "all fraud, hypocrisy, and delusion" as Margaret herself said? Thousands of Spiritualists refused to believe it—and the movement grew on.

The Fox Sisters Become Mediums

Above: Sir William Crookes in 1884. A physicist, Crookes went into psychic research in 1870 when he announced his intention to make a thorough investigation into Spiritual phenomena.

found themselves in demand. Although she had not been involved in the original rappings at the Hydesville home, the eldest sister Leah became the first professional medium. She gave private seances from November 28, 1849, and within six months her younger sisters had followed her example. Then the sisters set out on a propaganda tour that took them to Albany, Troy, and New York City. In Troy their lives were threatened, but they continued because, they said, the strange raps had asked them to "proclaim this truth to the world."

In New York in 1850 the influential newspaperman Horace Greeley, editor of the *New York Tribune*, was their first sitter. Fearing for their safety, he advised them to charge an extremely high admission fee to deter potential trouble makers. Four years later in 1854 America's first Spiritualist organization, the Society for the Diffusion of Spiritual Knowledge, was founded in New York by a wealthy merchant. It sponsored free public sittings given by Kate who received $1200 a year—a very large sum for the time—for her mediumistic services. Greeley, speaking on behalf of a number of sitters, affirmed: "Whatever may be the origin or cause of the 'rappings,' the ladies in whose presence they occur do not make them. We tested this thoroughly and to our entire satisfaction."

This was in contradiction to a theory put forward in 1851 that the Fox sisters had produced the raps by snapping their knee or toe joints, although the noises were often said to have emanated from walls or doors some distance from the girls. Critics of Spiritualism were given further ammunition from an unexpected source. In April 1851—just three years after the first rappings— an alleged confession of fraud by Margaret Fox was published by one of her relatives. Surprisingly, Margaret's guilty admission had no effect on the progress of Spiritualism. Converts were joining the ranks every day, mediums were springing up everywhere, and the phenomena were becoming more remarkable.

When Margaret married and Leah remarried in the 1850s, they both retired from public mediumship temporarily. Their youngest sister Kate not only continued to be a medium, but also began to produce spirit forms at her seances as well as raps. In 1861 she was engaged to conduct seances exclusively for Charles F. Livermore, a rich New York banker. Livermore wanted to contact his wife Estelle, who had died a year earlier. In her five years as Livermore's private medium, Kate is reported to have given nearly 400 seances, most of them in Livermore's home. Prominent persons were among the sitters. Doors and windows were locked before each sitting commenced, and careful records were kept. It was during this period that Kate began to produce spirit forms, but it was not until the 43rd seance that the spirit was recognized as Estelle. According to the reports, Kate remained conscious as a form slowly materialized. The materialization became more substantial as time went on, but it was never able to speak more than a few words. Communication took place mainly through raps and writing. Estelle and another spirit form, described as Benjamin Franklin, wrote on cards brought by Livermore. To avoid fraud, Kate's hands were held by one of the sitters while the banker's dead wife wrote her messages. The writing on the card was said to be the same as

Estelle's when alive. At the 388th sitting Estelle announced that it was her last appearance. Livermore never saw her again.

The banker showed his gratitude to Kate by giving her a trip to England in 1871. By then the English Spiritualist movement was well established. Kate gave seances for a number of eminent men including Sir William Crookes, who later became one of the foremost investigators of Spiritualist phenomena. She also gave joint sittings with two other famous mediums, Mrs. Samuel Guppy and Daniel Dunglas Home.

There was an astonishing story in connection with Mrs. Guppy. It seems that two other mediums, Frank Herne and Charles Williams, were once holding a joint seance with eight sitters. They were in a house near the center of the city, and Mrs. Guppy was at her own home three miles away. One of the sitters jokingly suggested that the spirits try to bring Mrs. Guppy to their seance—a tremendous feat considering how large Mrs. Guppy was. Suddenly there was a heavy bump on the table, and one or two screams. When a match was struck, Mrs. Guppy was there, on top of the table.

Three of the sitters, including the editor of the weekly newspaper *The Spiritualist*, accompanied Mrs. Guppy back home. After questioning those in Mrs. Guppy's household, they were satisfied that the medium had been at home until the time of her sudden appearance in the seance room across town.

The story was understandably treated with scorn by the daily

Mrs. Guppy Just Drops In

Two London mediums, Frank Herne and Charles Williams, were holding a joint seance with a respectable circle of sitters. The voices of the spirits John King and his daughter Katie were heard, and Katie was asked to bring something to the sitters—which she willingly agreed to do. One sitter perhaps jokingly suggested that Katie produce Mrs. Guppy, a well-known medium of majestic dimensions. Katie chuckled and said she would. John King shouted out, "You can't do it, Katie," but she declared "I will." The sitters were all laughing when there came a loud thump on the table, and a couple of them screamed. Someone lit a match—and there was Mrs. Guppy, her considerable bulk deposited neatly on the seance table. She was in trance and held a pen and an account book.

When Mrs. Guppy was gently awakened, she was somewhat upset. The last she remembered she had been sitting comfortably in her own home—about three miles away—writing up her accounts. Several sitters escorted the medium to her house, where an anxious friend waited. According to the friend, the two had been in Mrs. Guppy's room together when, suddenly, Mrs. Guppy was gone "leaving only a slight haze near the ceiling."

Left: a picture by an English spirit photographer. It includes the medium Mrs. Guppy (on the right) with friends. These pictures, apparently normal photographs in which psychic shapes appeared when developed, became a great fashion among 19th-century photographers.

Above: Victorian medium Daniel Dunglas
Home. The most famous physical medium,
Home produced a wide range of phenomena
that included levitation and partial
materialization. He worked in full light, and
was never caught in any kind of trickery.

press, but Spiritualists counted it simply as another seance
wonder. They recalled that three years earlier D. D. Home—the
medium with whom Kate Fox held joint sittings in England—
was reported to have defied the laws of gravity three stories above
a London street. Home performed this feat on December 13,
1868, in the presence of three witnesses, one of them Lord Adare.

In a trance, Home told the three men not to be afraid and not
to leave their places. He then went out into the hallway and into
a room next door. The three heard a window being thrown
open, and a few moments later Home appeared outside their
window standing upright. He opened the window from outside
and came in to join his dumbfounded sitters. He laughed at the
thought of what a policeman would have done had he seen him
"turning round and round along the wall in the air." Then he
asked Lord Adare to go and close the window in the next room.
When Lord Adare returned, he said that the window had been
open only a foot, and he could not imagine how the medium
had squeezed through the opening. "Come and see," said Home.
According to Lord Adare, this is what happened next:

"I went with him; he told me to open the window as it was
before. I did so; he told me to stand a little distance off; he then
went through the open space, head first, quite rapidly, his body
being nearly horizontal and apparently rigid. He came in again,
feet foremost, and we returned to the other room. It was so dark
I could not see clearly how he was supported outside. He did not
appear to grasp, or rest upon, the balustrade, but rather to be
swung out and in. . . . When Home awoke he was much agitated;
he said he felt as if he had gone through some peril, and that he
had a most horrible desire to throw himself out of the window;
he remained in a very nervous condition for some time, then
gradually became quiet."

Modern researchers have found minor discrepancies in the
reports of the witnesses to this apparently miraculous feat, but
the discrepancies are not weighty evidence against the possible
genuineness of the act. Almost the only scientific explanation
that would fit all the aspects of this case is that Home hypnotized
the others into believing they had seen him levitate.

D. D. Home, born in Scotland in 1833, was one of the most
outstanding mediums in Spiritualist history. An illegitimate
child, he claimed to be the natural son of Alexander, tenth Earl
of Home. He was adopted by a childless aunt, Mrs. McNeill
Cook, who took him to America. As a youth he lived in Green-
ville, Connecticut, and Troy, New York. During this period he
saw his first vision—that of a childhood friend who had died.
Four years later came a second vision in which the exact hour of
his mother's death was predicted.

Next, rappings began to occur in Home's presence. This was
just two years after the Hydesville rappings. His aunt thought he
was possessed and called in Congregationalist, Baptist, and
Methodist ministers for exorcism. When the rappings continued,
she turned the boy out of the house. From that time on he
appears to have lived on the hospitality of those attracted by his
unusual psychic gifts. Returning to Europe, Home gave seances
for aristocrats and royalty including Napoleon III of France. As
far as is known, Home was never detected in fraud.

Among his remarkable feats was the ability to grow taller under spirit guidance. Lord Adare reported one such incident when Home said that the spirit present was strong and tall. Said Lord Adare: "Home grew, I should say, at least six inches. Mr. Jencken, who is a taller man than Home, stood beside him, so there could be no mistake about it. Home's natural height is, I believe, 5 feet 10 inches. I should say he grew to 6 feet 4 inches or 6 feet 6 inches. I placed my hands on his feet, and they were level on the ground. . . . He appeared to grow also in breadth and size all over, but there was no way of testing that."

The Mr. Jencken mentioned in this account married Kate Fox in 1872 during her trip to England at her patron's expense. In the next years, bitter personal problems divided the three Fox sisters. Kate and Margaret allied themselves against Leah, who had returned to mediumship, and tried to ruin her career.

On May 27, 1888, Margaret Fox for the second time publicly confessed to fraud in a sensational letter to the *New York Herald*.

The Outstanding D.D.Home

Left: one of Home's levitations. Many of the phenomena he produced were of a most spectacular nature.

Spiritualism Starts to Spread

She denounced Spiritualism and promised a complete exposure. She kept her promise with a series of interviews and lectures. In an appearance at New York's Academy of Music, she produced raps on stage and explained how they were achieved by snapping her toe joints. Two months later, Kate Fox returned to New York and made a similar confession of guilt, joining her sister in the exposure meetings. Possibly Margaret and Kate hoped to make money from their confession, but if so, they were disappointed. This may explain why, just over a year later, Margaret Fox completely retracted her confession in an interview reported in the New York press. According to the *Encyclopaedia of Psychic Science*, "she spoke of her great financial difficulties at the time, of an excitement that almost upset her mental equilibrium and blamed the strong psychological influence of persons inimical to Spiritualism for her action."

These confusing confessions and retractions were not to continue much longer. One after the other the Fox sisters died: Leah in 1890, and her two younger sisters while they were still in their fifties—Kate in 1892 and Margaret in 1893. Although the scandal caused by the confessions of Margaret and Kate had shaken Spiritualism, the movement was too well established to be destroyed by it. Spiritualism had become worldwide in the nearly 50 years since the rappings at Hydesville. Many famous people had witnessed psychic phenomena and testified to their authenticity. Even if the Fox sisters had been fraudulent, there were many other remarkable mediums who were not so proved.

Early converts of Spiritualism had lost no time in spreading the good word. Within five years of Hydesville, Spiritualism had leaped the Atlantic. The first Spiritualist church in England was established in Keighley, Yorkshire in 1853. Two years later the *Yorkshire Spiritual Telegraph*, first Spiritualist newspaper in Britain, was published in the same town.

The creation of a Spiritualist movement in Britain is attributed to two visiting American mediums, Mrs. W. R. Hayden and Mrs. Roberts. The latter advertised her gifts in *The Times* of London in 1853, saying: "Spiritual Manifestations and Com-

Right: Emma Hardinge Britten actively promoted Spiritualism.

Far right: Robert James Lees. According to his daughter Eva Lees, he was only 13 or 14 when he delivered his first spirit message to Queen Victoria from Prince Albert. Miss Lees says the messages went on until the Queen's death. Lees also reportedly helped the police to identify and locate the dreaded London killer, Jack the Ripper. Controversy about the truth of that goes on vigorously even now.

munications from departed friends, which so much gratifies enlightened minds, exemplified daily."

Britain soon produced its own mediums. One of the earliest and most impressive pioneers in the field was Emma Hardinge Britten, a talented musician. She was converted to Spiritualism in the 1850s while on a professional visit to America.

Emma Hardinge Britten and her mother had sailed to the United States on the steamship *Pacific*. They had become friendly with some of the ship's officers, whom they continued to meet whenever the ship came into port. One of these officers figured in Emma Hardinge Britten's first mediumistic experience. According to her own account, the *Pacific* was due to arrive in New York again in February 1856. Expecting a parcel from England to be brought personally by a ship's officer, she went to the docks, but the overdue ship had not yet arrived. The delay was not considered serious for storms often slowed down winter crossings.

That night, however, just as she and her mother were about to retire, Emma Hardinge Britten felt a chill coupled with an impression of a spirit presence. "A sensation as if water was streaming over me accompanied the icy chilliness I experienced, and a feeling of indescribable terror possessed my whole being," she said. Her mother, who was already interested in Spiritualism, persuaded her to try to communicate with the spirits, and suggested the use of a method that had been told to her by the medium Mrs. Kellogg. On a table the young woman arranged slips of paper bearing the letters of the alphabet. Seemingly controlled by an unseen power, her hand spelled out the words: "Philip Smith, *Pacific*." Then she felt an ice-cold hand laid on her arm, and the message continued: "My dear Emma, I have come to tell you I am dead. The ship *Pacific* is lost, and all on board have perished; she and her crew will never be heard from more."

Next morning, after an almost sleepless night, Emma Hardinge Britten hurried to the home of Mrs. Kellogg. Despite the power of the message, she still doubted its authenticity. She ran up the two flights of stairs to the medium's apartment, and was astonished to find her coming out of her room with a fixed glazed look in her eyes as if in a trance. In a forced unnatural voice the medium greeted her visitor with chillingly familiar words: "My dear Emma, I have come to tell you I am dead. The ship *Pacific* is lost, and all on board have perished. She and her crew will never be heard from more." In time, the sad news was confirmed: the *Pacific* and its crew were never heard of again.

Emma Hardinge Britten traveled all over the United States, Canada, Australia, New Zealand, and Britain for many years in the cause of Spiritualism. She was a brilliant speaker and tireless organizer. She also founded and for five years edited *Two Worlds*, a Spiritualist publication that is still in existence.

A few years after Emma Hardinge Britten's conversion to Spiritualism in America, something happened to boost Spiritualism in her native England. Thirteen-year-old Robert James Lees of Leicester began to develop great powers as a medium. In the year 1861, soon after the death of Queen Victoria's husband Prince Albert, the Lees family had a seance in their home. While young Lees was in a trance, the spirit of a man claiming to be

Above: Queen Victoria with John Brown, her personal manservant. He reportedly was also a medium who enabled the widowed Queen to communicate with her beloved Albert. The evidence for Brown's mediumship is mixed, but the Queen certainly believed that he had genuine premonitions of the future, and relied on him greatly.

Mediums and National Leaders

Below: Mary Todd Lincoln in a spirit photograph by W. Mumler. She had arrived for the sitting incognito and veiled in mourning. When the print was taken, the photographer recognized the late President. Mary Lincoln agreed and added, "I am his widow."

Prince Albert sent a message to Queen Victoria, expressing a desire to communicate through Lees' mediumship. A newspaper editor who was at the seance published the request, which was brought to Her Majesty's notice. Queen Victoria, who already had an interest in psychic matters, sent two members of her court to a seance in Lees' home. The Queen's representatives gave false names. According to witnesses, the Prince Consort communicated through Lees when the young medium went into his trance. The Prince greeted the visitors as his friends and called them by their correct names.

Also while in a trance, Lees wrote a letter to the Queen. He signed it with a private name used only between the Queen and Prince Albert. The Queen was so impressed that she sent for Lees in order to speak to her dead husband through him. She wanted Lees to remain permanently at court but, it is said, the Prince Consort expressed a preference for another medium. This was John Brown, a servant at Balmoral, the Queen's estate in Scotland. Queen Victoria's long—and, some say, intimate—friendship with the lowly servant of rough character has been the subject of conjecture and controversy for over a century. Spiritualists argue that Brown's influence over the Queen was due entirely to his mediumship—that she tolerated his rude and outspoken nature because he made it possible for her to speak to her beloved husband.

At the same time that Robert James Lees is said to have been receiving spirit messages from Prince Albert, President Abraham Lincoln was taking an interest in Spiritualism.

If we believe a story told by Colonel Simon F. Kase—a lobbyist for railroad interests who moved freely in the highest government circles—messages from the spirit world changed the course of American history. In his book *The Emancipation Proclamation. How, and By Whom It Was Given to President Lincoln in 1861*, Colonel Kase gives an eye-witness account of the extraordinary events. He says that he first met the President about a railroad project. During subsequent meetings the two men discussed Spiritualism which, given the wide interest in it at the time, seems plausible.

It was some four weeks after his original meeting with Lincoln that, according to Kase, he was in the visitors' gallery of the House of Representatives. An old lady approached him, gave him her card, and said, "Call me when it suits you."

Kase saw his friend Judge Wattels nearby, and asked him who the lady was. The judge identified her as Mrs. Laurie. When Kase asked for more information, he said: "Well, sir, I have been twice to her house; she lives in Georgetown, and she has a daughter, now married to a Mr. Miller. She plays a piano with her eyes closed, and the piano rises up and beats the time on the floor as perfectly as the time is kept upon the instrument, and they call it Spiritualism." Kase said he would like to attend a seance, and Judge Wattels offered to accompany him that evening.

"The arrangement being perfected," Kase wrote, "we went and arrived there about eight o'clock in the evening. Who should we meet there but President Lincoln and his lady. After speaking and passing the courtesies of the day, perhaps ten minutes intervening, I saw a young girl approaching the President with a measured step, with her eyes closed, and walking up to . . . the President, accosted him as follows:

" 'Sir, you have been called to the position that you now occupy for a very great purpose. The world is in universal bondage; it must be physically set free, that it may mentally rise to its proper status. There is a Spiritual Congress supervising the affairs of this nation as well as a Congress at Washington. This Republic is leading the van of Republics throughout the world.' "

The teenage girl was Nettie Colburn Maynard, a medium known to the Laurie seances. The young girl, in trance, lectured the President for an hour on the importance of emancipating the slaves. Her argument was that the Civil War could not end until slavery was abolished because God destined all men to be free. "Her language was truly sublime," Kase reported, "and full of arguments, grand in the extreme, that from the time his proclamation of freedom was issued there would be no reverse to our army. As soon as this young girl came out of the trance she ran off, frightened to think that she had been talking to the President.

"Immediately, Mrs. Miller [daughter of the hostess Mrs. Laurie] commenced playing the piano, and the front side of it commenced to beat the time by rising off the floor and coming down with a heavy thud, beating the time of the tune played. I got up and requested the privilege of sitting on it that I might verify to the world that it moved. 'Yes,' the medium said, 'you, and as many more as see proper may get on it.'

"Judge Wattels, the two soldiers who accompanied the President, and myself, got on the instrument. The medium commenced to play, the instrument commenced to go with all our weight on it, rising four inches at least. It was too rough riding; we got off whilst the instrument beat the time until the tune was played out."

Kase reported a second visit to Mrs. Laurie's home two evenings later, when the President and his wife were again present. He said that Lincoln was once more addressed by the young medium on the subject of freeing the slaves.

"Thus it was," wrote Kase, "that President Lincoln was convinced as to the course he should pursue; the command coming from that all-seeing Spirit through the instrumentality of the angel world was not to be overlooked. He, like a faithful servant, when convinced of his duty, feared not to do it, and to proclaim freedom by the Emancipation Proclamation to four million slaves. The proclamation was issued on September 22, 1862, to take effect the first day of January, 1863. In the intermediate time the backbone of the rebellion was broken, the Union army had, in diverse places, 26 battles, every one of them except two being a success upon the Union side. Thus, the prediction of the medium was verified."

There is no confirmation from Lincoln that Spiritualism influenced his decision. However, it is startling enough that, within a few years of Spiritualism's obscure beginnings, the President of the United States and the Queen of England were taking a keen interest in the new movement. And if the Spiritualist version of Abraham Lincoln's historic freeing of the slaves is believed, Spiritualism was already influencing a nation's destiny.

President Lincoln and the Dancing Piano

During the presidency of Abraham Lincoln the vogue for the new Spiritualism was at its height among fashionable people. Even the President—a far from fashionable man—was drawn into it. Colonel Simon F. Kase, a lobbyist who had several times met Lincoln to discuss a railroad project with him, tells of encountering the President at a seance in the home of Mrs. Laurie and daughter Mrs. Miller. She was known for making a piano beat time on the floor as she played while in trance.

Kase said of the occasion that Mrs. Miller began to play, and the front of the piano in truth rose off the floor and beat the time of the tune with heavy thuds. Kase asked if he could sit on the instrument so that he could "verify to the world that it moved." The medium composedly answered that he and as many others as wished could sit on the piano. Four men did: Kase, a judge, and two of the soldiers who were accompanying Lincoln. Mrs. Miller again began to play and the piano—heedless of its load—began to rise and thump, lifting at least four inches off the floor. Kase concluded ruefully: "It was too rough riding; we got off while the instrument beat the time until the tune was played out."

Chapter 10
Man's Immortal Spirit

Each of us must die—but then what? All people since human life began have wondered, and chosen their explanation. Do we need to go into the afterlife equipped with food and tools from this world? Do we exist on a vast wheel of circling incarnations, our conduct now determining what we shall be in the next life? What difference does our virtue or wickedness make for the progress of our souls? If we do survive death to move onto some kind of astral plane, what will we do there—or will it be our turn to attempt to communicate with those who come after us on this earth?

The belief that death is the end of the personality is, in the context of human history, a novel one. Almost all people since the beginning of the human race have believed in some form of life after death. Only in recent times, and only in Western countries, have a large number of people maintained that death is oblivion. It may be this disbelief in the afterlife that provoked the growth of Spiritualism in the West. For Spiritualism is unflagging—and at times desperate—in its efforts to prove survival. To ancient Egyptians (or, in fact, to modern devout Christians), for example, the Spiritualist preoccupation with life after death would seem irrelevant. They take an afterlife for granted.

Nonetheless, while taking survival for granted in the sense of believing in it without proof, people have gone to some pains to prepare for it. For believers in the great religions the preparation is spiritual or ethical, such as doing good works. Among ancient peoples it often took a practical form. Some 50,000 years ago Neanderthals were burying their dead equipped with food and tools—reflecting a belief that the afterlife was similar to the earthly life. The tombs of the Etruscans, who flourished in Italy before the Romans, have been found to contain furniture and chariots for the use of departed spirits.

In ancient civilizations the death of a royal personage required elaborate preparations so that his spirit could live in the next world in the style to which he was accustomed on earth. In the 1920s archaeologists excavating the royal death pits of Ur, in

The mysterious problems of death and what happens afterward has absorbed and obsessed men ever since the Neanderthals made careful provision for the needs of their dead with foods and tools.

Opposite: a 15th-century French manuscript shows the soul of a dying man warred over by angels and demons. God, holding the sharp sword of justice, looks on.

Ancient Beliefs about Afterlife

what is now Iraq, were astonished to find the remains of Queen Shubad surrounded by 68 other people—women of the court and soldiers armed with spears. The evidence indicated that these royal attendants had gone to their deaths voluntarily for the archaeological team found no apparent signs of struggle or violence. The bodies were laid out in orderly rows. It is possible that the royal servants of the queen either took poison or narcotics before the pits were covered. This mass sacrifice, which took place 4500 years ago, was based on the belief that the souls of the attendants would continue to serve the queen in death.

About 500 years ago the Inca peoples of South America practiced a similar kind of sacrifice for the benefit of their dead emperor, whom they believed to be a god—though apparently those who were sacrificed were unwilling victims. When the emperor died, his body was mummified and wrapped in beautiful cloth. His preserved remains were carefully attended by retainers, and produced at festivals as an object of veneration. The Incas believed that the emperor's soul had journeyed to another world. Therefore, during the funeral ceremonies for him, his favorite wives and servants, strangled after being intoxicated, were sent with him in death.

Other peoples held similar beliefs but expressed them without human sacrifice. In the tomb of Meketre, an Egyptian nobleman of Thebes, excavators found painted wooden models of the man's servants. It was believed that, in the other world, the dead man would use magic to bring them back to life to serve him again.

More than any other ancient peoples, the Egyptians were concerned with the afterlife. It is mainly through the elaborate preparations they made for the survival of their pharaohs and notables that we have obtained our knowledge of their way of life, craftsmanship, and culture. The great pyramids in which the pharaohs were entombed contained beautiful paintings, furniture, and jewelry intended for the enjoyment of the spirit of the god-kings. A basic part of Egyptian belief was the idea that in order for the spirit, or *ka*, to survive, the body must also survive. That is why the corpse was so carefully mummified and offerings of food were left at intervals in the pharaoh's tomb.

In time Egyptian beliefs about the afterlife became more democratic, and the idea of immortality was extended to include ordinary people as well as rulers. It was believed that every soul had to face judgment, and in order to do so, had to take a long and wearisome pilgrimage to the seat of the god Osiris, ruler of the underworld. There, in the presence of Osiris and 42 judges, the dead person's heart would be weighed on the scales of justice. The soul had to be able to say that in life the person had not been guilty of any one of a long list of sins, including the mistreatment of cattle and the stealing of food from the dead.

Zoroastrianism, the religion of the ancient peoples of Persia, also conceived of the afterlife as involving a journey and a judgment. On the fourth day after death, a person's soul crossed the Bridge of Parting. The middle section of this structure was like a wide sword blade. The sharp bridge stayed flat for a righteous soul so that it could easily walk across. Then it was met on the other side by a beautiful maiden who was a spiritual embodiment of the soul's good deeds while on earth. The righteous ones en-

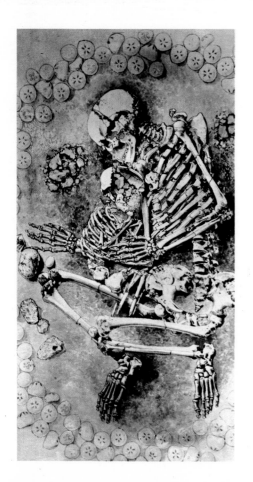

Below: the Stone Age grave of a mother and child. The broken pottery on each side of the skeletons were storage jars that held the food provided for afterlife.

tered paradise, "the Abode of Song," where luxurious gifts were bestowed upon them. When a wicked man tried to cross the bridge, however, its midsection turned on its edge, causing the evildoer to plunge into a stinking abyss below.

According to the Aztecs, the way in which a person died—not his actions during life—determined the kind of existence he would have in the next world. Those who were sacrificed to the gods in the Aztecs' gory ceremonies would enter the paradise of the sun god, and would be transformed into butterflies or hummingbirds. Women who died in childbirth shared this idyllic afterlife. Others were destined for afterlives of a rather colorless type.

A graphic conception of a luxurious Paradise is contained in the Koran, the sacred book of the Islamic religion. Those chosen by Allah "shall recline on jeweled couches face to face, and there shall wait on them immortal youths with bowls and ewers and a cup of purest wine . . . with fruits of their own choice and flesh of fowls that they relish. And there shall be the dark-eyed houris [pure maidens], chaste as hidden pearls. . . . There they shall hear no idle talk, no sinful speech, but only the greeting, 'Peace! Peace!' " In contrast, the spirits of the wicked are condemned by Allah to hellfire and a diet of boiling water and "decaying filth."

The ancient Greeks held a number of views about the afterlife. One of the most widespread was that the soul of the deceased journeyed to an underworld called Hades, ruled over by the god of that name. This was a gloomy place where the spirits existed as vague shadows, somewhat similar to the Sheol, or "place of de-

Above: funerary honors for an Inca emperor. The dead man, under a canopy, has life breathed into him through a tube—a tradition still practiced in parts of South America—while his successor watches. Wives and servants of the dead emperor were buried alive to serve him in the next world.

Below: an Egyptian model of a boat carved in about 1400 B.C., placed in a tomb to provide a safe passage to the next world.

Reincarnation: the Cycle of Rebirths

Below: *The Last Judgment* by the 15th-century painter Jan van Eyck. The Christian belief of the afterlife holds that the good will go to Heaven for their just reward, and the bad will go to Hell for their just punishment. Unhappily for Christian followers, ministers much more often stressed the torments of Hell than the joys of Heaven.

parted spirits," of the Jewish faith. The Greeks also had their hell, called Tartaros, and heaven, known as the Elysian fields. In heaven the chosen few enjoyed eternal spring. Great emphasis was put on attaining this reward by the Orphic sect. The Orphics took their name from the singer Orpheus who, according to mythology, descended into Hades and persuaded the god to release his dead wife Eurydice. On the journey back to earth, Orpheus could not resist turning his head to make sure that Eurydice was still following him. This was against Hades' strict command and, as punishment, Orpheus lost both his and Eurydice's lives.

Another influential Greek belief was Pythagoreanism, which was based on the teachings of the mathematician-philosopher Pythagoras. He believed that the soul had "fallen" into a bodily existence, and would have to migrate through or be reincarnated in other human and animal bodies before being set free. Pythagoras himself claimed to have had previous existences, including one as a soldier in the Trojan war.

The belief in reincarnation is strongest in Asia. In Hinduism, the religion of the majority of Indians, a person's soul is considered to be a reflection of the world-soul, and the goal of one's existence is to become one with this all-pervading divine principle, the Brahma. Before attaining this unity the soul must go through various reincarnations, both human and animal. The whole cycle of rebirths is known as the wheel of Sansara, and its turning—like the universe itself—is without beginning and without end. The Hindu believes that he can influence the nature of his next rebirth through his *karma*, the sum total of his actions in his present life. Bad karma will bring punishment in the form of reincarnation as a low caste person or a despised animal, such as a dog, or in various misfortunes during the next life. Good karma will be rewarded by reincarnation as a highly regarded animal—perhaps as a cow, the sacred animal of the Hindus—or as a Brahmin, the highest of all castes.

In between reincarnations, the soul may spend time in various heavens and hells. Some of the hells are ice cold, some boiling hot. The lot of the damned in one hell is to be boiled in oil and dismembered. The heavens provide many pleasures including music, dancing girls, and gambling houses. Of course, these fleshpot heavens have nothing to do with the soul's ultimate achievement of spiritual bliss.

Buddhism, like Hinduism out of which it developed some 25 centuries ago, teaches that humans must undergo a series of reincarnations. In the course of these various lives, some of which may be in other universes, the soul gradually learns to avoid the suffering inherent in life by giving up its craving for happiness—in fact, its craving for life itself. When one has shed all his earthly desires and achieved a state of indifference toward both pain and pleasure, he is said to have reached Nirvana. Having attained this state of supreme detachment, the soul is free from the cycle of rebirths. In fact it is no longer an individual soul as Westerners conceive it, for the whole idea is to lose the sense of self.

Such a concept takes us a long way from the idea of the spirit as an individual, which is fundamental to most Western creeds. It is almost the total opposite of Spiritualism, which holds that

Left: *Charon Crossing the Styx* by the
16th-century artist Joachim Patinir. The
theme of this painting comes from one of
the beliefs of the ancient Greeks about
afterlife. This view maintained that the souls
of the dead went to a gloomy underworld,
Hades, where they existed as vague
shadows. To get to Hades over the Styx
river, souls had to pay the ferryman
Charon. The needed coin was thoughtfully
placed under the tongues of the dead so
they could pay their way.

Below: this painting of *Dante and His Poem*
was done by a 15th-century artist. Dante's
Divine Comedy shows the afterworld as it
was believed to be in the Middle Ages.

Recollections of Earlier Lives

Right: a young Buddhist monk of Tibet
who is different from all others of his age.
He is an Incarnate Lama, which means that
he is the reincarnation of a head of a
monastery and will in turn become the
head. He was chosen as an Incarnate by
certain signs of revelation shortly after his
birth, which closely followed the death of
the monastery's chief lama. The Dalai
Lama, Tibet's supreme religious leader, is
also chosen by this system of reincarnation.

Above: a statue of Buddha in Kamakura,
Japan. Buddhism was founded by the Hindu
Prince Gautama who preached that
enlightenment could be reached only by
renouncing all desires. By this he meant the
material, sensual, and even the spiritual
cravings of all human beings.

the spirit retains all its earthly characteristics from tone of voice
to birthmarks. Whether Spiritualist, Christian, Jew, or atheist,
however, the Westerner would not readily be attracted to the
concept of losing his individuality.

One aspect of Eastern religions that has enjoyed some popularity in Europe and America—though not normally as part of a
religion—is the belief in reincarnation. However, the fascination
of this idea is, predictably, that in a sense it extends the personality. There is a time-travel aspect to it that fascinates anyone
interested in the past, while those who find their present existence

painful or simply dull can find solace in the possibility that they may have had a more interesting life in the past—or will have one in the future. Not all European or American believers in reincarnation are simply indulging in wishful thinking. Some have arrived at this belief through their conversion to Eastern religions. One such was the late English writer Aldous Huxley who died in 1963. In another instance, several psychiatrists practicing today have come to believe in reincarnation because some of their patients under hypnosis have recalled experiences of times before their own birth. Often the events are of such a violent nature that, according to the theory, they are traumatic enough to be retained hidden in the memory. Other more commonplace memories are entirely lost or buried too deeply to come to the surface. One man recalled being hanged for stealing by his neighbors in Colonial Massachusetts. In another case a patient recalled in great detail a previous life as a member of the Cathars, a medieval religious sect. Her recollections were full of violence, culminating in a terrifying memory of being burned at the stake for heresy.

Despite the wealth of detail that often comes from such hypnotic communications, it is usually impossible to verify the stories by referring to historical sources. When possible, investigation may disprove the case. In the 1950s a Colorado housewife, Virginia Tighe, claimed under hypnosis to have had a previous existence in Ireland as a girl named Bridey Murphy. The case received tremendous publicity until it was discovered that childhood memories, long forgotten by her conscious mind, had surfaced in the form of a "previous incarnation."

Other cases are not so easily dismissed. Some of the remembered details have been checked against reference books—in certain cases obscure enough that the person would not have read them—and found to tally with fact.

Spiritualism was, of course, a product of a mainly Christian society whose beliefs about the afterlife, though differing slightly from one denomination to another, share the idea that the individual survives death as an individual. The Christian creed affirms "the Resurrection of the Body, and the Life Everlasting." Central to the faith is the belief that Christ rose from the dead and appeared to his disciples. Interpretations of this act vary. Some people believe that Christ appeared to them in his actual earthly body. Some interpret the story symbolically, saying that Christ was present among his followers in spirit. Still others believe that he appeared in his spiritual body, which resembled his earthly body but was subtly different from it. This difference would account for the story of the "Road to Emmaus," in which Christ walked and talked with two of his disciples for some time before they recognized him.

Christianity in its various forms has always been concerned with the life everlasting. For most of its existence, the Church held—and parts of it still hold—graphic and vivid ideas of heaven and hell, salvation and damnation. Dante's *Divine Comedy* is the outstanding expression and elaboration of these ideas. Today many theologians are less inclined to theorize about the exact nature of the afterlife, except to affirm that it is progress toward the "Vision of God." As for the nature of the body in which the soul will survive, they can quote St. Paul: "All flesh is not the

Who Was Gretchen?

Mrs. Dolores Jay is an ordinary American housewife, married to a minister and the mother of four children. But when she is deeply hypnotized, Dolores Jay moves back through time past the time of her childhood and her infancy—deeper and deeper back until she whimpers in German. (When she is conscious, she neither speaks nor understands any German).

It is 1870. She is Gretchen Gottlieb, a 16-year-old Catholic girl, terrified and in hiding from anti-Catholic fanatics in a forest. "The man made my mother dead," she says. She complains that her head aches, she talks about a glittering knife, and then, desperately, evades questions. "Gretchen can't," she finally wails. And there it ends. Gretchen presumably was killed, and Mrs. Jay remembers nothing until her own life began in 1923.

Dolores Jay herself can't account for it. She doesn't believe in reincarnation. She has only heard fragments of the taped hypnosis sessions, but she can't understand the language. She has never been to Germany. She has never heard of the little town of Eberswalde where Gretchen says she lived, and which exists in what is now East Germany close to the Polish border. But Eberswalde was the scene of Germany's last stand against the Soviet Union in 1945, and the town was almost completely razed. The records that once might have proved whether or not there was such a person as Gretchen Gottlieb have been destroyed.

Who can explain it? Not the modern middle-aged woman who, under hypnosis, becomes the young 19th-century German girl—a girl who remembers her dolls, her home, and her own death.

Many Questions Still Unanswered

Below: *The Resurrection* by Ferrair Gaudenzio, done in the 16th century. The resurrection of Christ—and the promise of resurrection for his faithful followers—is a fundamental teaching of Christianity. It is mentioned in all four Gospels, and in the epistles of Paul.

same flesh: but there is one kind of flesh of men, another flesh of beasts, another of fishes, and another of birds. . . . So also is the resurrection of the dead. It is sown in corruption: it is raised in incorruption: it is sown in dishonor; it is raised in glory: it is sown in weakness; it is raised in power: it is sown a natural body; it is raised a spiritual body. There is a natural body, and there is a spiritual body." (1 Corinthians 15:39, 42–44)

What does this spiritual body look like? To this inevitable question Christianity does not offer a precise answer. It is suggested that in some fundamental way it will resemble one's earthly body so as to preserve a person's individuality, but without age or sex. More than this, few theologians would care to specify.

Many, however, have been highly critical of the Spiritualist conception of the afterlife. "I should be very disappointed," commented one Anglican clergyman, "if the afterlife were so concerned with trivia as the Spiritualists believe." To state the Christian point of view rather bluntly, we will have better things to do in afterlife than play guessing games and indulge in reminiscences with those we have left behind.

Not that all Christians would rule out the possibility of some communication from the beyond, but they would expect it to occur only for some important reason—as in some of the cases in which saints are said to have appeared to certain people. The story of Joan of Arc and her voices is probably the outstanding example of this kind. Only certain people are afforded such glimpses of the next world. Most Christians, while encouraged to prepare themselves spiritually for eternal life, are not encouraged to become preoccupied with it.

It is not surprising that some people find it difficult to adopt an attitude of patient faith. In particular those who have lost someone they love can be extremely anxious to know without a shred of doubt that that person continues to exist. Others may simply become intrigued by the possibility of discovering the truth by scientific or quasi-scientific means. Because science has solved so many of the mysteries of the universe, some people expect it to solve the mystery of possible existence beyond the grave.

After more than 125 years of gathering evidence for life after death, Spiritualism still has not arrived at a clear conception of that life. Most Spiritualists believe that there are various planes or spheres so that each spirit goes to an astral plane or sphere best suited to the stage of spiritual development the living person had reached. They also believe that there is subsequent spiritual progress open to every soul. Some Spiritualists hold that this progress entails reincarnation, while others feel that it takes place entirely in spiritual worlds. The main innovation of Spiritualism in the long history of belief in immortality is the idea that communication between the inhabitants of our world and those of the next is not only possible but relatively easy—if we on this side of the divide follow the correct procedures.

Right: *The Doubt: Can These Dry Bones Live?* This painting by a mid-19th-century artist draws on that period's deep interest in religion and death. An answer is perhaps suggested by the sprouting chestnut lying on the grave marker which is inscribed "Resurgam" — "I shall rise again".

Chapter 11
The Scientists Investigate

Were the mediums capable of producing genuine physical materializations during their seances? Here is the evidence, with the reports of the investigators who risked their reputations (usually gained in other more generally recognized disciplines) to discover if spirits were not only speaking from the grave but actually appearing in ectoplasmic form. Certainly the seances they attended were often spectacular, with tables flying, apparitions materializing and disappearing, and even flowers and miscellaneous objects formed out of thin air, as mediums in trance groaned and shuddered. How were the scientists able to carry out serious research in the gloomy darkness of the seance room? What were their discoveries?

On a midwinter evening in England just about 100 years ago a small group of psychic investigators were sitting in a small, warm, gaslit room, eager to witness the phenomena produced by a powerful young medium named Agnes Nichol. The seance lasted for four hours, and at the end of it, a most astonishing manifestation occurred. On a bare table in the center of the room there suddenly appeared a quantity of flowers. Anemones, tulips, chrysanthemums, Chinese primroses, and ferns lay in a heap on the table.

"All were absolutely fresh as if gathered from a conservatory," wrote one of the witnesses. "They were covered with a fine, cold dew. Not a petal was crumpled or broken, not the most delicate point or pinnule of the ferns was out of place."

It would be easy to dismiss this report as beyond belief, and to assume that the researcher was inexperienced and gullible and the medium a brilliant fraud. However, the man who wrote those words cannot be so easily dismissed. It was Dr. Alfred Russel Wallace who, with Charles Darwin, had developed the theory of evolution. Wallace was one of the first scientists to investigate Spiritualism. The seance described was held in his own home. This fact tends to rule out the possibility of the medium having brought the flowers into the room through secret panels or doors in the ceiling, as some critics have suggested.

Dr. Wallace, like many leading scientists of his period, was strongly attracted by the idea of doing research on psychic and

By the 1860s psychic phenomena were becoming so widespread that some scientists began warily to investigate the claims made by the Spiritualists and mediums.

Opposite: the materialization of Katie King, the spirit control of medium Florence Cook. This is a photograph taken by Crookes.

Early Tests on Mediums' Powers

occult phenomena. More than a decade earlier, when he had been an unknown teacher in England's industrial heartland, he had taken a great interest in hypnosis—then known as mesmerism and considered as part of the occult. Later, during the 12 years of tropical travel, exploration, and study that led to the formulation of his theory of evolution, Dr. Wallace learned about the Spiritualism boom at home through letters. He resolved that, on his return to England, he would investigate the powers that produced the knocks, movements, and other spirit manifestations of the seances.

Dr. Wallace started his experiments in the summer of 1865. After attending a dozen seances he became convinced of, as he put it, "an unknown power." In September of that year he participated in seances with one of England's first professional mediums, Mrs. Mary Marshall. She was able to produce the raps, table levitation, and spirit writings typical of the time. Wallace is reported to have witnessed these phenomena in broad daylight, apparently satisfying himself that there was no fraud. He was particularly impressed by spirit messages spelled out through Mrs. Marshall's mediumship. Although a stranger to him, Mrs. Marshall was able to tell him his brother's name, where he died, and the last person who saw him alive.

Perhaps with the idea of ruling out fraud completely, Wallace decided to carry on his investigations in his own home. Starting in November 1866 he arranged to study at close range the extraordinary powers of young Agnes Nichol, later the well-known Mrs. Guppy. In the seances with her, levitation was a common occurrence—but in an uncommon way. Sometimes the medium was lifted chair and all onto the table. An even more astonishing aspect of her power was the ability to make delicate flowers and other objects materialize out of the thin air, in perfect form. This happened on hundreds of occasions. To confound the skeptics who insisted that the objects must have been secreted in advance, Agnes Nichol often produced specific items on request.

It is said that when a friend of Wallace asked for a sunflower, a six-foot-tall sunflower with earth clinging to its roots fell onto the table. Such experiences led Wallace to state that the existence of genuine Spiritualist phenomena did not require further confirmation. Such phenomena "are proved," he wrote, "quite as well as any facts are proved in other sciences."

The public was understandably confused by the claims and counterclaims surrounding the new Spiritualist movement in the late 19th century. Many people hoped that science would eventually step in to settle the matter once and for all. The London Dialectical Society, formed in 1867, was an early attempt to do just that. Among its first minutes we find a decision to appoint a committee of eminent members "to investigate the phenomena alleged to be Spiritual manifestations, and to report thereon."

The committee's report was presented to the Society's Council on July 20, 1870, and published privately in 1871. It concluded that raps and knocks occurred without mechanical contrivance, that movements of heavy objects occurred without contact or connection with any person, and that these sounds and movements "often occur at the time and in the manner asked for by persons present, and by means of a simple code of signals

Left: Alfred Russel Wallace, the naturalist who with Darwin enunciated the principles of evolution. He was also one of the earliest scientists to investigate Spiritualism, and tested Agnes Nichol (later Mrs. Samuel Guppy) at seances in his own house.

Left: Mrs. Guppy with one of her children. When a child herself, she was able to see phantoms, and her mediumistic development proceeded rapidly. First she could produce table movements and raps, then levitations in which she would be lifted from the seance table still sitting in her chair, and finally, materializations.

Far left: a six-foot Golden Lily that suddenly appeared at a seance. A spirit control named Yolande reportedly materialized it, and then was unable to dematerialize it for a week. This distressed her, for she had "only got the plant on condition she brought it back." She finally managed to dissolve it, leaving only two flowers that had fallen.

Scientists Begin Psychic Research

Above: Allan Kardec who wrote the basic text of Spiritism in France. He was born as Hypolyte Leon Denizard Rivail, but took as his pseudonym two names he believed he had used in his previous incarnations. In South America today his writings are the basis of a greatly vigorous and popular form of Spiritualism.

answer questions and spell out coherent communications." The committee urged that the subject was worthy of more serious attention than it had hitherto received.

These conclusions did not meet with enthusiasm from the general press. For example *The Times*, then as now one of England's most influential newspapers, dismissed the report as "nothing more than a farrago of impotent conclusions, garnished by a mass of the most monstrous rubbish it has ever been our misfortune to sit in judgment upon."

Among those who wrote to the committee during its investigation was the young French astronomer Camille Flammarion, the man who is credited with having coined the word "psychic." He had embarked on a study of Spiritualism in 1861 at the age of 19 after encountering the philosophy of Allan Kardec in a book called *Le Livre des Esprits* (*The Book of the Spirits*). Kardec believed that spiritual progress can be achieved only by a series of reincarnations. He founded the Society of Psychological Studies in Paris to propagate his beliefs. Flammarion joined Kardec's Society to study psychic phenomena, and after some practice, acquired facility in automatic writing. The long-lived Flammarion believed in the immortality of the soul but, in his early days of psychic research, maintained that Spiritualist phenomena did not prove the case. By 1923, however, when he became President of the Society for Psychical Research, his views had changed. In his presidential address, Flammarion summed up his 60 years of research stating that he had been forced to moderate his views by the weight of evidence. "There are unknown faculties in man belonging to the spirit," he declared, ". . . exceptionally and rarely the dead do manifest, there can be no doubt that such manifestations occur, telepathy exists just as much between the dead and the living as between the living."

In the same month that the Dialectical Society committee gave its report—and well before publication of that 400-page document—a scientist as distinguished as Dr. Alfred Russel Wallace publicly declared himself ready to investigate Spiritualism. This was Sir William Crookes, one of the greatest physicists of the 19th century. The report and Sir William's announcement of July 1870 not only focused public attention on the field of psychical research, but also created a favorable climate in which other scientists could explore this new territory. In the 15 years after 1870, Sir William Barrett and Sir Oliver Lodge—like Sir William Crookes well-known physicists—were actively engaged in investigating the unexplained.

Crookes' decision to delve into Spiritualism was greeted with wide approval. The press felt sure that Crookes, creator of several important scientific inventions and discoverer of the element thallium, would soon show Spiritualist claims to be humbug. Crookes appeared to share that view. When he announced his investigation he stated that he had no preconceived notions on the subject, and then added: "The increased employment of scientific methods will produce a race of observers who will drive the worthless residuum of Spiritualism hence into the unknown limbo of magic and necromancy."

This statement was taken as a disclaimer of belief in Spiritualism. But, if Crookes' private beliefs had been better known, it could have been interpreted that he intended only to disprove the "worthless residuum"—perhaps the frauds—without prejudice to the basic beliefs. Crookes had first come in contact with Spiritualism in 1869 at sittings with Mrs. Marshall. He had also been intrigued by the psychic powers of another medium, J. J. Morse. In his book *Crookes and the Spirit World*, R. G. Medhurst reveals that an entry in the scientist's diary in December 1870 shows he was a firm believer in Spiritualism within months of announcing his intention of studying it. Crookes wrote: "May He [God] also allow us to continue to receive Spiritual communications from my brother who passed over the boundary when in a ship at sea more than three years ago."

Whatever his private beliefs, Crookes applied strict scientific controls during his research with the famous D. D. Home, whose levitations and other physical phenomena were celebrated throughout Europe. Crookes' meticulous testing of Home failed to produce any evidence of fraud. Though his work with Home is without doubt the most important part of Crookes' psychical investigations it is overshadowed by the more doubtful and controversial seances with Florence Cook, a young Londoner barely into her teens. Whereas Home submitted to Crookes' tests in what were virtually laboratory conditions, most of the Florence Cook seances—at least in the beginning—were held in situations in which it was far more difficult to rule out fraud. Crookes recognized this and wrote during the early days of his investigation: "On a few occasions, indeed, I have been allowed to apply tests and impose conditions; but only once or twice have I been permitted to carry off the priestess from her shrine, and in my own house, surrounded by my own friends, to enjoy opportunities of testing the phenomena I had witnessed under less conclusive conditions."

Florence Cook was an extraordinary girl, and the first English medium to produce materializations of a whole human body in the light—which at that time was gaslight. In accordance with normal Spiritualist practice, Florence sat in a dark curtained recess—usually called a "cabinet"—to protect her from the light. (Spiritualists say that bright light can be harmful to a medium during a physical seance.) After a while, a spirit form who called herself Katie King emerged from this cabinet.

During tests the medium was sometimes tied to her chair, and other elementary controls were introduced, but they seldom satisfied the skeptics. The disbelief was supported by the evidence of the sitters' eyes. Florence Cook and her materialization Katie King were remarkably similar in appearance. What was needed was proof that the two girls were different, and that they could both be seen simultaneously. Crookes was aware of this, and eventually furnished what he regarded as the necessary evidence. He wrote in one of the Spiritualist journals of the day that throughout the seance, while watching the materialized Katie King, he had distinctly heard "a sobbing, moaning sound . . . from behind the curtain where the young lady was supposed to be sitting." Not surprisingly, his critics were not impressed. Soon, however, Crookes furnished what he regarded as "absolute proof." In a letter to *The Spiritualist*, dated March 30, 1874, he wrote:

Below: Camille Flammarion, the astronomer and psychic researcher, is cartooned among the stars. Although he was close to Kardec as a young man, he was skeptical about the phenomena of Spiritism as then manifested. Practicing automatic writing with Kardec's Society for Psychological Studies, he succeeded in obtaining words and phrases on astronomical subjects signed by Galileo. But he was firmly convinced that the scripts were the product of his own mind, and that Galileo had nothing to do with them. Later in his life, Flammarion softened his viewpoint, and apparently believed that some manifestations were genuine.

LES HOMMES D'AUJOURD'HUI

DESSINS DE GILL

CAMILLE FLAMMARION

Right: the young Florence Cook.

Far right: Katie King, the materialized spirit guide of Florence Cook. The two girls looked very alike, as this picture shows, but Crookes found differences in them. For example, Florence wore earrings for pierced ears, but Katie could not. Katie King was also much taller.

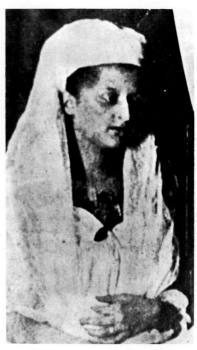

"On March 12, during a seance here [at his home in Northwest London] after Katie had been walking amongst us and talking for some time, she retreated behind the curtain which separated my laboratory, where the company was sitting, from my library, which did temporary duty as a cabinet. In a minute she came to the curtain and called me to her, saying, 'come into the room and lift my medium's head up, she has slipped down.' Katie was then standing before me clothed in her usual white robes and turban headdress. I immediately walked into the library up to Miss Cook, Katie stepping aside to allow me to pass. I found Miss Cook had slipped partially off the sofa, and her head was hanging in a very awkward position. I lifted her onto the sofa, and in so doing had satisfactory evidence, in spite of the darkness, that Miss Cook was not attired in the 'Katie' costume but had on her ordinary black velvet dress, and was in deep trance. Not more than three seconds elapsed between my seeing the white-robed Katie standing before me and raising Miss Cook onto the sofa from the position into which she had fallen."

However, Crookes had still not seen the two together. The opportunity came on March 29, he said, when Katie invited him into the cabinet after he had turned out the gaslight in the laboratory. He carried with him a phosphorus lamp, by whose dim light he could see adequately.

"I went cautiously into the room it being dark [continued Crookes' letter], and felt about for Miss Cook. I found her crouching on the floor. Kneeling down, I let air enter the phosphorus lamp, and by its light I saw the young lady dressed in black velvet, as she had been in the early part of the evening, and to all appearances perfectly senseless; she did not move when I took her hand and held the light quite close to her face, but continued quietly breathing. Raising the lamp, I looked around and saw Katie standing close behind Miss Cook. She was robed in flowing white drapery as we had seen her previously during the seance. Holding one of Miss Cook's hands in mine, and still kneeling, I passed the lamp up and down so as to illuminate Katie's whole figure, and satisfy myself thoroughly that I was really looking at the veritable Katie . . . and not at the phantasm of a disordered brain. She did not speak, but moved her head and smiled in recognition. Three separate times did I turn the lamp to Katie and examine her with steadfast scrutiny until I had no doubt whatever of her objective reality. At last Miss Cook moved slightly, and Katie instantly motioned me to go away. I went to another part of the cabinet and then ceased to see Katie, but did not leave the room till Miss Cook woke up, and two of the visitors came in with a light."

In the same letter Crookes pointed out some important differences in the appearance of the medium and the spirit materialization. Katie was six inches taller than Florence, he asserted. The spirit girl's skin was smooth on her neck, while the medium's neck was rough and had a large blister on it. Katie's ears were unpierced, but Florence Cook habitually wore earrings. The spirit's complexion was very fair, whereas the medium's was dark. Katie's fingers were longer than Florence's, and her face was larger.

Spiritualists distrusted scientists, and Crookes realized this. He and his family therefore befriended Florence Cook and gradually gained her confidence. The young girl was a regular visitor to the Crookes' house and occasionally stayed with the family, sometimes for a week at a time. The trust that developed between the scientist and the medium enabled Crookes to take a

The Spirit and the Scientist

Below: Katie King appearing at a seance in Philadelphia in 1874. At this time the London Katie and Florence Cook were in the midst of hectic seances with Crookes because Katie had said she was going to take her leave in a week's time. (She had said at the start that she would only manifest herself for three years.) When Crookes saw a photograph of the Philadelphia Katie, he declared her a fraud.

Photographs Show Spirit in Action

series of 44 photographs that must be among the strangest in the annals of science. They show Katie King walking around Crookes' laboratory, in one case arm-in-arm with the scientist. Five cameras were used, including two stereoscopic ones. All were operated simultaneously so as to capture the spirit from various angles.

When Katie had first communicated through Florence Cook she said it would only be for a three-year period. In 1874 she announced her intended departure. The week before she was to leave for good, Crookes took the photographs. During the photographic sessions Katie is said to have covered Florence Cook's head with a shawl to protect her from the flashes.

"It was a common thing [during the photographic sessions] for the seven or eight of us in the laboratory to see Miss Cook and Katie at the same time, under the full blaze of the electric light," Crookes testified. This happened when he was asked by Katie to hold the curtain open. "We did not on these occasions see the

Right: this drawing of Crookes shows him looking at Katie King and Florence Cook with a phosphorus lamp while the medium is in trance. The scene is the library of Crookes' home, used as a cabinet during seances. Most mediums used cabinets to condense the psychic energy necessary for manifestations, they explained.

Private Seance by Miss Florence Cook,
OF LONDON.

Admit *Mr Bowles*

3 Waverley Rd

Preston

to private Séance on *Monday April 17-9*

at *7-45* o'clock p.m. prompt,

to be held at *Mrs Searl's*

43 Ormus St New Hall Lane

note the No make no inquiries

This Ticket not transferable

face of the medium because of the shawl, but we saw her hands
and feet; we saw her move uneasily under the influence of the
intense light, and we heard her moan occasionally. I have one
photograph of the two together, but Katie is seated in front of
Miss Cook's head."

During the photography sessions the scientist was able to see
the features of the materialized Katie in the light of the flash, and
he vouched for the fact that several small marks on the medium's
face were not on Katie's. He took the spirit's pulse one evening
and found it beating steadily at 75 per minute, close to normal.
The medium's pulse, taken a little while later, was going at its
usual rapid rate of 90. He also found Katie's lungs to be sounder
than Florence Cook's at a time when the medium was under
treatment for a severe cough.

More proof that Florence and Katie were not one and the
same had been provided by Cromwell Varley, the famous consultant electrician who worked on the Atlantic cable. An ardent
Spiritualist, Varley devised a test designed to prove that Florence
Cook was inside the cabinet when Katie paraded around the
seance room. Florence was placed in an electrical circuit with
wires connected to coins placed on her arms so that a small
current was running through her body. A large *galvanometer*—an
instrument that detects and measures small electric currents—
was placed 10 feet away from the cabinet. It was placed on a
mantelpiece in full view of the sitters so that the flow of the
electrical current could be monitored. If the medium broke the
circuit in order to leave the cabinet dressed as Katie, the galvanometer would register violent fluctuations. Katie appeared
as usual, and there was no change in the current. Crookes asked
Katie to plunge her hands into a chemical solution that would
cause a change in the current flow if Florence managed to dress
as Katie and leave the cabinet without removing the wires.
Again the galvanometer showed no significant fluctuation of
current.

At her last materialization Katie allowed Crookes to witness
the touching farewell between her and her medium Florence

Above: a photograph by Crookes showing
himself with Katie King on his arm. He
took many photos of Katie, but few now
survive.

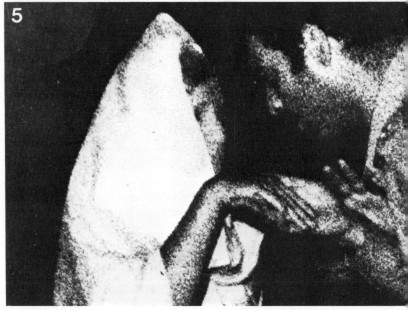

Cook. Crookes sent an account of this to *The Spiritualist*:

"After closing the curtains she conversed with me for some time, and then walked across the room to where Miss Cook was lying senseless on the floor. Stooping over her, Katie touched her and said, 'Wake up, Florrie, wake up! I must leave you now.' Miss Cook then woke and tearfully entreated Katie to stay a little time longer. 'My dear, I can't; my work is done. God bless you,' Katie replied, and then continued speaking to Miss Cook. For several minutes the two were conversing with each other, till at last Miss Cook's tears prevented her speaking. Following Katie's instructions I then came forward to support Miss Cook, who was falling onto the floor, sobbing hysterically. I looked round, but the white-robed Katie had gone. As soon as Miss Cook was sufficiently calmed, a light was procured and I led her out of the cabinet."

Was Sir William Crookes the victim of an extremely clever fraud? He was fully aware that many people assumed so, but he

"The White-Robed Katie Had Gone"

After the reports Crookes made of his sensational work with Florence Cook and Katie King, Katie became a kind of psychic celebrity. It was claimed that she appeared not only at the Philadelphia seance, but in Winnipeg as well. More recently, she reportedly materialized in Rome in July 1974, appearing to a circle of 23 sitters. The seance was held under strong red light that made strange photo lighting. The medium was Fulvio Rendhell. Katie materialized gradually (2), and then walked around the outside of the circle touching several sitters and kissing a few. She materialized gladioli and rose petals (3 & 6), which she held during the full half hour of her appearance. Katie permitted a doctor to check her heartbeat and temperature; both were normal. Then she embraced her medium, and dematerialized on his chest, leaving an empty chair (7) and the flowers behind.

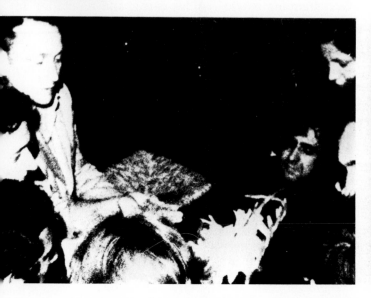

Scientists Found Research Society

Below: Sir Oliver Lodge, another early scientific investigator who became a Spiritualist. He wrote an influential book about his communications with the spirit of his dead son.

felt that he was not. He defended his experiences with these words:

"Every test that I have proposed she [Florence Cook] has at once agreed to submit to with the utmost willingness; she is open and straightforward in speech, and I have never seen anything approaching the slightest symptom of a wish to deceive. Indeed, I do not believe she could carry on a deception if she were to try, and if she did she would certainly be found out very quickly, for such a line of action is altogether foreign to her nature. And to imagine that an innocent schoolgirl of 15 should be able to conceive and then successfully carry out for three years so gigantic an imposture as this, and in that time submit to any test which might be imposed upon her, should bear the strictest scrutiny, should be willing to be searched at any time, either before or after a seance, and should meet with even better success in my own house than at that of her parents, knowing that she visited me with the express object of submitting to strict scientific tests—to imagine, I say, the Katie King of the last three years to be the result of imposture does more violence to one's reason and common sense than to believe her to be what she herself affirms."

Crookes' experiments with Florence Cook were not as rigidly controlled as today's psychic researchers would demand. Nonetheless they leave few areas of doubt. There are three possible conclusions: either Katie King was in fact a spirit being, in which case Crookes' research is probably the most important on record; or Florence Cook deceived everyone about her mediumistic powers, in which case she must be regarded as the most accomplished imposter in Spiritualism's history; or Crookes and the young medium were in collusion. The third alternative touches the distinguished scientist with scandal. It is based on a statement by a man named Anderson, who claims that Florence Cook made a confession of fraud to him during her later life. According to Anderson, she also said that Crookes was having an affair with her. This statement was not made public until after Anderson's death. Most researchers regard it as flimsy evidence either of fraud or of a sexual alliance between Florence Cook and Sir William Crookes. It seems unlikely that a scientist of Crookes' standing would risk his career and reputation by fabricating evidence. However, his predisposition to believe in Spiritualism must be taken into consideration. Whatever the explanation, the story of the scientist, the medium, and the spirit girl remains one of the most fascinating and puzzling enigmas in the Spiritualist saga.

While Crookes was photographing Katie King, another prominent scientist was embarking on a study of psychic phenomena. This was Sir William Barrett, professor of physics at the Royal College of Science in Dublin. His first experiments centered on hypnotic trances, but he went on to study many aspects of Spiritualism including physical phenomena. During the course of his research, he heard raps in broad daylight in circumstances that ruled out fraud. After that he was inclined to consider raps as possible indication of spirit activity. But he still at first dismissed the more dramatic phenomena—such as levitation—attributing them to hallucination. He later revised his thinking on the subject when he discovered that some of his friends possessed mediumistic powers that caused levitation. They were above suspicion, and with their help he carried out tests in daylight which satisfied him that such powers were genuine.

In January 1882 Barrett called a conference in the offices of the British National Association of Spiritualists. Out of this was born the Society for Psychical Research (SPR). Its objectives were to examine a variety of phenomena including telepathy, hypnotism, apparitions, and the physical phenomena of Spiritualism, and to collect and collate material on these subjects. The SPR, still active today, holds no corporate view on any of these phenomena, but many of its members, and its own publications, have been responsible for presenting much of the best-authenticated evidence for Spiritualist phenomena. Professor Barrett was one of the original members of the Society, along with other eminent researchers and Spiritualists. Three years later, during a visit to the United States, Barrett gave impetus to the foundation of the American Society for Psychical Research.

Crookes once wrote that he "intended only to devote a leisure month or two to ascertain whether certain marvelous occurrences . . . would stand the test of close scrutiny." He discovered, however, that "the subject is far more difficult and extensive than it appears," and those months soon became years. The same was probably true of Barrett, who spent over half a century investigating Spiritualism and similar subjects. In a paper included in the SPR's *Proceedings* in 1924 entitled "Some Reminiscences of Fifty Years of Psychical Research," Barrett summed up his conclusions. He stated that there is evidence for the existence of a spiritual world, for survival after death, and for occasional communications from those who have died—or "passed over" as Spiritualists say.

As the founders of the SPR were launching a systematic study of the psychic world, the world-famous physicist Sir Oliver Lodge was independently becoming involved in experiments in telepathy. While teaching at Liverpool University, Lodge was asked by a local merchant to supervise some tests of two of his salesgirls who had shown telepathic powers. The tests were conducted along lines suggested by the SPR, and Lodge submitted a report of the findings to the Society. Soon afterward he became a member of the organization.

His interest in psychical research having been aroused, Lodge continued such study for the remaining 56 years of his life. He became convinced of the existence of thought-transference. He also encountered convincing evidence of the continued existence of the personality after death—called "survival" by Spiritualists —in the work of the remarkable Boston medium Mrs. Leonore Piper. This American medium visited England in 1889-90 purposely to give test seances for the SPR. She and her daughters, who were met in Liverpool by Lodge, stayed with the Lodge family for some time. During seances in their home she went into trance and produced information about distant and deceased relatives of Lodge. She included details that she could not have learned merely from talking to the Lodge family, or even from family letters and records. Lodge became, in his own words, "thoroughly convinced not only of human survival, but of the

Above: the American medium Mrs. Leonore Piper. Almost all her work was done under strict scientific control. Her powers were almost entirely mental, her one physical accomplishment being to withdraw scent from flowers which then withered.

Below: an example of automatic writing as done by Leonore Piper.

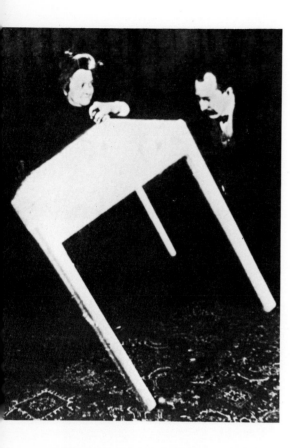

Above: a table levitating at one of Eusapia Paladino's seances. When her feet were not held, she would lift the tables with her knees. However, even when she was put under tight restraint, the tables still unquestionably rose.

power to communicate, under certain conditions, with those left behind on the earth."

Having satisfied himself about the value of Spiritualism, Lodge became a crusader, sharing his findings with any who would listen to him or read his words. It was not until World War I that his belief in communications with the spirit world received its greatest publicity, however. This was through a very personal book, *Raymond, or Life and Death*. In it Lodge related the events surrounding the tragic loss of his son Raymond, who was killed in action in September 1915. He said that, before learning of his son's death, he had received a cryptic message in automatic writing from Mrs. Piper, then on her third visit to England. The message was from Dr. Richard Hodgson, a pillar of the SPR who had died in 1905. Through Mrs. Piper he wrote in part: "Myers says you take the part of the poet and he will act as Faunus. Faunus. Myers. Protect." (Frederick Myers, one of the founders of the SPR, had been dead since 1901). A classical scholar recognized the reference to Faunus as coming from a poem by the Roman writer Horace. In his poem, Horace describes how the woodland god Faunus saved his life by cushioning the blow when a tree fell on him. Shortly afterward Lodge received the news of his son's death. He then interpreted the message as both a prediction of the event and as an effort by the spirits to cushion him from the blow. Lodge gave other examples in his book of the numerous communications he and his wife received from their dead son through mediums.

Before he died Lodge left a sealed message with the SPR. He let it be known that the message contained details he had never revealed to anyone, and that he hoped to reveal from beyond the grave. Although many messages were allegedly received from the great physicist after his death in 1940, none has been the one Lodge intended to communicate as the proof of survival.

Whereas scientists usually accept the conclusions of their colleagues on scientific matters, they have always been reluctant to concur on psychic matters without having personal experience. This is probably partly because the evidence violates well-established natural laws, and partly, no doubt, because emotional factors can influence the evaluation of evidence. And so, although Dr. Alfred Russel Wallace, Sir William Crookes, Sir William Barrett, and Sir Oliver Lodge had all accepted the evidence in favor of Spiritualist claims after their own research, other scientists scoffed at their findings.

For example, Professor Cesar Lombroso, a famous Italian criminologist, wrote an article in 1888 in which he ridiculed Spiritualism. As a result, he was publicly challenged to a seance with a famous medium, and in 1891 he accepted the invitation. He was accompanied by three other professors and five doctors. Afterward he wrote: "I am ashamed and grieved at having opposed with so much tenacity the possibility of the so-called spiritistic facts; I say the facts because I am still opposed to the theory. But the facts exist, and I boast of being a slave to facts."

Lombroso continued to investigate Spiritualism, and eventually accepted the idea that the dead could communicate through mediums. In his book *After Death—What?* he gave an account of a seance with the medium who had convinced him of the

THE KINK OF DENMARK.

Left: a 1909 cartoon from the *American Journal Examiner* during Eusapia Paladino's American tour, when she was detected in the act of producing fraudulent effects at her seances. Her exposure caused a sensation in the press.

Evidence for Psychic Powers

genuineness of psychic powers:

"The medium, who was seated near one end of the table, was lifted up in her chair bodily, amid groans and lamentations on her part, and placed (still seated) on the table, then returned to the same position as before, with her hands continually held, her movements being accompanied by the persons next to her."

The medium in question was Eusapia Paladino, an almost illiterate peasant woman of Neapolitan birth. For 20 years she was the center of intensive research by almost every psychical researcher of importance in Britain, in America, and on the Continent. She was often exposed in fraud, but nearly every scientist who investigated her came to the conclusion that she could also produce a wide variety of genuine manifestations. Sir Oliver Lodge was one of the scientists who sat with Eusapia Paladino. Another was Dr. Charles Richet, Professor of Physiology at the Faculty of Medicine in Paris. Professor P. Foa, Professor of Pathological Anatomy at the University of Turin, and several other Italian scientists also tested the medium and published a report of their findings.

The Spirit Hand that Slapped

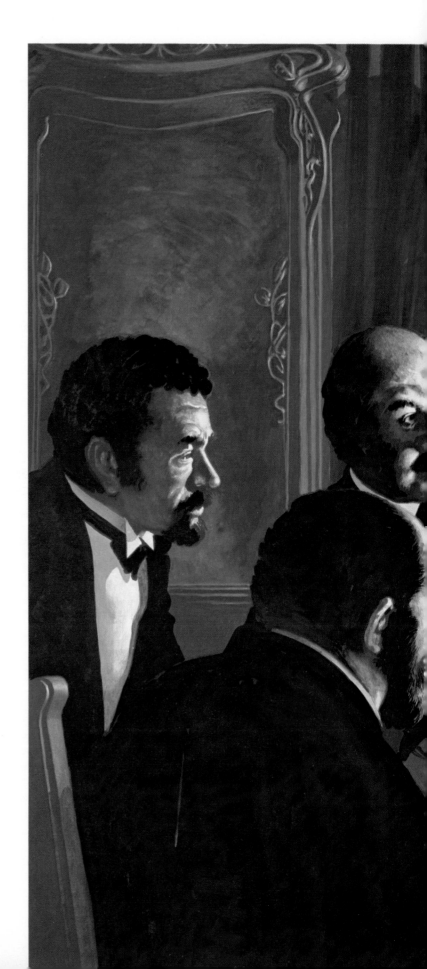

During his investigation of the powers of Eusapia Paladino, the Italian medium noted for bang-up seances, Professor P. Foa tried to use a photographic plate to register radiations. Eusapia Paladino's spirits apparently resented the interference. As the medium sat in trance outside the curtained cabinet, a hand shot out and tried to snatch the plate. Dr. Foa seized the hand as it retreated behind the curtains and felt the fingers, but the hand wriggled loose and hit him squarely.

The spirits then turned their attention to a table, which they sailed over the heads of the company. When one sitter attempted to approach it, the spirits whisked it behind the curtain where it began to break up noisily. Dr. Foa saw the table turn over on its side, and one leg snap off. At that point it shot back out of the cabinet and continued to break up noisily under the fascinated gaze of the entire circle. One of the sitters asked for a handshake, and Eusapia Paladino invited him to approach the cabinet. He had hardly reached it when he felt himself attacked by hands and pieces of wood.

The entire circle heard the noises of the blows, and saw the hand moving in the ghostly half-light.

Can Ectoplasm Be Flesh and Blood?

Below: Eva C. producing ectoplasm. Her hands are holding apart the curtains of the cabinet. The photograph was taken by flashlight.

Although a curtained cabinet was used by Eusapia Paladino, she always sat outside and the manifestations—hands and faces sometimes—appeared inside the cabinet. During the seance with Professor Foa and his colleagues, a photographic plate was used in an attempt to register radiations associated with the phenomena. The presence of this plate, according to the report, aroused the spirits' hostility:

"The 'hand' . . . made an effort to seize the plate by snatching it unexpectedly, and renewed this attempt repeatedly, but without success. Dr. Foa seized the hand which was covered with the curtain, and had the impression of pressing real fingers; the fingers escaped him, however, and gave him a blow . . . Dr. Aggazotti, who held another plate over the medium's head, had in his turn to struggle in order to prevent its escaping him.

"At this juncture the medium told . . . Foa not to be alarmed whatever might happen, and advised all present not to touch the objects which would be suspended in the air, otherwise she would be unable to restrain the movements and might hurt somebody.

"Table No. 1 rose in the air many inches high, and passed once over the head of Prof. Foa; returning to the ground and, keeping all the time outside the cabinet, it turned over, then stood up again. . . .

"After table No. 1 had stood upright, Dr. Arullani approached it, but the piece of furniture moving violently toward him, repulsed him; Dr. Arullani seized the table, which was heard to crack in the struggle . . . [the table] passed behind the curtain . . . Dr. Foa saw it turn over and rest on one of its two short sides, whilst one of the legs came off violently, as if under the action of some force pressing upon it. At this moment the table came violently out of the cabinet, and continued to break up under the eyes of every one present. Dr. Arullani asked for [a] handshake, and was invited by the medium to approach the cabinet. He had hardly reached it when he felt himself hit by pieces of wood and hands, and we all heard the noise of the blows."

No one slept when Eusapia Paladino was giving a seance!

All the European investigators of Eusapia Paladino knew that the medium sometimes used trickery, and also knew her tricks. However, when she went to the United States during 1909–10, she was given much bad publicity on being exposed in her well-known frauds, in spite of her performance of many genuine phenomena. Her defenders said that she was so fearful of her American investigators that she often did not allow herself to go into trance in case she might be hurt. She herself explained to one newspaper reporter: "Some people are at the table who expect tricks—in fact they want them. I am in a trance. Nothing happens. They get impatient. They think of the tricks—nothing but the tricks. They put their minds on the tricks and I automatically respond. But it is not often. They merely will me to do them."

Psychic magazine sums up Eusapia Paladino's extraordinary career in these words: "No scientist then or now . . . has been able to explain many of [her] dizzying feats in any way that does not of necessity imply the existence of some force as yet completely unknown to science . . . she is one of history's unresolved paradoxes."

The ability of mediums to produce physical manifestations has been attributed to a curious substance called ectoplasm. This substance, produced from the medium's body, is believed to be capable of assuming various forms. Sometimes, according to Spiritualists, it is able to cause raps and knocks though invisible. At other times, it takes on the appearance of a misty cloud floating around the room. Spiritualists believe it can also become as solid as a human being, taking on all the human characteristics of color and texture. Baron A. von Schrenk-Notzing, a Munich physician and psychical researcher, was able to obtain and preserve a small piece of ectoplasm and submit it for analysis. It was found to contain leukocytes—white or colorless blood cells —and epithelial cells—those from various protective tissues of the body. Ectoplasm was, he said, "an organized tissue which easily decomposes—a sort of transitory matter which originates in the organism in a manner unknown to us, possesses unknown biological functions and formative possibilities, and is evidently peculiarly dependent on the psychic influences of the medium."

Between 1917 and 1920, Dr. W. J. Crawford, lecturer in mechanical engineering at Queens University, Belfast, conducted many experimental seances with the Goligher family in an attempt to define the nature of ectoplasm. He discovered that during seances, the medium, Kathleen Goligher, and the sitters all lost weight. The medium's body shrank perceptibly. Placing the medium on a set of scales, he measured her loss of weight when ectoplasm was experimentally withdrawn in fluxes from her. The maximum loss was $54\frac{1}{2}$ pounds, nearly half her normal weight. By contrast, during table levitations her weight increased. Strict test controls prevented her from touching the table, so the increase could not be explained by her bearing the weight. Dr. Crawford put forward the theory that the medium threw out ectoplasmic supports, like cantilevers. He was able to take flash photographs that appear to show ectoplasmic rods issuing from Kathleen Goligher, some of them reaching to the table. Dr. Crawford had reached no final conclusion at the time of his death on July 30, 1920.

Sir William Barrett was a witness at one of the Goligher seances. He described later how he had seen the table suspended 18 inches in the air with no one touching it. He was unable to press the table down, using all his strength. When he climbed onto it to force it down, he was promptly thrown off. After this the table turned upside down on the floor. He was asked to lift it up, but was unable to move it. It "appeared screwed down to the floor," he attested.

It is now many years since these eminent scientists investigated Spiritualism and, although many of them declared themselves 100 percent convinced of the authenticity of some of the psychic phenomena, we are today no nearer a scientific understanding of what really happens at a seance. The case for the authenticity of physical phenomena rests largely on the research of these early pioneers, for today there are few mediums who claim power to produce such phenomena. Mediums at some Spiritualist camps still offer to give materialization seances, but the ease with which the manifestations appear makes their genuineness more than a little suspect.

Above: some of the spirits materialized by Eva C. had a distinctly flat, two-dimensional appearance, and skeptics suggested they were simply pictures on cardboard. This seems possible in the above materialization.

Chapter 12
Frauds and Fraud-hunters

Do all mediums cheat, given the opportunity? The history of fraud would suggest that might be true. Skeptical researchers, armed with the increasingly sophisticated equipment of developing science, acquired a formidable battery of techniques to trap the medium trying to pretend that theatrical tricks were spirit manifestations. How did they catch the unwary? What tricks were uncovered? What part did magicians such as Houdini play in unmasking the frauds? Did the great Houdini himself succeed in communicating with his wife after his death—or if the message claimed to be received never existed, was it because she herself had entered into a conspiracy to hoodwink believers and gain publicity?

On a cold night in January 1880 Marie, a "spirit girl," was singing and dancing before some distinguished guests. Round and round the darkened seance room she danced. Suddenly one of the guests reached out and grabbed her by the wrist. Surprisingly, the spirit struggled and fought with him—and the seance ended abruptly when gaslight revealed that Marie was really the medium herself, dressed only in undergarments.

An even more embarrassing aspect of the exposure was the fact that the medium was the same Florence Cook whose Katie King materialization had walked arm-in-arm with Sir William Crookes a few years earlier. That famous scientist had affirmed his belief in the genuineness of the phenomena Miss Cook had produced under his supervision. Even now, when she was caught in an act of fraud, he continued to believe in her psychic powers. Others, too, continued to believe in her. As for Florence Cook's reaction to the exposé, she was apparently untroubled by it, for she gave another seance the following day.

All professional mediums cheat. That was the view of Camille Flammarion, the French psychic researcher. However, Flammarion was also convinced after nearly 60 years' study of psychic phenomena that mediums could be genuine. His views on fraud were shared by many of his fellow researchers. "It is unfortunately true," wrote the English psychic investigator Hereward Carrington, "that many genuine mediums will frequently resort to fraud when their powers fail them, or when

As Spiritualism developed, the phenomena became more dramatic and the opportunities for fraud more abundant. Investigators of a skeptical turn of mind looked for cheating, and found it.

Opposite: an illustration from the *London Graphic* in 1880, showing the famous seance where the spirit girl Marie turned out to be the medium in her underwear.

Above: a contemporary drawing showing
Henry Slade's trial. The man testifying in
the witness box is Professor Lankester, who
had seized Slade's slate and found writing
already prepared. Slade asserted that just as
the slate was snatched he heard the spirit
writing, and said so, but his words were
lost in the commotion.

Right: a slate used in seances with its red
wax seals visible. (The College of Psychic
Studies).

phenomena are not readily forthcoming." He said that the Italian medium Eusapia Paladino, whom he considered to possess genuine powers of a high order, "would constantly trick whenever the occasion for her to do so was presented."

Spiritualists learned to live with a certain amount of fraud as, one after another, even the most respected mediums were caught impersonating spirits. Like some of the scientists, they believed a single case of fraud was not enough proof that a medium had no genuine powers. This permissive attitude toward occasional fraud explains why, even after an exposure, most mediums were able to continue filling their seance rooms.

Although many researchers could easily detect even clever fraud, and could take it into account in their conclusions, it was disputed whether the careful investigator could never be fooled. A lively debate on this subject arose during discussion of Sir William Crookes' paper on mesmerism and Spiritualism, read before the British Association for the Advancement of Science in 1876. Crookes was confident that the controls he applied in testing mediums would make fraud impossible. Sir William Barrett of the SPR disagreed, arguing that a skilled magician or fraudulent medium could be equipped with devices which, whatever the conditions imposed, could be used to deceive.

In spite of the fact that controls in the early days of psychical research were rather slack by modern standards, a great many mediums were exposed in fraud. In 1876—the same year that Crookes and Barrett debated the subject—three British mediums who had attracted large followings were caught red-handed.

Francis Ward Monck, a clergyman turned medium, was challenged by a magician who insisted on searching the medium during a seance in Huddersfield, England. Monck ran into a room, locked himself in, and escaped through a window. Later a pair of stuffed gloves were found among his belongings. Monck was apprehended and put on trial for fraud. Dr. Alfred Russel Wallace, the scientist who had investigated Agnes Nichol and others, was one of the defense witnesses. He claims to have seen Monck produce the spirit form of a woman without trickery. However, Monck had been caught in a flagrant fraud before by none other than Sir William Barrett. On that occasion Sir William found Monck simulating a partially materialized spirit with a piece of white muslin on a wire frame. On the present occasion, Monck was found guilty of fraud and sentenced to three months in prison.

Dr. Henry Slade, an American medium known for spirit writing on slate blackboards, visited Britain in the same year. Professor Ray Lankester was determined to expose Slade as an imposter. Together with another investigator he visited the American medium and observed his techniques. During his second visit to Slade, Lankester suddenly seized the small blackboard before the writing was to take place. He found a message already written on it and secreted. After exposing Slade in a letter to *The Times* on September 16, 1876, Lankester brought an action against the medium for obtaining money under false pretences. The case was heard on October 1. Once again, as in Monck's trial, Dr. Alfred Russel Wallace was a witness for the defense. Despite this distinguished support,

Mediums Tried for Fraud

Challenges from Magicians

Below: contemporary drawings exposing the methods of fraudulent mediums to produce startling fake effects at their sittings. Almost all seances were held in the dark, since strong light was believed to be harmful to mediums in trance, but the darkened rooms offered a perfect opportunity for the fraudulent medium and his tricks.
1. Simulating levitation. The medium creeps around the circle, pretending he is floating above the sitters' heads as he knocks a few with the heels of shoes.
2 and 3. Two views of a "spirit hand" at work mystifying the credulous would-be believers.

Slade was found guilty and sentenced to three months' imprisonment with hard labor. In the course of the appeal the sentence was quashed on technical grounds, and Slade left England quickly for the Continent before Lankester could obtain a fresh summons. When he returned to London two years later he did so under the assumed name of Dr. Wilson.

William Eglinton was the third medium to be revealed as a fraud in 1876. The accounts of his seances are among the most dramatic in the annals of psychic science, and include a number of materializations that occurred out of doors in bright daylight. Eglinton was exposed by Thomas Colley, the Archdeacon of Natal in Southern Africa and the Rector of Stockton in England. The Archdeacon, an eager psychical researcher, cut off pieces of the white robe and beard of a spirit materialized by Eglinton. Later investigation showed that these exactly matched some muslin and a false beard found in the medium's suitcase. His exposure of Eglinton did not make Archdeacon Colley discredit all mediums. He was a firm believer in the genuineness of Monck, for example, and challenged J. N. Maskelyne, a famous magician and anti-Spiritualist, to duplicate Monck's materialization performances by trickery. Archdeacon Colley offered a large sum of money if the magician were successful. Maskelyne attempted to produce a materialization, but failed.

This underlines the enigma of mediumship—that although three well-known mediums such as Monck, Slade, and Eglinton were exposed in fraud, many scientists and investigators of repute did not doubt that all three were also capable of extraordinary mediumistic feats without evidence of trickery.

From the earliest days of Spiritualism there has been a running battle between mediums and magicians. In 1853, just five years after the Hydesville rappings had taken the public by surprise, the first challenge was issued by magician J. H. Anderson of New York. He offered a handsome monetary reward to "any poverty stricken medium" who could produce raps in the public

1   2   3

hall where he gave his performances. The Fox sisters were among those who accepted Anderson's challenge, but Anderson backed out and, amid hisses from the audience, refused to allow the mediums on the stage.

The magician-medium rivalry reached a peak in the case of the Davenport brothers. Their home in Buffalo, New York, had had an outbreak of raps, bumps, and assorted other noises in 1846—two years before the more publicized Hydesville rappings. In 1850 the two boys, Ira and William, and their young sister Elizabeth, tried table turning. The table moved, conveying messages, and some force caused Ira's hand to write automatically. Some witnesses at the same session claimed that the three children levitated simultaneously.

The two young Davenport brothers decided to go professional and give theater performances. They used a special cabinet that had three doors at the front and a bench running lengthwise inside. The center door had a small diamond-shaped opening covered by a curtain, through which various phenomena could manifest. Before each performance members of the audience were free to inspect the cabinet, and also to check that the Davenports, who sat astride the bench facing each other, were securely tied and immobile. Within seconds of the doors being closed, the brothers were able to produce raps, musical sounds, and a variety of other phenomena. During part of the performance a member of the audience was allowed to sit on the bench between the brothers.

Although the phenomena were typical of Spiritualist seances of the day, the brothers maintained an ambiguous stance in regard to their powers. They never presented themselves as Spiritualists; on the other hand, they insisted on the genuineness of the phenomena. In 1857 they responded to a challenge from the *Boston Courier*, which had offered a big prize to anyone producing genuine physical phenomena. A committee of professors from Harvard University conducted the tests. The

Seance procedure was usually for the members of the circle to hold—or at least touch—hands. This not only united their psychic energies, but could also serve as a rudimentary control on the medium. However, it was easily bypassed by any deft and unscrupulous medium, as many exposures have shown.
4. The medium starts out with both hands in contact with those of the sitters on either side.
5. Note the hands. One is now free for banging the tambourine.
6. The trustful sitters, still hand in hand, are duly impressed by the amazing spirit activity.

5 6

brothers were tied in their cabinet with no thought for their comfort; the ropes around them were drawn through holes bored in the cabinet, firmly knotted outside, and tied again with linen strips. Professor Benjamin Pierce, a committee member, sat in the cabinet between the brothers. According to the brothers' biographer, as soon as Professor Pierce entered an invisible hand shot the bolt, the din of musical instruments filled the tiny room, and a phantom hand moved in and out of the diamond-shaped window in the center door. The professor also felt the hand touching his face. At the end of the session the brothers were found released from their ropes, and the ropes were found twisted around the professor's neck. This last statement was hotly denied by the sponsoring newspaper, but it was neither verified or denied by the committee. Aside from a brief negative statement, it never published a report of its findings. However, the prize money was not awarded, so we may surmise that the professors were unconvinced.

In 1864 the Davenports went to England where they soon became a center of controversy. They held seances every night for more than two months in a public hall in London. Various committees studied these demonstrations without finding evidence of fraud. Nevertheless, there was widespread public opposition and even hostility. The Davenports were not helped by the fact that the long ropes and other paraphernalia they used were typical of magicians' acts.

When the Davenports visited Liverpool two members of an inspection committee selected by the audience used a complicated knot to secure the brothers. The Davenports protested that the knot was too tight and inhibited their circulation, but a doctor who examined them disagreed. They refused to sit, and asked one of their helpers to cut the knot. The following night a riot broke out, and the Davenports hastily left Liverpool.

In Hull, Huddersfield, and Leeds, the brothers encountered openly threatening and antagonistic audiences. Feeling that police protection was inadequate, they broke off further en-

Davenports Face Public Hostility

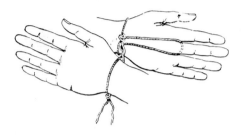

Above: the Davenport knot as explained by W. E. Robinson, a contemporary investigator. He claimed that the Davenports always used a smooth hard-finished rope, which made it impossible for a really secure knot to be tied. The brothers would also influence the person who did the tying to use a particular procedure. This was to tie the left hand first with two or three good knots around the wrist as the two faced the audience. Then, as the brothers put their left hands behind their backs and turned their backs to the audience, the person tying them up was to tie the right hands to the left hands with as many knots as he or she saw fit. But—according to Robinson—they had always managed to catch a little slack between the two hands. Once safely in the cabinet, they simply bent the fingers and, with enough slack to get one hand free, untied the other and produced the noises.

Opposite: a poster advertising one of the performances by the two Davenport brothers. Their public seances were well advertised and well attended.

Left: a rare lithograph of the Davenport brothers in 1864. Ira and William produced phenomena on stage together for some years.

Houdini Wages War on Mediums

gagements. Writing of these events to an associate, the Davenports said: "Were we mere jugglers we should meet with no violence, or we should find protection. Could we declare that these things done in our presence were deception of the senses, we should no doubt reap a plentiful harvest of money and applause. . . . But we are not jugglers, and truthfully declare that we are not, and we are mobbed from town to town, our property destroyed and our lives imperilled."

Life was not all unpleasantness for the Davenports. They went to France where, after some initial opposition from the authorities, they gave a number of successful performances. Before leaving Paris they were summoned to appear before Emperor Napoleon III and Empress Eugénie at the Palace of St. Cloud. There they performed for an astonished gathering of the nobility. They went on to Belgium and then to St. Petersburg, now Leningrad, where the Czar received them in the Winter Palace.

The brothers must have had their private beliefs about the nature of the phenomena they produced, assuming that they were not fraudulent, but they remained resolutely noncommittal in speaking of them. One obvious reason for such a policy was that the speculation and controversy on their attitude created tremendous publicity—and therefore larger audiences. In a letter to Harry Houdini, one of the world's most famous magicians, Ira Davenport said: "We never in public affirmed our belief in Spiritualism. That we regarded as no business of the public, nor did we offer our entertainment as the result of sleight-of-hand or, on the other hand, as Spiritualism. We let our friends and foes settle that as best they could between themselves, but, unfortunately, we were often the victims of their disagreement."

Houdini believed that he could produce all the Davenport's amazing effects by trickery. He claimed that in 1911 he tracked down the surviving brother, Ira, then in his 70s to discover the secret behind one puzzling aspect of their performance. One of the conditions sometimes imposed on the brothers by a member of the audience was that they had to hold flour in their hands throughout the performance. They were able to produce the phenomena without spilling the flour. Houdini claimed that Ira admitted to fraud, revealing that they simply held the flour in the palms of their hands while using their teeth and thumbs to manipulate the ropes and musical instruments. However, there is only Houdini's word for this.

Houdini rode to stardom on the Spiritualist bandwagon, throwing out challenges to mediums wherever he went. According to the British Spiritualist weekly *Psychic News*, Houdini was himself a fraudulent medium for five years before achieving fame as a magician. His subsequent campaign against mediums was accompanied by a wealth of publicity. Part of his act was to give a seance in which he duplicated by trickery the effects presented as genuine by mediums.

Houdini said he believed it was his mission to protect the public from fraudulent mediums. But it also seems that he would go to any lengths, fair or foul, to prove trickery in psychic phenomena. In 1922 he agreed to be a committee member for the

Below: Ira Davenport in his old age with Harry Houdini. (William died in 1877 during a tour of Australia.) Houdini claimed that in 1909 Ira had quite willingly explained to him exactly how the brothers had faked their effects.

Scientific American, which offered a huge prize for proof of genuine mediumship. Margery Crandon, wife of a professor of surgery at the Harvard Medical School, was one of the mediums to be tested. She conducted several convincing seances for the committee in Houdini's absence, and it seemed that they were about to award her the money in 1924.

Houdini hurried back to challenge the decision. Three more sessions were arranged, during which Houdini imposed strict conditions. He designed a cabinet in which the medium could be enclosed with only her head and hands visible. This was used for two of the seances. During the second seance Mrs. Crandon's spirit control Walter accused Houdini of planting incriminating evidence in the cabinet. When the session came to an end, a folding rule was found in the cabinet. Houdini in turn accused Margery Crandon of having smuggled it into the cabinet so that she could use it to manipulate a small box containing a bell which, supposedly, was rung by spirit hands. After Houdini's death in 1926, his assistant confessed that he himself had put the ruler in the cabinet on Houdini's instructions. Whether Houdini exposed Margery Crandon or whether the spirit control exposed Houdini is still a matter for debate.

When the famous illusionist died in 1926, he left a code word with his wife Beatrice in order to prove his identity if anyone claimed to get messages from him. Just over two years later, Beatrice Houdini announced that she herself had received a message from her dead husband through a young medium named

Below: a spirit photograph faked to show the spirit of Lincoln and Houdini brooding together. It became part of the collection of Harry Price, an amateur conjurer and a respected investigator into dubious psychic phenomena.

A Publicity Stunt?

Arthur Ford. In sworn testimony she declared:

"Regardless of any statements made to the contrary, I wish to declare that the message, in its entirety, and in the agreed-upon sequence, given to me by Arthur Ford, is the correct message prearranged between Mr. Houdini and myself."

The witnesses to the statement were H. R. Zander of the United Press; Mrs. Minnie Chester, a lifelong friend of Mrs. Houdini; and J. W. Stafford, associate editor of the *Scientific American*.

Beatrice Houdini had not accepted Ford's mediumship without prior evidence, and had arranged a seance with him only after a previous series of sittings attended by Houdini's mother. In those seances separate words were given, presumably by Houdini, through Ford's spirit control or guide—which is a spirit that relates principally to one medium and introduces other spirits wanting to communicate with the living through that medium. First came "Rosabelle." Four weeks later, the word "lock." Then, after various other clues, Ford declared the entire message as: "Rosabelle — answer — tell — pray — answer — look — tell — answer — answer — tell." The dead magician asked the sitter to convey the message to his widow, adding, "I know she will be happy because neither of us believed it to be possible."

After the message was given to her, Beatrice Houdini arranged a sitting with Ford. During this seance, Ford conveyed intimate information to her from Houdini. Mrs. Houdini released the affidavit the next day, only to be greeted by sneers and abuse from Houdini's former colleagues, who accused her of fraud. This upset her so much that she wrote a long letter to newspaper columnist and radio reporter Walter Winchell, who published it.

"This letter is not for publicity," she began. "I do not need publicity. I want to let Houdini's old friends know that I did not betray his trust. I am writing because I wish to tell you emphatically that I was no party to any fraud. Now, regarding the seance: for two years I have been praying to receive the message from my husband; for two years every day I have received messages from all parts of the world from people professing to have received them. I have got the message I have been waiting for from my beloved, how, if not by spiritual aid, I do not know."

Years later, the truth of the affidavit and of the letter to Winchell came into question. When the British Broadcasting Corporation made a television film of Houdini's life in 1969, it referred to his interest in Spiritualism, but made no mention of his widow's sworn testimony. When a reporter for the *Guardian* newspaper asked the program's producer the reason for this omission, the producer replied: "We spent months researching the subject in America, but Mrs. Houdini's sister, Marie, told us that Houdini's widow had admitted to her that the affidavit was a complete fabrication; that she had signed it because Arthur Ford, her boyfriend at that time, had persuaded her to do so for personal publicity." By this time, Beatrice Houdini had died, and was unavailable for comment on this statement. However, if she had lied in issuing the affidavit, she was certainly guilty of a Spiritualist fraud as great as any of those of a similar nature exposed by her crusading husband during his lifetime.

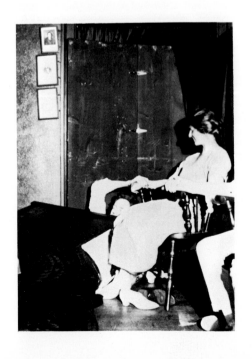

Below: a Margery Crandon seance. Malcolm Bird has been thrown to the ground by a panel of the seance cabinet which the spirit control had apparently ripped off, although it had been secured with three strong angle brackets.

Above: the fraud-proof wooden cage which
Houdini devised to test Margery Crandon.
It was uncomfortable and restrictive for
anyone.

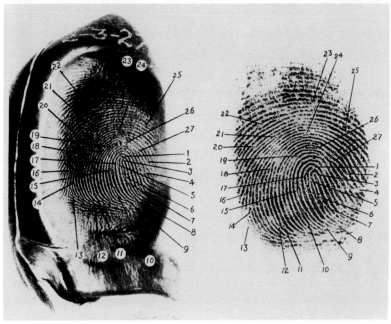

Left: a technique was developed to make a
thumb print in dental wax of Walter, spirit
guide of Margery Crandon. One of the
investigators on checking Walter's print
(left) against those of the sitters, found it
was identical to that of Margery's dentist
(on the right), who had helped her develop
the method of taking the prints. It was
believed that the dentist was innocent of any
part in the business, and it was never
decided who was guilty.

Another member of the Houdini team, press agent Cal Harris, also signed a statement that he had heard Houdini's voice at a seance with medium Frank Decker. "I am satisfied the medium was not speaking," said Harris, "because I had one hand over his mouth." The message Harris received was said to be personal. In the years since Houdini died, the magician Joseph Dunninger has gained valuable free publicity by holding a seance every year on the anniversary of the great man's death. Houdini never communicates—but his silence might be due to the fact that Dunninger is not a medium.

The medium who is said to have broken the Houdini code, Arthur Ford, became America's most famous mental medium— that is, one who contacts the spirits through mental processes without producing physical phenomena. The peak of his career came in a televised seance with Bishop James Pike, the former Episcopal Bishop of California. It was conducted for Toronto TV by Allen Spraggett, and was shown throughout America and in Britain. It caused a sensation. In the seance, the Bishop's dead son, James Jr., apparently communicated with his father via Ford. Later, the seance was proved to have been fraudulent. Spraggett and Canon William V. Rauscher, Ford's confidant, wrote a biography entitled *Arthur Ford: The Man Who Talked With the Dead*. In it they revealed damning evidence found in Ford's private papers after his death in January 1971.

Although he had been convinced of the genuineness of the televised seance, Bishop Pike had admitted that much of the evidence could have been obtained through the most elementary research. He was impressed mostly by obscure details in messages said to come from his predecessor, the Right Reverend Karl Morgan Block, fourth Bishop of California, and the Reverend Louis W. Pitt, former rector of an Episcopal church. All of these particular details were found in obituaries cut from newspapers and kept among the medium's private papers. Ford's biographers say that he had a remarkable memory, and used it to memorize masses of details from obituaries he collected. Yet in surveying Ford's career, Spraggett concludes: "I think the evidence supports the hypothesis that Arthur Ford was a genuine gifted psychic who, for various reasons, scrutable and inscrutable, fell back on trickery when he felt he had to."

Harry Houdini made people believe that his campaign against mediums was a trail-blazing effort to dispel public ignorance about fraudulent mediumship. But in fact, exposure had been done effectively and earlier by two books that must have been essential reading for psychical researchers in those days. days. In 1907 Dr. Hereward Carrington published his *The Psychical Phenomena of Spiritualism*, and in the same year David P. Abbott his *Behind the Scenes with the Mediums*. They did a thorough job of revealing the conjuring techniques used by fraudulent mediums to produce a variety of effects. Between them the two books gave no less than 100 versions of trickery in slate writing alone.

Abbott, a magician and a member of the American Society for Psychical Research, based his book on personal observation of many fraudulent mediums. In one example he describes the seemingly astonishing performance of a woman medium who

"Fell Back on Trickery"

Opposite: a poster announcing the fabulous feats of Harry Houdini, one of the most famous magicians of all time. He conducted a campaign to expose mediums as frauds.

Below: Arthur Ford, the medium who claimed to have communicated the code that Houdini had given his wife before his death with the idea that it would, if transmitted correctly, prove that his spirit had survived death. Like most mediums, Ford seems to have resorted to unethical means to create fake paranormal effects, mainly by memorizing published information which he later presented as transmitted from those in the spirit world.

Ingenious Ways of Fooling People

Below: a catalog of fakery for mediums in need of earthly assistance for their miracles in the seance room. According to Harry Price, the investigator, this catalog was available only on loan to mediums who had to return it when they had made their choice of goods. There were both effects, which were illustrated, and secrets. For the complete novice, there was a kit—the "Complete Spiritualistic Seance"—which included slate writing; table turning, rapping, and lifting; fire-resisting effects; and reading of sealed letters, all at a bargain price.

gave seances in a theater. She asked her audience to write questions and sign their names on bits of paper, and to keep the papers in their possession. Then, from the stage, she answered the questions. The effect was startling, but Abbott revealed that it was relatively easy to do with the aid of accomplices. Because many members of the audience had not brought paper, assistants handed out pads of paper for their use. These pads were scored into sections so that each person could tear off the square on which he had written his question, keep it, and pass the pad to someone else. These tablets were especially prepared with wax so that the base could be easily developed and the impression left by the pressure of a pen or pencil read.

Assistants collected the pads and apparently placed them in front of the medium on the stage. In fact, however, they switched the pads, giving her blank ones and smuggling the used ones under the stage. These were quickly developed and handed to a confederate with a telephone. The medium had a small receiver hidden in her hair, which was connected to carefully concealed wires running down to copper plates in her shoes. When she stepped on two nails hammered into the stage floor, she was able to complete the telephone circuit and hear her accomplice read the questions. In addition, other assistants in the hall picked out the people who wrote questions on their own paper, and read their questions while collecting the pads throughout the audience. At the earliest opportunity they wrote out the questions they had spotted, and sent them below stage to be read with the others. Most people came away convinced that the performance was supernormal.

A similar trick was used to astound some theater audience members. The audience was invited to write questions on pieces of paper, addressing the questions to a dead friend or relative. They were also asked to sign their names. Each question was sealed in an envelope, and given to a blindfolded medium. She or he would remove the piece of paper, read the message without removing the blindfold, and convey an answer from the spirit world. This trick is extremely simple, because even with adhesive tape and absorbent cotton beneath a blindfold, a person can see a sufficiently large area down the sides of the nose to be able to read what is written on a piece of paper. Many gullible people are convinced by this demonstration, never dreaming that in this case they themselves could do the same.

Fifty years after Abbott wrote about the question-and-answer trick, a British medium was making a fortune with the same method but more sophisticated equipment. William Roy has been described as the most audacious Spiritualist crook of modern times. Before his exposure in 1955 he was the best-known medium in Britain. He was denounced as a fraud by the Spiritualist publication *Two Worlds*. The following account of his methods is taken from Simeon Edmunds' book *Spiritualism, A Critical Survey:*

"Much of Roy's success in duping quite critical sitters was due to his clever development of the microphone-relaying technique whereby he was able to demonstrate the 'direct voice' in full light, an achievement quite beyond the capabilities of his rivals. To do this he ran wiring under the carpet from the microphone and amplifier to two brass tacks, the heads of which protruded through the carpet and were ostensibly securing it to the floor. He adapted the hearing aid as a miniature loudspeaker and attached it to his cuff, running wires from it up his sleeve, inside his jacket and down his trouser legs into his shoes. Here they connected through the soles with two metal plates, one on each shoe, so that when he stood on the tacks a circuit was completed and the confederate could produce voices from the loudspeaker." The voices would issue from the area around Roy's wrist—far enough away from his mouth to avert suspicion.

Roy, whose real name was William George Holroyd Plowright, was paid handsomely by a British newspaper, the *Sunday Pictorial*, for a five-installment confession in 1958. He posed for photographs with his ingenious apparatus, which eventually found its way into the museum at the Metropolitan Police Detective Training School. He also boasted that he had made wealth out of grief-stricken people. The success of his performance was partly due to the thoroughness with which he researched his victims. He examined voters' lists, visited the National Registry office to pore over records of births, marriages, and deaths, and gleaned a wealth of information from wills. All this information he kept in a card index file. Some details were supplied by fellow frauds. "We phony mediums traded information—like swapping stamps," he confessed.

When sitters arrived for a seance they were asked to leave their coats and handbags outside in the hall. Roy listened to their conversation via a concealed microphone before he entered the seance room. Meanwhile a confederate searched handbags and coat pockets for further clues in letters, tickets, or notebooks. The phony phenomena usually started with the movement of a light cardboard trumpet coated with bands of luminous paint—a prop commonly used to condense the voice in producing direct voice phenomena. He achieved the voices by attaching a telescopic tube, invisible in the darkness, through which he spoke. He would then remove a hearing aid from his pocket and plug it into what looked like a normal wall socket. This linked him to the confederate who supplied him with information. Roy, in turn, gave the information to the sitters in the guise of a trance message from his American Indian spirit guide, Tinka. Next, by using the hearing aid as a miniature loudspeaker attached to the end of the trumpet, he was able to relay voices from his confederate, while continuing to speak at the same time through another trumpet. The sitters were greatly impressed to hear two spirit voices speaking simultaneously. Masks and cheesecloth were also used by Roy to create materializations.

Spiritualists knew Roy was a fraud as early as 1951 but agreed not to reveal it in return for his promise to stop conducting seances and to leave the country. Roy did so, but soon returned and continued his fraudulent practice. After *Two Worlds* labelled him a fraud in 1955 he issued a writ for libel. Once the matter went to court, the newspaper was prevented from making further comment. When Roy abandoned the lawsuit in February 1958, he agreed to pay the court costs in 24 monthly installments to the editor, Maurice Barbanell. Immediately afterward the newspaper published all its evidence for fraud. At first Roy

139. Spirit Rapping Table.

This is particularly for mediums who have their own apartments, yet is easily used in any room where the table can be placed. In appearance it is an ordinary finely finished library table, bears minute examination, and is portable. When circle is formed around table it emits raps as desired. Can be used at any time, no previous preparation necessary. Infallible in every respect. Price......$50.00

140. The 20th Century Rapping Hand.

This creation is certainly the most wonderful effect of its kind; the equal of it has never yet been devised. A fine model of a

—20—

Above: a page from *Gambols with the Ghosts*, the marvelous catalog issued by Ralph E. Sylvestre & Co. of Chicago in 1901. Notice at the bottom of the page item 140, the 20th-century Rapping Hand.

Below: the self-rapping hand. It was used at many fraudulent seances to produce spectacular effects undetected in the customary dark. It was probably controlled pneumatically by rubber tubing.

Some Magicians Become Converts

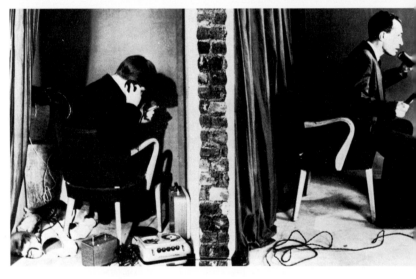

Right: two pictures of William Roy taken to illustrate his confession. After making a fortune as a fraudulent medium, Roy got a handsome fee for his personal story, run in five parts by a newspaper. Above Roy is shown in the black darkness in which he conducted his seances. Behind him, and separated by a brick wall, is his accomplice. The picture below shows the same scene with the lights on. Roy is producing one voice from the trumpet (invisible in the gloom). The accomplice does the second voice with a microphone in his hand connected by wires through what looks like an ordinary wall socket to a speaker hung on Roy's telescopic rod. The confederate also has an earphone connected to a microphone behind the curtains to pick up voices in the seance room. Among the other equipment in his room is an amplifier, a tape recorder, and a pile of stage props.

Below: demonstration of a fake medium at work. Her hands and legs are tied to the stool, but a spring releases a section of the stool and gives her free movement to use instruments and the trumpet on the table.

denied the charges. Then, having been offered a substantial fee by the *Sunday Pictorial* for his story, he cheerfully confessed. By the time the story was published Roy had left the country again.

His final remark in the series of *Pictorial* articles was: "Even after this confession, I know I could fill seance rooms again with people who find it a comfort to believe I am genuine." Ten years later in 1968 those words were proved right. A medium using the name Bill Silver and working under a wealthy man's patronage was discovered to be William Roy. Once again it was a Spiritualist newspaper, *Psychic News*, that exposed him. Moreover, the paper revealed that some of the sitters knew the real identity of Silver as Roy, but were still convinced by his phenomena, which were said to include voice communications from beings living on Venus. The sitters included a bishop and the Beatles. When challenged by another Sunday newspaper, William Roy had the gall to claim that his earlier confession had been a pack of lies, and that he had always been genuine.

Not all mediumistic fraud is as coldly calculated as that practiced by Roy. Some, in fact, seems to be unconscious.

Professor James Hyslop, an American psychical researcher, discovered a woman medium who, in complete darkness, made tambourines play and bells ring. She willingly agreed to his taking flash photographs of these phenomena. When the pictures were developed she was dumbfounded to see that she was producing these effects with her own hands. They plainly showed her ringing the bells and banging the tambourine. Subsequent investigation showed that her hands and arms were completely numb during seances, and she had no conscious knowledge of their movements and actions.

The long contest between mediums and magicians has included many challenges and counterchallenges. Many, if not most, of these encounters served to confirm the magicians' disbelief in Spiritualism. In some cases, however, magicians have become convinced that spirits could communicate through mediums, and some have even become Spiritualists themselves.

In 1930 the British psychical researcher Harry Price challenged any magician who could duplicate the phenomena of medium Rudi Schneider under the same conditions. Schneider, an Austrian, was subjected to extensive testing. During his seances, held in the National Laboratories of Psychical Research, he produced levitation of various objects, musical sounds, and partial materializations in a cabinet some five feet away from where he was sitting. Various controls were imposed to eliminate any contact between Schneider and the manifestations. No one came forward to accept Price's challenge—perhaps because of the strings attached. Although he offered a large money prize to the successful challenger, Price made it part of the deal that any unsuccessful ones contribute the same sum to his organization.

Will Goldston, one of the greatest professional magicians in Europe, said after witnessing Schneider's phenomena: "I am convinced that what I saw at the seance was not trickery. No group of my fellow magicians could have produced these effects under such conditions." Goldston told the story of his conversion to Spiritualism in his book *Secrets of Famous Illusionists* published in 1933.

The great exposés are, for the most part, a thing of the past. This is mainly because physical phenomena, the featured attraction of most late 19th century seances, are now rarely produced. Although advancing technology has provided fraudulent mediums with more sophisticated methods of duping the public—as in the case of William Roy and his voice-up-the-sleeve act—it has also provided investigators with more sophisticated means of detection. Infrared photography in particular has made it possible to reveal the machinery behind physical phenomena without affecting the darkness of the physical seance room. Technological expertise, say the skeptics, is the reason behind the virtual disappearance of old-style physical mediumship. The recent emergence of spiritual healing, including psychic surgery, will no doubt call forth a new breed of investigators, bent on discovering the tricks—if they are tricks—behind some of today's astonishing manifestations. In the meantime, most Spiritualists look to a different kind of medium—the kind who relies entirely on mental processes to establish that link between this world and the next that Spiritualists continually seek.

Above: Harry Price, the psychic investigator, with a trick blackboard used by fraudulent mediums. Two apparently plain slates are placed together by the medium. When taken apart, one slate has a spirit drawing on it and the other some writing. The secret is a strong hidden spring, which releases a previously prepared surface and conceals the blanks. Price was the director of the National Laboratory of Psychical Research, and spent a great deal of time and money on the testing and exposure of fake mediums.

Chapter 13
The Medium and the Message

If physical manifestations can be faked with reasonable ingenuity, what about the problem of mental mediumship? Are there gifted psychics who can communicate with the spirits of the dead not by simple rappings and bangings, but with evidential messages, full of facts which can be checked and verified? How are these mediums able to produce these detailed accounts, and what methods can the investigators use to make sure that more subtle deception is not taking place? Who are these strangely gifted individuals who seem capable of looking into the past and the future when caught up in a mysterious trance?

Two days after the huge British airship, the R101, had crashed in flames on a hillside in Beauvais, France—killing 48 of its 54 passengers—the hesitant, anxious voice of a man claiming to be its captain spoke through the lips of a medium in London. In short disjointed sentences he described the horrifying last moments before his incineration. His account of the crash included a wealth of technical information that was confirmed six months later by an official inquiry. The disaster, which occurred on October 5, 1930, included two high ranking aviation officials among its victims. It shook the government's confidence in dirigibles, and ended British efforts to develop the lighter-than-air craft for commercial use.

The seance in which the dramatic communication was received took place at the National Laboratory of Psychical Research set up four years earlier by Harry Price, a well-known psychic investigator. Price, his secretary, and journalist Ian D. Coster, had arranged a sitting with the talented young medium Eileen Garrett. The purpose was to attempt a spirit contact with the recently deceased writer Sir Arthur Conan Doyle, the report of which was to be published in a magazine. Sir Arthur, the creator of Sherlock Holmes, was also a Spiritualist.

Shortly after the sitters had gathered in the seance room, Eileen Garrett went into a trance. Instead of making contact with the novelist, however, the sitters heard a voice announcing himself as Flight Lieutenant H. Carmichael Irwin. In

Opposite: the charred wreckage of the R101, the dirigible developed by the British for passenger service, which crashed in early October 1930.

Seance that Made Psychic History

anguished tones, the voice said: "I must do something about it . . . The whole bulk of the dirigible was entirely and absolutely too much for her engines' capacity. Engines too heavy. It was this that made me on five occasions have to scuttle to safety. Useful lift too small. Gross lift computed badly—inform control panel. And this idea of new elevators totally mad. Elevator jammed. Oil pipe plugged . . . Flying too low altitude and never could rise. Disposable lift could not be utilized. Load too great for long flight . . . Cruising speed bad and ship badly swinging. Severe tension on the fabric which is chafing . . . Engines wrong—too heavy—cannot rise. Never reached cruising altitude—same in trials. Too short trials. No one knew the ship properly. Weather bad for long flight. Fabric all waterlogged and ship's nose is down. Impossible to rise. Cannot trim. Almost scraped the roofs of Achy. Kept to railway. At enquiry to be held later it will be found that the superstructure of the envelope contained no resilience and had far too much weight in envelope. The added middle section was entirely wrong . . . too heavy, too much overweighted for the capacity of engines . . . ."

The reporter who took this amazing communication in shorthand at first resented the intrusion of Irwin, captain of the R101, when he had expected the voice of Sir Arthur Conan Doyle. But he was soon to realize that he had unwittingly been part of a dramatic moment in psychic history. He published the story, and it was read by, among others, a Mr. Charlton,

Below: an aerial view of the R101 wreck on the hillside in Beauvais just north of Paris.

Far left: Eileen Garrett, medium at the extraordinary seance in which the spirit of the captain of the R101—which had crashed just two days before—broke into the sitting.

Left: a newstand poster advertising one newspaper's account of the R101 seance. Because of the worldwide interest in the crash of the airship, the seance also attracted worldwide attention. A reporter present at the seance had put the news story out at once.

who had been involved in the R101's construction. Charlton asked Harry Price for a copy of the seance report. After studying it he and his colleagues described it as "an astounding document," containing more than 40 highly technical and confidential details of what occurred on the airship's fatal flight. "It appeared very evident," said Charlton, "that for anyone present at the seance to have obtained information beforehand was grotesquely absurd."

Charlton was so impressed by the evidence that he began his own psychic investigation, and ultimately became a Spiritualist. The only hypothesis that he could put forward to explain all the evidence was that "Irwin did actually communicate with those present at the seance, after his physical death."

Before the official enquiry into the crash, Major Oliver Villiers of the Ministry of Civil Aviation participated in a seance with Eileen Garrett. Through the medium he heard the testimony of others who had lost their lives in the disaster. Here is part of the verbatim account of the conversation during the seance between Villiers and crew member Scott, one of the victims:

"Villiers: What was the trouble? Irwin mentioned the nose."

"Scott: Yes. Girder trouble and engine."

"Villiers: I must get this right. Can you describe exactly where? We have the long struts numbered from A to G."

"Scott: The top one is O, and then A, B, C, and so on downward. Look at your drawing. It was the starboard of 5C. On our second flight after we had finished we found the girder had been strained, not cracked, and this caused trouble to the cover . . ."

Later Villiers asked Scott if the girder had broken and gone through the airship's covering:

"Scott: No, not broke, but cracked badly and it split the outer cover . . . The bad rent in the cover on the starboard side of 5C brought about an unnatural pressure, forced us into our first dive. The second was even worse. The pressure on the gas bags was terrific, and the gusts of wind were tremendous. This external pressure, coupled with the fact that the valve was weak,

Below: the Court of Inquiry, chaired by Sir John Simon, "to hold an investigation into the causes and circumstances of the accident which occurred on October 5th, 1930, near Beauvais in France, to the Airship R101."

The New Era of Mental Mediums

blew the valve right off, and at the same time the released gas was ignited by a backfire from the engine."

The Court of Inquiry report showed that practically every one of these statements was correct; none were incorrect.

One important aspect of Eileen Garrett's work is that she respected psychical investigators and actively encouraged their work. In fact, she founded the New York-based Parapsychology Foundation, which was financed by a wealthy woman politician, Congresswoman Frances Payne Bolton of Ohio. On Eileen Garrett's death in 1970 at the age of 77, Archie Jarman, a researcher and writer who had known her for nearly 40 years, paid tribute to her in the columns of *Psychic News*. He revealed that she had asked him to "dig into the famous R101 airship case as deep as I could delve." He agreed to do so and pledged he would take neither fee nor expenses, so that whatever his investigation disclosed, it would be seen that he had worked "without fear or favor." He continued:

"The completed saga, so often briefly mentioned, turned out

Right: a *Punch* cartoon of Sir Arthur Conan Doyle chained to his creation Sherlock Holmes, but with his head in the Spiritualist clouds. After he tired of his popular detective hero, he tried to kill him off, but the outcry was so tremendous that Conan Doyle reluctantly resurrected him.

to be a pretty massive affair. It took nearly six months and finally filled 455 pages of typescript and blueprints. It involved two trips to France, seeking the few remaining witnesses at Beauvais where the R101 crashed. There were conferences with aeronautical experts, such as the designer of the R101's heavy diesel engines (which were partly responsible for the fatal crash), and with the aging but active captain of the sister-ship, R100.

"Technical witnesses were interrogated; ordnance maps scrutinized; Eileen's own aeronautical knowledge investigated (result, nil, she knew hardly enough to float a toy balloon). At close range I became familiar with meteorology, geodetics, with prewar political maneuvering and with certain conspiracy at a Ministry, with aerodynamics and with scandalous decisions which took nearly 50 brave men to their deaths.

"It was the technical aspect of this case which makes it unique in psychic history—and I mean *unique* . . . My opinion is that greater credulity is demanded to believe that Eileen obtained her obscure and specialized data by mundane means than to accept that, in some paranormal manner, she had contact with the remembering psyche of the 'dead' Captain Irwin to the moment of his incineration with his vast airship."

No one materialized in Eileen Garrett's presence. There were no physical manifestations such as raps or levitations, so beloved of early Spiritualists and psychical investigators. Why, then, is the R101 case so important to the Spiritualist case? The reason is that many of the scientists who risked ridicule by declaring their belief in materialized figures were equally adamant that these seance phantoms were not proof of an afterlife. They felt that mental mediumship might provide the proof.

Professor Charles Richet, a French physiologist and psychical researcher, for example, eventually came to believe in the genuineness of some physical phenomena—after having first ridiculed the idea. But Richet found it difficult to believe in life after death. He described materialization phenomena as "absurd but true," and argued: "Even if (which is not the case) a form identical with that of a deceased person could be photographed I should not understand how an individual 200 years dead, whose body has become a skeleton, could live again with this vanished body any more than with any other materialized form."

Baron A. von Schrenck-Notzing, German pioneer in investigation of psychic phenomena, conducted experiments with every leading medium until his death in 1929. He discovered the amazing powers of Willi and Rudi Schneider. One hundred formerly skeptical and often hostile scientists who witnessed his tests with Willi Schneider signed a statement that they were convinced of the reality of telekinesis—the moving of objects by mental power—and of ectoplasm. Yet the Baron maintained: "I am of the opinion that the hypothesis of spirits not only fails to explain the least detail of these processes, but in every way it obstructs and shakes serious scientific research."

Other scientists accepted materializations as proof of an afterlife. But who was to say they were right? Richet and Schrenck-Notzing believed that, in a way we do not understand, and probably subconsciously, the medium shaped the phantom

Above: an illustration from one of Conan Doyle's stories, which was serialized in an English magazine. Called "The Land of Mist," it had a theme of Spiritualists and seances. Here the hero is astonished by the materialization of his dead mother. Conan Doyle himself desperately wished to communicate with his own dead mother or with his son, killed in World War I.

Materialization
of Silver Belle

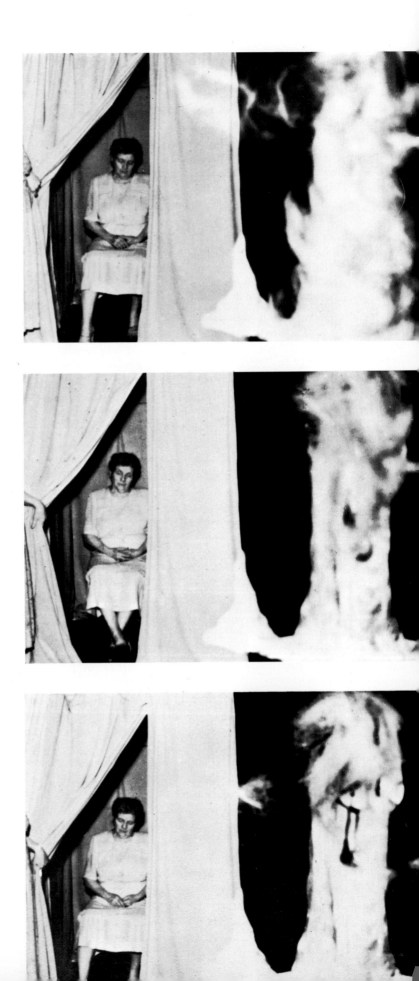

forms from the ectoplasmic material exuding from his or her body, controlling it through an extension of the nervous system. That may seem to be a far-fetched or fantastic theory, but to some it is more satisfactory than to admit the existence of a soul—and the far-fetched idea of a soul materializing itself.

If, however, a medium were to communicate information known only to the dead person and to the sitter, this would be more convincing evidence that the person's spirit had survived death. Still, many investigators would maintain that the medium received the information from the sitter, either from a hint given unconsciously by the sitter or by telepathy. More conclusive would be information *unknown to both medium and sitter, and later established as known to the dead person when alive*. One of the most gifted mediums for such phenomena was Mrs. Leonore Piper, and one of her most extraordinary contacts was George Pelham.

"The case of George Pelham," said Richet, "though there was no materialization, is vastly more evidential for survival than all the materializations yet known."

Pelham was the pseudonym of George Pellew, a young New York lawyer who had given up the law to become a writer. He had known Dr. Richard Hodgson of the SPR—a brilliant researcher who devoted much of his life to the study of Mrs. Piper's mediumship—and the two men had often discussed survival. Pelham argued that the idea of life after death was not only improbable but inconceivable. Hodgson said that if it was not probable it was at least conceivable. Pelham then promised that if he died first, he would return and "make things lively." He apparently kept his promise, and much sooner than he could have anticipated; for in February 1892 at the age of 32, he was killed in a fall from his horse.

A month later the first of a series of communications from Pelham began. Dr. Hodgson had arranged a sitting with Mrs. Piper for an intimate friend of Pelham's, using the pseudonym "John Hart" for the sitter. Mrs. Piper went into a trance; her spirit control Phinuit made various vague statements before announcing that there was a "George" present who wanted to speak. According to Dr. Hodgson, who took notes,

Materializations are not usual in seances today, but they still occur. Here is the materialization of a spirit, Silver Belle, photographed by infrared light at 50-second intervals, during a seance that took place at a Spiritualist summer camp in Ephrata, Pennsylvania, in 1953. The medium, sitting in her curtained cabinet, is Ethel Post-Parrish. Silver Belle was her spirit control or guide. During this manifestation, Silver Belle was reportedly witnessed by 81 people. Some of them apparently walked arm-in-arm with her.

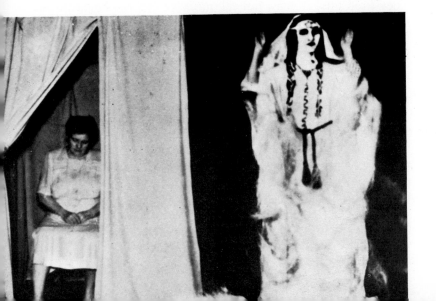

Leonore Piper Passes the Tests

Below: Dr. R. Hodgson shown in a faked photograph he had taken to demonstrate the ease of fakery. He was a very capable, but skeptical, investigator who undertook a systematic study of the medium Mrs. Leonore Piper.

Pelham took over the seance, giving his real name in full as well as the first names and surnames of several of his most intimate friends, including the one under an assumed name at the seance. He mentioned in particular a Mr. and Mrs. Howard and gave a message to Katherine, their daughter. When the Howards were told of the message, it was instantly recognized by the family as a reference to a conversation he had had with the girl some years earlier. The Howards later attended sittings with Mrs. Piper, and plied George Pelham with questions. His answers were full and detailed in most cases, but Mr. Howard pointed out that Pelham had failed to answer some points. This failure caused him to have doubt about the identity of the alleged spirit. He therefore challenged George Pelham to "tell me something in our past that you and I alone know."

Mrs. Piper's hand then began writing a message which Dr. Hodgson later said contained too much of the personal element in Pelham's life to be made public. Hodgson watched as the medium's hand rapidly covered the paper, and Mrs. Piper allowed him to read what was written until the word "private" appeared. At that point she gently pushed Dr. Hodgson away.

"I retired to the other side of the room, and Mr. Howard took my place close to the hand where he could read the writing," Dr Hodgson recounted. "He did not, of course, read it aloud, and it was too private for my perusal. The hand, as it reached the end of each sheet, tore it off from the block book and thrust it wildly at Mr. Howard, and then continued writing. The circumstances narrated, Mr. Howard informed me, contained precisely the kind of test for which he had asked, and he said he was 'perfectly satisfied, perfectly.'"

Having apparently established his identity, George Pelham stayed on as one of Mrs. Piper's regular spirit controls along with Phinuit. During a six-year period he spoke to 150 sitters, 30 of whom were old friends. He recognized all 30, although each had been introduced to the medium under a pseudonym. He not only addressed them all by name, but also used with each the tone and manner he was accustomed to use with that person when alive. Never once did he mistake a stranger for a friend. When his father and stepmother heard of Pelham's alleged posthumous activities, they decided to attend a seance. They used false names, but the moment George Pelham spoke through the medium he said, "Hello, father and mother, I am George." The conversation that followed was, according to the father, exactly what he would have expected from his living son.

Dr. Richard Hodgson was one of the mainstays of the SPR in its early days. He had a reputation as a talented investigator with a critical and skeptical mind. In 1887 he was sent to America by the SPR to act as secretary for the American Society for Psychical Research in Boston—a post he held for the rest of his life. He became a close friend of the American philosopher and psychologist William James, who brought him and Leonore Piper together. Professor James had been persuaded to attend one of Mrs. Piper's seances by some female relatives who had been greatly impressed by her. James expected to be able to explain the medium's feats logically, but was soon convinced that she possessed supernormal powers. He began a systematic study of Mrs. Piper, and introduced her to Hodgson. When James had to terminate his studies temporarily because of pressure of other work, Hodgson took up the project. Being extremely skeptical, he had Mrs. Piper watched by private detectives to learn whether she tried to collect information she could use at seances. He also took every precaution to prevent her from acquiring knowledge about her sitters in advance, and introduced them anonymously or by pseudonyms to protect their identities. Hodgson finally became convinced not only that Leonore Piper was genuine but also that spirit beings were communicating through her mediumship.

Typical of the evidence which helped him reach this decision was that provided at a seance attended by Professor Herbert Nichols of Harvard University. The sitting with Mrs. Piper was arranged by Hodgson at the request of Professor James. Professor Nichols was extremely skeptical at the outset. After the seance he wrote a letter of praise to James declaring, "she is the greatest marvel I have ever met ... I asked her scarcely a question, but she ran on for three-quarters of an hour, telling me names, places, events, in a most startling manner. Then she suddenly stopped talking and began writing—this was far less satisfactory and about an entirely different set of matters— mostly about Mamma (who recently fell and was killed) and messages to her grandchildren. One thing here, however, will interest you. Mamma and I one Christmas exchanged rings. Each had engraved in their gift the *first word* of their favorite proverb. The ring given me I lost many years ago. When Mamma died a year ago the ring I had given her was, at her request, taken from her finger and sent to me. Now I asked Mrs. Piper, 'What was written in Mamma's ring?' and as I asked the question I held the ring in my hand and had in mind *only that ring*, but I had hardly got the words from my mouth till she slapped down on paper the word on the *other ring*—the one Mamma had given me, and which had been lost years ago while traveling. As the word was a peculiar one, doubtfully ever written in any ring before, and as she wrote it in a flash, it was surely curious."

Time and again, Dr. Hodgson witnessed similar astonishing phenomena produced by Mrs. Piper. In his second report on her mediumship, published in 1897, he stated:

"At the present time I cannot profess to have any doubt that the chief communicators to whom I have referred in the foregoing pages are veritably the personages that they claim to be, that they have survived the change we call death, and that they have directly communicated with us whom we call living, through Mrs. Piper's entranced organism."

On Hodgson's death in 1905 the investigation into Leonore Piper's psychic powers was continued by James Hervey Hyslop, Professor of Logic and Ethics at Columbia University, New York. Within days of taking up the task he was studying communications received from his former colleague Dr. Hodgson, who became a regular communicator. Professor Hyslop had first encountered Mrs. Piper in 1888, and his initial skepticism about her mediumship soon dissolved. After 12 sittings, the personalities of the communicators who spoke through Mrs.

Eastern Miracles by Western Hands

It was evening in Benares, India. The legendary Madame Blavatsky—the small dumpy Russian mystic and medium with a strangely magnetic personality—was surrounded by several Indian scholars, a German professor of Sanskrit, and her devoted disciple Colonel Olcott.

The professor observed with regret that the Indian sages of old were supposed to have been able to perform amazing feats, such as making roses fall from the sky, but that people said the days of such powers were over. Madame Blavatsky stared at him thoughtfully. "Oh, they say that, do they?" she demanded. "They say no one can do it now? Well, I'll show them; and you may tell them from me that if the modern Hindus were less sycophantic to their Western masters, less in love with their vices, and more like their ancestors in many ways, they would not have to make such a humiliating confession, nor get an old Western hippopotamus of a woman to prove the truth of their Shastras!"

She set her lips together firmly, and made a grand imperious sweep of her right hand. With a swish, exactly one dozen roses came cascading down.

Madame Blavatsky returned calmly to her conversation.

Above: William Stainton Moses, English medium who had been a clergyman. He produced a famous series of automatic scripts, which he wrote while in trance. They were interspersed with words written by the spirits themselves.

Below: a sample of automatic writing by William Stainton Moses. (The College of Psychic Studies)

Piper—and the evidence they provided—were so strong that he declared: "I have been talking with my father, my brother, my uncles. Whatever supernormal powers we may be pleased to attribute to Mrs. Piper's secondary personalities, it would be difficult to make me believe that these secondary personalities could have thus completely reconstituted the mental personality of my dead relatives. To admit this would involve me in too many improbabilities. I prefer to believe that I have been talking to my dead relatives in person; it is simpler."

The same conclusion was reached by the vast majority of Mrs. Piper's sitters. Because her mediumship was so accurate and detailed, and because men with critical and skeptical natures believed that fraud had been ruled out, the case of Mrs. Leonore Piper has become one of the most significant in psychic history. It established within 40 years of Spiritualism's beginnings that evidence for an afterlife could be provided through the mind of a medium, without the need for darkness, raps, levitations, or spirit forms. What is more, the quality of the evidence was in most cases far superior to the laboriously spelled out messages that were banged out by tilting tables, or the indistinct materializations that appeared at many seances.

At its best, mental mediumship appears to offer a kind of psychic telephone link between this world and the next, using the medium as a receiver. In some cases, the medium goes into a trance and speaks with the voice of the communicator. More often mediums remain conscious and relate in their normal voice what they are hearing mentally. The telephone analogy is a useful one, for it points to some of the difficulties that can occur. Suppose, for example, that you had been abroad for 20 years and, on returning home, decided to call up some friends. They would not be able to see you, so to establish that it really was you, you would probably talk about events in your life before you had left, and about which they knew or in which they had shared. This is what most spirit communicators do.

This raises an immediate objection, however. The communications seem trivial, and the sitters usually know the facts that are given to establish identity. Therefore, telepathy between sitter and medium is postulated as the explanation. Also, sometimes the evidence provided is not right, dates or names are wrong, and doubt is thrown on the authenticity of the entire communication. Here is where the comparison with telephoning breaks down, for conveying information through a medium is not as simple as the telephone analogy indicates. F. W. H. Myers, an early SPR researcher, is supposed to have spoken through a famous medium to give this posthumous description of his efforts to communicate:

"The nearest simile I can find to express the difficulties of sending a message—is that I appear to be standing behind a sheet of frosted glass which blurs sights and deadens sound—dictating feebly—to a reluctant and somewhat obtuse secretary. A feeling of terrible impotence burdens me—I am so powerless to tell what means so much."

We are used to atmospheric interference in television and radio communications and more or less accept it. So perhaps we should allow for distortions through mediumistic communication. Spirit communicators indicate that—in a way we do not understand—they have to use the medium's mind to control vocal cords or move a hand to write a message. The medium's own mind can therefore color the communications. It seems reasonable that if contact really is established between the living and another realm of existence, then difficulties could easily arise. If we accept this, the wonder is not that inaccuracies and misunderstandings creep into many seance messages, but that on occasion a communicator is able to convey accurate information at length—as in the R101 seances.

A set of seance messages called the Cummins-Willett Scripts provide us with the best evidence of this kind. They were received through the mediumship of one of the best modern exponents of automatic writing, an Irishwoman named Geraldine Cummins. The presumed sender of the messages was Mrs. Winifred Coombe Tennant who, during her life, also produced automatic writing under the pseudonym of "Mrs. Willett." Her real name came to light as a result of what she wrote through Geraldine Cummins.

Mrs. Winifred Coombe Tennant was an energetic, practical, and highly intelligent person. She was appointed a Justice of the Peace in 1920, and was the first woman magistrate to sit on the Glamorganshire, Wales, County bench. In 1922 she ran unsuccessfully as a Liberal Party candidate for Parliament. Later, however, she became the first woman to be appointed by the British Government as a delegate to the League of Nations Assembly. With this background, it is perhaps not surprising that she kept her psychic talents secret, and her work as a medium, under the name Mrs. Willett, became known only when she communicated with Geraldine Cummins.

Mrs. Winifred Coombe Tennant died in August 1956. A year later W. H. Salter, honorary secretary of the SPR, wrote to Geraldine Cummins asking if she would cooperate in an experiment. She agreed to do so, but only after she had returned to her home in County Cork, Eire. Two weeks later Mr. Salter sent a second letter to her in Ireland. In it he gave her the name of Major Henry Tennant, who hoped to receive a message from his mother.

During the next two years Geraldine Cummins received 40 scripts, ostensibly from Mrs. Tennant, Major Tennant's mother. Most of them she included in her book *Swan on a Black Sea*, published in 1965 and edited by Signe Toksvig. These scripts represent one of the most important contributions to psychical research in the last few decades. In them, the spirit of Mrs. Tennant discusses her life, her relationships with others, and her involvement in psychic work. The writings are peppered with names, dates, and details which, with few exceptions, were found to be accurate.

Skeptics might claim that Geraldine Cummins could have researched all or most of this material when she got the name of Major Tennant, or that she was acquainted with the family. Either theory is questionable in view of comments in a letter that Geraldine Cummins wrote to Signe Toksvig on August 31, 1957, a few days after receiving Salter's second letter. She refers to the experiment, saying in an aside that the letter from

Famous Scripts by Two Mediums

Below: during her life Mrs. Winifred Coombe Tennant was a Justice of the Peace—and, under the secret name Mrs. Willett, a medium who produced automatic writing while fully conscious. After her death she sent a series of detailed communications.

A Description of Life as a Spirit?

Below: Geraldine Cummins, an Irish medium whose automatic writings on mainly theological themes have shown remarkable knowledge. She was asked by the bereaved son of Winifred Coombe Tennant (Mrs. Willett) to try for a message, and for three years after received scripts that were full of details only the immediate family had known.

Salter contained the name of a major. "The name meant nothing to me. But I realized I must tackle the job the next day. Otherwise these critical people would say I spent time making inquiries about this blasted major." The first communication from Mrs. Winifred Coombe Tennant was received on August 28, 1957, five days after Salter's second letter. The medium was not happy with the result, and she commented: "I don't care if it's all wrong. It seemed to me an impossible task." She referred to the test scripts in another letter four days later adding, "I'm sure the script message is a failure." In her introduction to *Swan on a Black Sea*, Signe Toksvig observes: "It can be seen that Miss Cummins is by no means an automatic believer in her automatic or transmitted scripts."

Professor C. D. Broad, Fellow of Trinity College, Cambridge, wrote a long and masterly foreword to the Cummins/Toksvig book. He examines many alternative explanations for the scripts and comments: "I found them of great interest, and I believe that these automatic scripts are a very important addition to the vast mass of such material which *prima facie* suggests rather strongly that certain human beings have survived the death of their physical bodies . . ."

The scripts are too long and complicated to condense meaningfully. Instead, here is part of one of the scripts addressed to her son Major Tennant, dated October 29, 1958:

"I am back again in my married life. It is different, though in appearance to my perceptions it is the same outer world of reason, order, and sensible arrangements. But it is different, humanly speaking. I am much with Christopher [another son], who is a darling, while your father pairs off with Daff [her daughter]. That is a new experience to me.

"What is novel also is that I appear to be in a kind of kindergarten, and in my working hours I relive in memory what earth time has snatched away from me. So in the study of memory I do not remain at Cadoxton [their home in Gloucestershire]. I enter the film of past events and make excursions into different times in my past earth life so as to assimilate it.

"I perceive again my budding public life, my immense enthusiasm for the Welsh Wizard, Lloyd George. He has even visited me in the disguise of his past earthly personality so blazing with fire and force when in its prime. . . ."

Major Henry Tennant, initially a skeptic, wrote to Geraldine Cummins after receiving the first communication to say, "The more I study these scripts the more deeply I am impressed by them." He pointed out only one incorrect name and added, "every other name and reference is accurate, and to me very evidential and at times surprising. There was no tapping of my mind because much appears that I never knew."

Geraldine Cummins was highly critical of her own gift. She admitted shortly before her death in 1969 that it was not until she had received the Willett scripts that she felt she had produced what she demanded as irrefutable proof of survival. It had taken her 35 years of mediumship to achieve that goal.

Above: Grace Rosher, who does automatic writing with a pen lying lightly on her hand. Her gift first made itself manifest after her fiancé died when, pausing after finishing a perfectly normal letter, she discovered to her surprise that the pen was moving by itself. The handwriting was that of her dead fiancé Gordon Burdick.

Left: Miss Rosher comparing a spirit message she claimed to receive from Sir William Crookes with a facsimile of his normal handwriting during his life.

Chapter 14
Mediums and Machines

Is it possible to take a picture that actually documents the aura which psychics for centuries have claimed to see? Are there ghostly voices in the atmosphere which can be caught and recorded on tape? Traditional tools for communicating with the dead have been the ouija board and the planchette; the illuminated trumpet also played an important role in many seance rooms. One popular mechanical tool was the camera, which proved suddenly capable of capturing a likeness not only of a living sitter but of someone dead. Was it possible for a spirit to make a ghostly impression upon a photographer's plate? Can the unseen be made visible?

Friedrich Jurgenson switched on his tape recorder one day in 1959 expecting to hear the recording of bird calls he had made in a Swedish forest. Suddenly the voice of his dead mother addressed him. He heard her saying: "Friedel, my little Friedel, can you hear me?" That was all. Astonished, Jurgenson replayed the tape to check that his ears had not deceived him. His mother's voice was distinct and unmistakable. Jurgenson, a Russian-born writer, painter, and film producer living in Sweden, began a long series of experiments to record spirit voices following his first experience. Since then, hundreds of voices mysteriously appeared on his tapes. Usually they uttered just a word or two at a time. After Jurgenson received his first tape phenomena, other experimenters also began receiving spirit voices on tape. The most notable of these was Dr. Konstantin Raudive, a Latvian-born psychologist who was living in Sweden at the time of Jurgenson's first tape voices.

Spirit recording had arrived—and it seemed to be what psychical research had been waiting for: a simple, fraud-proof means of contacting the next world without the vagaries of mediumship. The phenomenon, whatever it proves in the long run, is one of the most exciting manifestations of recent years.

For 14 years Jurgenson let it be thought that the startling voice of his mother on the bird-call recording was an unexpected event. He now admits that he had been experimenting for several months before with the aim of receiving "something" on electro-

As the technology of the 20th century has developed, ingenious minds have found ways to employ it in the search for a method to prove the existence of a dimension to life beyond those we are normally aware of.

Opposite: this dead nettle leaf, seen photographed by the Kirlian method, is visibly surrounded by a glowing corona.

Unknown Voices on Tape

magnetic tape. "Somehow, and completely without any known reason," he has said, "there grew in me an overwhelming desire to establish electronic contact with somebody unknown. It was a strange feeling, almost as if I had to open a channel for something which was still hidden and wanted to get into the open. At the same time I remember feeling skeptical, amused, and curious."

When the late Dr. Raudive heard about Jurgenson's mysterious phenomena, he began his own experiments. He used various techniques from simple recording with a microphone to more complex electronic systems for which he had certain equipment especially designed. The results in numerical terms alone have certainly been impressive. By 1968 Raudive had recorded more than 70,000 voice effects. He wrote about these in his book published that year. Known as *Breakthrough* when it appeared in the United States and Britain in 1971, it was originally entitled *Unhorbares wird Horbar* (*The Inaudible Becomes Audible*.) As a result of the publicity surrounding Dr. Raudive's work, voice phenomena have been dubbed "Raudive voices."

"In one 10-minute recording I got 200 voices," Raudive once said. "With patience there is no reason at all why anyone cannot tape the voice phenomena. But the experimenter must develop his hearing by constant listening to tapes. What at first seems like atmospheric buzzing is often many voices. They have to be analyzed and amplified, of course."

Raudive was convinced that the voices were of the dead, as the voices themselves claimed. "There is no doubt that we have established communication with another world," he said. He was also fascinated by the mixture of languages the voices used. Often, he said, one message would be made up of words from more than one language. Since Raudive spoke Latvian, Russian, German, Swedish, French, and Spanish, and could understand most Slavonic dialects, he was usually able to interpret the most curious sounds into meaningful messages.

The problem is that different individuals listening to the recordings seldom hear the same words. Often the listener has to be told what the voice allegedly is saying before he can make out the words. This subjective factor is well illustrated in a message that Raudive claimed came from Sir Winston Churchill. Raudive wrote down the message as "Te Mac-Cloo, mej dream, my dear, yes"—a combination of Latvian, Swedish, and English words. Two British researchers thought the message was entirely in English, which is more plausible inasmuch as Churchill did not speak either Swedish or Latvian. One of them thought he said, "Hear, Mark you, make believe, my dear, yes," while the other thought the British leader was saying, "Mark you, make thee mightier yet." In either case the message is something of a stylistic deterioration for a man who was arguably the greatest master of rhetoric of our time.

Churchill is not the only famous personality alleged to have communicated on Raudive's tapes. The spirits of Tolstoy, Nietzche, John F. Kennedy, Hitler, and Stalin have also come through electronically according to Raudive.

Many of the voices seemed to want to communicate specifically with Raudive, and would address him by name: "The dead live, Konstantin;" "Kosti we are;" "Please believe." At times when

Above: the Swedish film maker and painter Friedrich Jurgenson with his tape recorder, on which he is convinced he has captured multilingual voices of the dead.

Left: Konstantin Raudive with the goniometer, a recording device built especially for him by an interested electronics engineer to receive the voices Raudive believed were coming from the dead. Raudive himself had no technical background, and reportedly relied entirely on his collaborators to develop and supply recording equipment.

Below: Dr. Hans Bender, the German parapsychologist who has investigated both Jurgenson and Raudive, believed that the tape voices were genuine, even if they were not spirits.

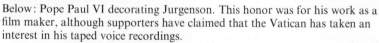

Below: Pope Paul VI decorating Jurgenson. This honor was for his work as a film maker, although supporters have claimed that the Vatican has taken an interest in his taped voice recordings.

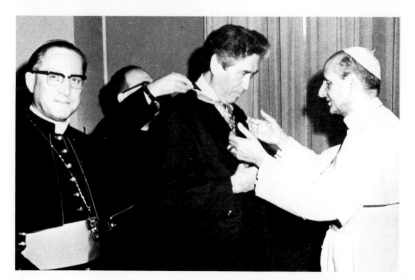

But Are They Spirit Voices?

another researcher was doing the taping, the voices would ask for Dr. Raudive: "We need Kosti."

David Ellis, an English college student who received a special grant from Cambridge University to study recorded voice phenomena, spent two short periods with Dr. Raudive in Germany in 1970 and 1971. Although inclined to believe in the possibility of spirits communicating electronically, Ellis expressed some reservations about the actual source of some of the voices he heard on Raudive's tapes. Writing in an article for *Psychic* magazine in February 1974, Ellis said that he thought many of the sounds could easily have been radio transmissions. "The air is full of broadcast transmissions—commercial and amateur radio, radio telephony, scrambled speech—no wavelength in the normal range can be guaranteed to be clear . . ." Ellis reported that one message was eventually translated as some chat from a Radio Luxembourg program: "Hello, this is Kid Jenson reminding you about Dimensions. Later on tonight on 208: soft rock, hard rock, jazz, and blues . . ."

Not all of the voices can be accounted for in this way. There are many instances when they apparently reply to questions put by the experimenter. Ellis thinks that in some way, Raudive may have himself telekinetically produced the voices. "How else," he asks, "could the extraordinary mixture of languages, many of which the purported communicators did not know in their earthly life, be explained?"

Ellis says that his theory of telekinesis would not necessarily rule out the possibility that the messages *originated* with spirits. But, he goes on, it does mean that, instead of speaking directly onto the tape, the spirit voices would first be received telepathically by the experimenter and then "clothed in words from his own unconscious mind before being imparted to the tape."

Below: Sir Arthur Conan Doyle (on right) sitting with a friend and listening to a repeat of one of his Spiritualist lectures on the radio, then in its infancy. At the time the radio was seen by those interested in aspects of psychic contact as offering a possible future method of communication with the dead.

The Ellis theory is similar to that of Dr. Hans Bender, a German professor of psychology who studied the voices received by Jurgenson. He is satisfied that the voices are genuine, but not necessarily spirits. He believes that the operator's subconscious mind somehow imprints the messages on the tape.

Another experimenter in the field of taping spirit voices is Raymond Cass, a British hearing aid specialist. On June 18, 1974, he recorded a voice which is reputed to have said, "Raudive, man of oak, toward the tomb." He sent copies of this cryptic message to three researchers who were also studying the phenomena. Three months later, at the age of 63, Raudive died.

The possibility of a form of spirit radio was predicted in 1936

Left: Guglielmo Marconi. He was another notable scientist—the inventor of the wireless radio—who believed modern technology would hold the key to expanding man's knowledge and understanding of time and the universe. He hoped to find a way to capture Christ's last words on the cross.

Below: Thomas A. Edison, inventor of the phonograph and the light bulb. He shared the enthusiasm of many of his generation for contact with unseen forces, and worked on a device that would locate a frequency between long and short waves to be used as a telepathic channel between the worlds of the living and the dead.

by Sir Oliver Lodge, a former President of the SPR. Lodge, whose work on wireless transmission formed a basis for Marconi's invention of the radio, believed that some way would be found to link this world with the spirit world. In 1930 a voice believed to be that of Sir Arthur Conan Doyle, speaking through the medium Eileen Garrett, had indicated that the initiative in experimenting with communication methods was being taken by spirit scientists. Today many people believe that the modern tape recorder has enabled spirits to establish contact.

Marconi and Edison both hoped to achieve some form of contact with the unseen through electronic means. In 1920 Edison was busily constructing a device that he believed would put him in touch with people who had died. He believed there would be a radio frequency between the long and short waves which would make possible a form of telepathic contact with the other world. Until his death in 1937, Marconi worked secretly on a highly sophisticated device that he hoped would receive voices from the past. A devout Roman Catholic, he wanted in particular to record the words spoken by Jesus on the cross.

Mechanical means of establishing a dialogue between the two worlds have been sought for many centuries. According to one historical account, Pythagoras, the famous Greek mathematician and philosopher, attempted spirit contact. He held many gatherings for his followers at which "a mystic table, moving on wheels, moved toward signs which the philosopher and his pupil, Philolaus, interpreted to the audience as being revelations supposedly from the unseen world."

Pythagoras' moving table was apparently an early ouija board (from the French *oui* and the German *ja*, both meaning

Below: another early method of contacting spirits. The sitters each place a finger on an upturned wineglass on a table with the letters of the alphabet written around the edge. (The most common early 19th-century table was a round one, with a central pedestal support). The glass whizzed around the table, spelling out the spirit message.

Mechanical Means of Spirit Contact

Left: the ouija board in use. Here Patience Worth, the spirit control of medium Mrs. John H. Curran, has materialized and is serving as the second guide for the board. Experts claimed that the spirits were able to speak exceedingly fast by means of the board, so perhaps a materialized spirit got even better results.

"yes"). The ouija is a small wooden pointer mounted on rollers. It is placed on a board marked with the letters of the alphabet and with the words "yes" and "no." The questioner's hand rests lightly on the pointer, which moves around the board, spelling out a message. Similar results can be obtained with the use of an inverted drinking glass on a table around which the letters and words have been arranged.

Compared to direct speech through the medium, ouija board communication is rather slow and laborious. However, in the hands of Hester Dowden, one of Britain's foremost automatic writing mediums of the early 20th century, the ouija board method produced some impressive results. According to one witness, "The words come through so quickly that it is almost impossible to read them, and it requires an experienced short-hand writer to take them down when the traveler moves at its maximum speed." Hester Dowden was usually blindfolded so that she could not see the letters and pointer.

In 1853 a French Spiritualist had devised an improvement on the ouija board, incorporating a pencil. Known as a planchette, this simple instrument was used to write messages automatically. The medium's hand would rest lightly on the planchette, which would then roll over the paper and write the message. However, mediums who produced automatic writing soon dispensed with the planchette and simply held a pen or pencil normally.

Adoption by the Ouija Board

At the turn of the century the ouija board craze swept the country. In St. Louis, the ouija board of medium Mrs. John H. Curran began spelling out a message in quaint English. The spirit said it was Patience Worth, a Puritan girl who had died 300 years before. She said she had always wished to write books and to be a mother, but had done neither.

Using the ouija board, Mrs. Curran produced four novels by Patience Worth.

Motherhood was more complicated. Patience Worth was determined that Mrs. Curran adopt a baby girl with red hair and blue eyes. The Currans finally found a young widow, due to deliver her baby, who agreed that they could adopt her baby if she did not survive childbirth. The baby girl—red-haired and blue-eyed—was born, and the young widow died. Patience Worth had her baby. The child was named Patience Worth Wee Curran.

Mrs. Curran died in 1938 and after that, Patience Worth never spoke again through any other medium. But mysteriously, the child Patience Worth Wee died of an apparently mild heart ailment five years later.

Had Patience Worth claimed her own?

All these forms of communication can be explained in terms of unconscious muscular movements. Though the people using the devices are not aware of their actions, their subconscious minds may be controlling the movements of their hands. This makes the resulting messages no more than a reflection of the thoughts stored in the deeper levels of the mind. Of course, this theory is slightly less believable in the case of several operators working with a glass on a table because each operator would have different subconscious thoughts that might tend to cancel each other out. Even in this case, however, one could suppose that one operator might be influencing the thoughts of the others.

The "subconscious mind of the operator" theory cannot satisfactorily explain a case in which the message contains information not known to anyone present. Dr. Reginald Hegy, a former ship's surgeon and founder member of the College of Physicians of South Africa, told about his early experiments with the glass and alphabet in his book *A Witness Through the Centuries*. He and a small group of friends tried the glass-and-table method of contact with spirits, and received a series of messages. Some were in English, but many others were in French, Hungarian, and various provincial German dialects—languages not known by the sitters. It took some time to have the messages translated and their information checked. Many of the messages to the questioners seemed to come from complete strangers, who helpfully gave their names and information about their deaths. "Among the hundreds of names, dates, and other facts given," Hegy reports, "not one proved to be incorrect on investigation."

To prevent unconscious control of the glass, the group appointed one person to rearrange the letters so that they would be out of order. The sitters were then led in blindfolded. During the seance they held their heads turned away from the table, probably to avoid seeing the board down the sides of their noses. The messages continued as before, just as accurate, but were given even more rapidly than usual.

These various mechanical methods of contacting spirits—the ouija board, planchette, glass and table—are fairly sophisticated compared to table turning, which was one of the most widespread methods in the early days of Spiritualism. In this technique, the participants sit or stand around a table and place their hands lightly on its surface, sometimes with their fingers touching so as to complete a human circuit around the table. The table then rocks, and by means of a simple code—one tilt for "yes," two for "no," for example—is able to answer questions or, if the alphabet is recited, to spell out messages.

This crude method is open to the same criticism of subconscious influence levelled at ouija boards and planchettes. In addition, fraud is relatively easy. Table turning is only occasionally used by Spiritualists today, and then generally as an elementary introduction to the subject of contact with the next world.

Early in Spiritualism's short history mediums dispensed with some of the cumbersome techniques, preferring to use trance control or direct voice. In the former method no mechanical device is involved, but the latter generally makes use of a trumpet or megaphone. The theory is that a spirit larynx can form itself out of ectoplasm and attach itself to the narrow end of the trumpet. The trumpet then acts as an amplifier and travels around the circle of sitters, pausing to allow a communicator to speak to particular individuals. Some witnesses claim to have heard voices so like the earthly voices of the communicators that they recognized them instantly. An explanation for this extraordinary phenomenon, allegedly from a spirit, was given by J. Arthur Findlay in his book *On the Edge of the Etheric*:

"From the medium and those present a chemist in the spirit world withdraws certain ingredients which for want of a better name is called ectoplasm. To this the chemist adds ingredients of his own making. When they are mixed together a substance is formed which enables the chemist to materialize his hands. He then, with his hands, constructs a mask resembling the mouth and tongue. The spirit wishing to speak places his face into this mask and finds it clings to him, gathers round his mouth, tongue and throat. . . . The etheric organs have once again become clothed in matter resembling physical matter, and by the passage of air through them your atmosphere can be vibrated and you hear his voice."

That was the spirit world's explanation according to Findlay. Another method of producing spirit voices was for the medium to crawl around on all fours in the darkness, whispering through the trumpet. More than one medium was caught in this fraud.

Below: a contemporary view of the courtroom during the highly publicized Cavendish case in 1903. The complainant was Henry Cavendish, a wealthy young man whose estate had fallen into the control of a Major and Mrs. Strutt. He told the court that Mrs. Strutt had given him planchette messages from his dead mother and three archangels, all persuading him to sign his property over.

Subconscious Influence

Below: a planchette, which is a ouija pointer equipped with a pencil so that instead of indicating letters to make up a message, the spirits can write out what they have to say directly. At first it was a fascinating novelty, but soon mediums turned to direct writing.

Paintings from the Dead

1.269

This was drawn on 8ᵗʰ Dee. but I did not know that Elsie Cameron, whom it resembles, was murdered until some days afterwards. A. Pearse

Right: a drawing executed in a trance by Captain A. Pearse on December 8, 1924. It resembled Elsie Cameron, a young London typist who had left home on December 5. Two days after the drawing was made, Mr. Cameron started to make inquiries of poultry farmer Norman Thorne, in whom his daughter had been interested. Thorne denied having seen her; but on January 15, the mutilated dead body of the girl was found buried under one of his poultry runs. Thorne was tried for Elsie Cameron's murder, found guilty, and hanged.

Opposite: one of the spirit paintings of Ethel Le Rossignol, a British artist. The most striking characteristic of most automatic artists is the tremendous speed with which they work, so capturing the power of their psychic visions.

However, there were some convincing direct voice seances. Mrs. Etta Wriedt of Detroit, Michigan often held seances in daylight. On these occasions the trumpet did not float on air to a sitter, but was held to the ear by the sitter, whereupon a spirit voice apparently issued from it. Mrs. Wriedt did not sit in a cabinet, nor did she enter a trance, so she was able to converse with the voices along with the sitters. Sometimes voices were heard independently of the trumpet. One sitter is said to have heard three voices together. One spoke in each ear, and the third addressed him through the trumpet.

During one of her visits to England, Etta Wriedt was invited by the Dowager Duchess of Warwick—who had been the mistress of the late King Edward VII—to visit Warwick Castle, which was troubled by strange phenomena. Mrs. Wriedt was taken directly to her room on arrival at the castle, but some of her luggages was left in the hallway outside her door. Among the pieces was her seance trumpet. While waiting for her guest, Lady Warwick noticed the trumpet. She picked it up out of curiosity and placed it to her ear. Immediately she heard the voice of King Edward speaking in his characteristic slightly German accent. She conversed with him, partly in German.

At later seances held by Etta Wriedt in the castle, the King often communicated, sometimes in German. He became so per-

Right: Mrs. Etta Wriedt, the American direct voice medium. She did not sit in a cabinet, did not go into a trance, and frequently entered into brisk conversation with the voices and her sitters. Although Etta Wriedt herself only spoke English, the voices were a multilingual lot, speaking just about every western European language, some eastern languages, and Arabic. (The College of Psychic Studies)

Far right: a seance trumpet. Often in the early days of Spiritualism they were painted with a luminous paint so that a ghostly shape seemed to float around the darkened seance room.

Below: Frances Evelyn, the Dowager Duchess of Warwick, dressed as the Queen of Assyria. A great beauty in her youth, she was one of the mistresses of King Edward VII. Nonetheless, she was not, apparently, overjoyed with his return as a disembodied spirit through Etta Wriedt's mediumship.

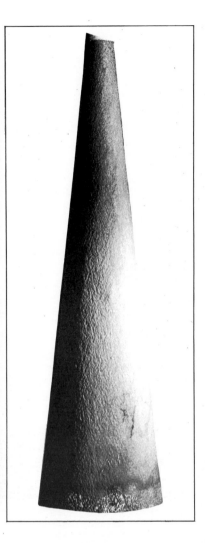

sistent that no other communicator was able to speak to Lady Warwick. Apparently resenting this possessiveness on the part of her deceased lover, Lady Warwick terminated the seances.

Foreign languages were a feature of Mrs. Wriedt's seances. On one occasion, two European sitters were addressed in their native languages of Serbian and Croatian. The medium herself appeared to have no interest in such communications. While the foreign spirits spoke she usually sat knitting.

Early in the 20th century, the English writer Dennis Bradley made an enthusiastic forecast regarding direct voice contact: "Communication with the spirits in their actual voices may, within this century, become as simple as the telephone or wireless. In fact, it seems to me that it is a new and phenomenal form of wireless communication."

As it turned out his prediction was wrong, for direct voice contact has virtually disappeared—along with other physical phenomena. Perhaps tape recording is the new improved method of tuning in the direct voice. It remains to be seen whether everyone who tries for long enough with a tape recorder and a blank tape will get the Raudive voices, or whether only those with psychic gifts—as Raudive himself seems to have had—will be able to do so.

Photography, which was in its infancy when Spiritualism was born, offered a unique opportunity to prove the existence of spirits by mechanical means. It also offered lucrative opportunities for tricksters, thanks mainly to the double exposure.

The first spirit photograph was produced by William Mumler in Boston in 1862. Mumler, an engraver by trade, tried to take a picture of himself by focusing a camera on an empty chair, and then jumping into a pose beside the chair after uncapping the lens. When developing the plate, he discovered the transparent figure of a young girl sitting in the supposedly empty chair. Below the waist, the figure seemed to dissolve into a mist. Mumler recognized the girl as a cousin who had died 12 years earlier. He repeated the experiment, and obtained other spirit images. Soon his work was attracting the interest of Spiritualists, and he set up a business producing photographs of the bereaved with their departed loved ones. The widowed Mary Todd Lincoln visited Mumler's studio under an assumed name, and obtained a photograph of herself with Lincoln by her side.

Later Mumler was accused of trickery. One spirit, for example, turned out to be the picture of a living man whom Mumler had photographed a few weeks earlier. Accusations of fraud must have hurt the business of the first psychic photographer, for he died in poverty in 1884.

Meanwhile, of course, other practitioners of spirit photography had appeared on the Spiritualist scene in America and Britain. Some sitters reported receiving pictures of long-dead relatives who had never had their photographs taken during their lifetime. A prominent English spirit photographer even succeeded in capturing the image of a spirit rabbit—perhaps a forebear of the rabbits that he kept in his backyard.

Despite the frequent errors to which these artists were prone—

The Seance Trumpet in Use

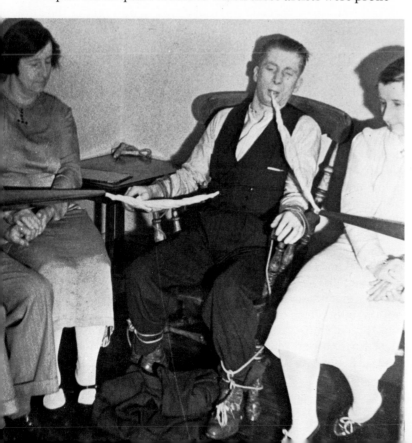

Left: a seance photo taken by infrared light of the physical medium Jack Webber, suspending two trumpets in midair by means of rods of ectoplasm. Webber, who operated in the 1920s and '30s—rather late for a physical medium—encountered considerable skepticism. It was believed that his trumpet voices were more likely simply clever ventriloquism.

Spirits Pose for the Camera

Below: the French photographer Buguet, who cashed in on the general enthusiasm for spirit photography. Buguet would place a plate in the camera and start waving his arms around, complaining of pains in his head from the spirits. Pains were soothed only when a convenient healing medium made "magnetic passes" at his head. After all this, the plate was developed, and with luck there would be a spirit lurking in the gloom. Buguet prudently insisted on prepayment, but in time the police took note of a multitude of complaints. When the studio was raided they found dolls to represent dead babies and 240 heads neatly cut out of photos made for ordinary clients. Buguet was sentenced to a year in prison.

Opposite: nine spirit photographs by Thomas Hudson, the first British psychic photographer. Like the others, he was detected in fraud. Apparently sometimes he used double exposures; other times he dressed up as the ghost himself.

occasionally the spirits appeared upside down, suggesting a certain carelessness in loading the camera—many people were convinced that the images could be genuine, particularly when they themselves imposed safeguards against trickery. The Marquess of Donegall, for example, carried out a test seance with John Myers, a former London dentist and one of England's well-known psychic photographers. In the presence of several witnesses, including a leading magician, Lord Donegall loaded Myers' camera—which he examined closely—with his own marked plates. He took six photographs in bright light while Myers simply stood by. Lord Donegall then developed the plates himself. Two of them showed extra, unidentifiable, nondescript men whose presence could not be accounted for. Lord Donegall published his findings in the *Sunday Dispatch* on October 9, 1932. The following week, however, he published the results of a further sitting with Myers in which he accused Myers of substituting plates.

While psychic photographers tried to capture the spirits of the dead, a doctor at St. Thomas' Hospital, London, was developing a method of making one aspect of a person's spirit visible *before* death. Dr. Walter J. Kilner was intrigued by the possible existence of the aura—a permanent radiation long believed to surround the human body. The belief that saints had a visible aura has been given expression by artists in many religious paintings. Clairvoyants often claimed to be able to use the colors of a person's aura to diagnose diseases or read character. Dr. Kilner thought that if such radiation existed, it should be possible to detect it by modern technology—and he set about experimenting with various techniques.

In 1911 Dr. Kilner published the results of his research in a book entitled *The Human Atmosphere*. Enclosed with each copy of the book was a special screen that was said to render the aura visible to normal sight. The screen consisted of two hermetically sealed pieces of glass enclosing some coal tar dye. By looking through this screen in daylight, and then looking at a naked person standing in front of a dark background in dim light, one could see three distinct radiations around the person's body. According to Kilner, these radiations lay in the normally invisible ultraviolet end of the spectrum. They varied in depth, with the outer aura extending as much as a foot from the body. Their depth could be affected by a magnet, and was also sensitive to electric currents. Illness was found to affect both the size and color of the aura. Mental deterioration caused a marked reduction, and the approach of death made the aura shrink to almost nothing.

Today some striking advances in the study of auras have been made by a Russian husband-and-wife team, Semyon and Valentina Kirlian. Some 30 years ago Kirlian, an electrical engineer, happened to see a demonstration of high frequency electrotherapy machinery at a research institute. As he watched, Kirlian noticed a tiny flash of light between the electrodes of the machine and the patient's skin. He wondered what would happen if he placed a photographic plate between the patient and the electrode. He knew that glass electrodes would fog the plate through exposure of light, so he decided to use a metal electrode. This was

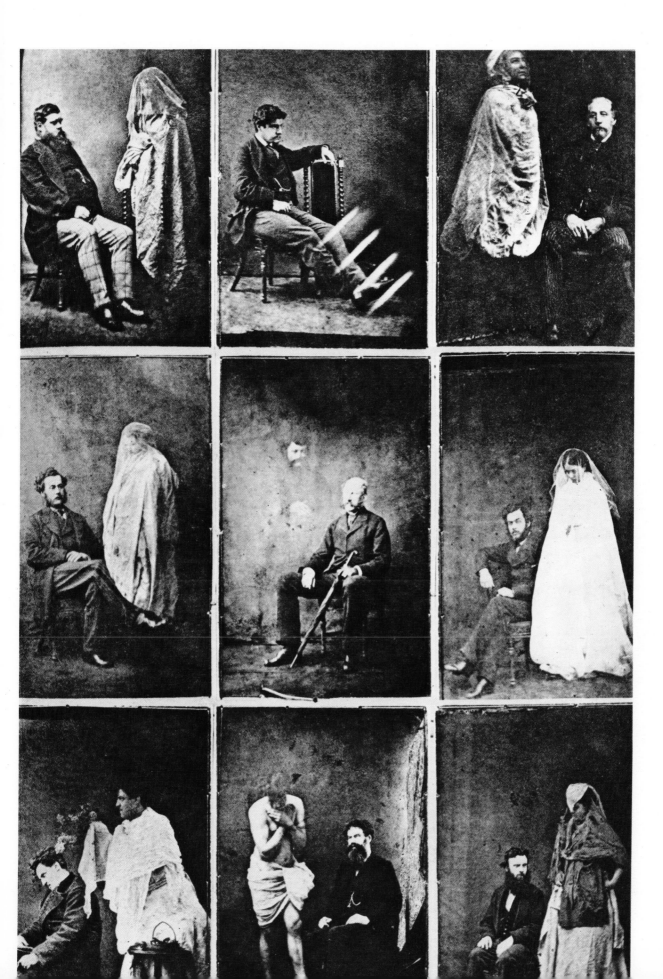

Photographic Way to Record Aura

Below: Semyon and Valentina Kirlian, the husband-and-wife team working in the USSR. They have experimented with high-frequency electrical current photography for over 30 years.

Opposite: two Kirlian photographs of a man's finger. The picture above shows the normal condition. In the bottom picture, the man has taken a drug that slows down his metabolism, and this makes the color of the corona around his fingertip change. Further Soviet research at the Kazakh State University in Alma-Ata has found that illnesses tend to show up in advance—before any symptoms appear—as a disordered play of flares.

risky, however, and for this reason, Kirlian used himself as a guinea pig. He placed his hand beneath the electrode and switched on the machine. For three seconds he withstood the stabbing pain in his hand, and then he hurriedly placed the plate in emulsion. On the developing plate he saw a strange luminescence in the shape of his fingers.

Kirlian and his wife set to work developing a more satisfactory method of recording the phenomenon. Eventually they invented and perfected a technique that achieves astonishing results. No camera is required for the process, which is now called Kirlian photography. The object to be photographed—which can be organic, such as a finger or a leaf, or inorganic such as a stone— is placed on photographic paper. The paper then goes underneath a specially constructed high frequency spark generator that produces 75,000 to 200,000 oscillations per second. When the generator is switched on, the radiation from the object is transmitted to the paper. The Kirlians also invented a special optical instrument so that they could observe the phenomenon in motion. A description of Kirlian's hand as seen through this instrument appeared in the book *Psychic Discoveries Behind the Iron Curtain* (1970), by Sheila Ostrander and Lynn Schroeder:

"The hand itself looked like the Milky Way in a starry sky. Against a background of blue and gold, something was taking place in the hand that looked like a fireworks display. Multicolored flares lit up, then sparks, twinkles, flashes. Some lights glowed steadily like Roman candles, others flashed out, then dimmed. Still others sparkled at intervals. In parts of his hand there were little dim clouds. Certain glittering flares meandered along sparkling labyrinths like space ships traveling to other galaxies."

Research by other Russian scientists revealed even stranger phenomena. They took a leaf and photographed it by Kirlian photography. Then they cut part of the leaf away and rephotographed it. To their astonishment the Kirlian machine produced a complete image of the leaf. It seems that this special energy— called "bioplasma" by the Soviet psychic researchers—will remain even though the physical object is mutilated.

The question immediately arises whether bioplasma proves the existence of a human spirit, capable of surviving death. On the face of it, the evidence seems to give a negative answer. If a leaf possesses bioplasma—not to mention inorganic objects —it seems likely that what the Kirlians have revealed is a purely physical phenomenon. On the other hand, it is possible that this energy field plays some part in telepathic, extrasensory, and physical phenomena such as poltergeist activity. At present, Dr. Thelma Moss of Los Angeles and other American investigators of paranormal phenomena are making important contributions to the field of Kirlian photography, and in the years ahead we can probably expect to hear of further developments in this new area of psychic research.

If man does possess a soul, it may well be that proof of its existence may one day be provided not by Spiritualists, but by people like Friedrich Jurgenson and the Kirlians—people who have stumbled on fascinating aspects of the unseen through the unconventional use of modern technology.

Chapter 15
Spiritualism Today

Are there still mediums in this day and age? What messages are they claiming to bring us from the world of those who have died? What protection does the law offer them, and what penalties await the medium caught in fraud? Are there spiritual healers who can produce miracles by the laying on of hands—or by psychic operations in which malignant tumors are extracted with bare fingers that heal the gaping wounds apparently with a touch? Do the artists of the past continue their creative work through the medium of sensitive psychics living today? Is Beethoven working on a new symphony with a musically uneducated English housewife?

Styles change in virtually all areas of life—from entertaining to child rearing—and Spiritualism is no exception. Today, illuminated trumpets and ectoplasm have disappeared along with gaslight, and table turning is about as fashionable as the polka. Certain aspects of Spiritualism, including its basic beliefs, remain the same, but it has lost most of the melodramatic trappings beloved in the late 19th century.

An experience recounted by Rosamund Lehmann, an English novelist, is typical of many people's first encounter with modern Spiritualism. The author's curiosity about Spiritualism grew out of the death of her daughter Sally. In her quest to discover whether her daughter had survived death Rosamund Lehmann went with a friend to a demonstration of mediumship at the College of Psychic Studies in London. She admits in her book *The Swan in the Evening* that she went to the meeting with a certain sense of guilt because her parents had strongly disapproved of Spiritualism.

The friend who accompanied her also had misgivings, but of a different kind. He told her after the meeting that he had dreaded the possibility of receiving a message from his dead father with whom he had not always seen eye to eye.

Their expectations were similar to those of most people attending a Spiritualist meeting for the first time. However, the very normality of the proceedings seems to put newcomers at ease. Rosamund Lehmann was fortunate in being one of the

Opposite: although the theatrical drama of the seance room has mellowed and changed, the seances go on. Spiritualism attracts 20th-century adherents determined yet to prove the survival of the human spirit.

Spiritualism in Modern Form

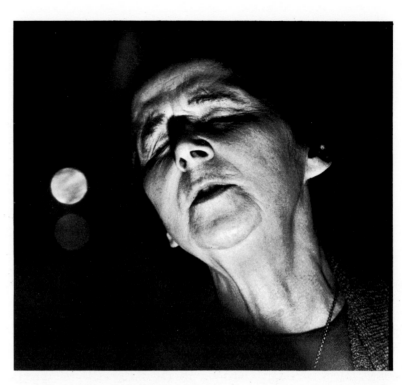

Right: the British medium Mrs. Ena Twigg in a trance. Mrs. Twigg is a minister of the Spiritualist Church and, like any British minister, she can officiate at weddings and at funerals—as well as at seances.

few people at the meeting to receive a message, and one that she found very convincing. She writes:

"I had heard that the demonstrator was a remarkable sensitive called Mrs. Ena Twigg. She is an attractive, charming looking person, and I saw her with surprise and relief . . . In short, I began to relax. But what followed startled me tremendously. Mrs. Twigg, whom I had never seen before, opened her demonstration by addressing me. Then she described Sally, whom she appeared to see standing behind me; then she put her hands to her temples and said: 'This is a very strange message. . . . Why is she talking about the War God? She is saying Wotan, Wotan, the War God. . . . She is saying she does wish the War God would believe she is alive. . . . Can you understand?' Another pause. 'Oh! Now she's saying I haven't got the name quite right. It's not quite right but it's the only way she could think of to get it through. She is laughing. She says you will understand. Do you understand?'"

The writer was startled and impressed by this message from a complete stranger. The Christian name of her husband—Sally's father—was Wogan, a most unusual English name. It was obvious that, in the spirit communication, one letter had somehow been changed, making the name sound like that of the Norse God of War.

In the course of a modern public demonstration of mediumship or clairvoyance, only about 10 or 12 people at most receive messages. Many therefore leave the meeting with a sense of disappointment, not having heard anything relevant to themselves, and not knowing whether or not the messages received by others were evidential.

To increase their chances of receiving a personal message, those interested can arrange a private sitting. The larger Spiritualist organizations in Britain have special rooms reserved for this purpose, but most mediums give seances in their own homes either in their living room or in a room set aside for spirit communication. Normally the seance room atmosphere is calm and restrained. Apart from the medium describing people invisible to the sitter, and conveying words that she or he alone can hear, the sitting resembles an informal chat. Most mediums now work without going into a trance. Some mediums are superb entertainers, describing the spirits so vividly and poignantly, and conveying the messages with such dramatic timing that they can reduce the sitters to tears. The majority of mediums, however, have a matter-of-fact approach, and let the content of the message speak for itself.

Today in Britain mediums can practice their calling with no fear of legal prosecution—provided that they do not do so "with intent to deceive" or use "any fraudulent device." This provision is part of the Fraudulent Mediums Act passed in 1951. Before that time, mediums were liable to prosecution under the Witchcraft Act of 1735. Under that law mediumship itself was illegal so police could raid any seance without prior evidence that fraud was being committed. Spiritualists were understandably upset by this state of affairs. In particular, they

Below: a modern seance, now often called a home circle. These present-day Spiritualists meet weekly to "complete a link" between themselves and the spirit world. The flowers are important because it is believed that "the spirit people like them." Most modern seances do not have showy displays of physical phenomenon.

Early Conflicts with the Law

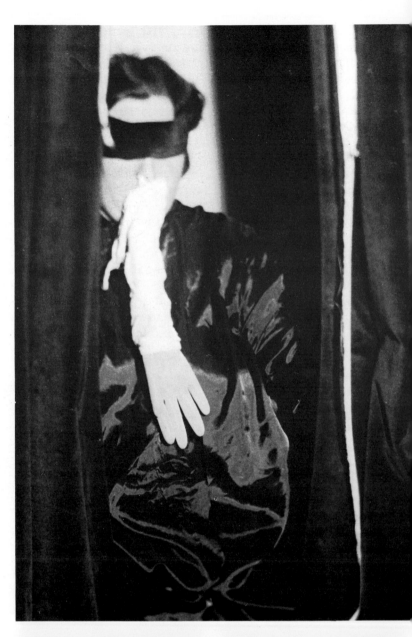

Right: Helen Duncan, the British physical medium. This picture, taken during a seance, shows her materializing a hand from her curtained cabinet. During his investigations with the Laboratory of Psychical Research, Harry Price obtained photos of a similar manifestation that was clearly a rubber glove.

Right: the rubber doll that masqueraded as Mrs. Duncan's child spirit guide Peggy in some of her fraudulent seances.

Far right: Miss Esson Maule in the hallway of the building in which the Peggy-chemise episode took place. Helen Duncan was arrested as a fraudulent medium and received a sentence to pay a small fine or serve a month in prison.

feared that mediums in trance could be injured by sudden interference during a physical seance.

The conflict between Spiritualists and the law in Britain came to the boil in 1944 with the trial of Mrs. Helen Duncan. One of the foremost physical mediums of her day, Helen Duncan had been investigated and exposed by the London Psychical Laboratory in 1931. Two years later she was convicted of fraud and given a small fine. It appears that her talents included the technique of swallowing and regurgitating items, and the ectoplasm she produced was shown on one occasion to be chewed-up toilet paper. In spite of her various embarrassments, this medium continued to enjoy great popularity, and many Spiritualists insisted that she could produce genuine phenomena.

Early in 1944 Helen Duncan gave a series of seances in Portsmouth, England. A young naval officer attended one of the seances and received a communication from his deceased aunt, of which he had none, and from his deceased sister, who was actually alive. The man returned for another seance with a plainclothes policeman. During one of the materializations they switched on a flashlight and grabbed the medium, who was veiled in some filmy white material. In the hubbub that followed someone snatched away the vital evidence—the veil—but the medium was arrested.

Helen Duncan's trial provided a little light relief from the war situation. For seven days readers of Britain's newspapers were treated to fascinating headlines such as "Spirit called Peggy liked lipstick," and "Spirit had 20-inch mustache." Despite an able defense financed by a Spiritualist fund, Mrs. Duncan was convicted of fraud and sentenced to nine months' prison.

This was not the end of her career, however. After her release she resumed work, and in 1956 one of her materialization seances was raided by the police. The medium fell ill and was taken to a hospital in Edinburgh. There she died at the age of 59, five weeks after the surprise raid. The death certificate attributed her decease to diabetes and heart failure. Since she weighed 280 pounds, it is probable that her heart would have given out before too long. However, the shock of the police

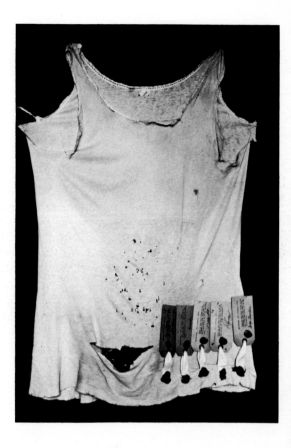

Above: Peggy the spirit guide again—this time in the shape of a woman's chemise. This Peggy appeared during a seance in 1933. One of the sitters was policewoman Esson Maule, who suddenly grabbed at the spirit as another sitter simultaneously put on the lights. The medium and Miss Maule had a brief tug of war over the garment— the tear is where Miss Maule briefly got her arm stuck through it. The seals were placed on it, with signatures, by most of the other sitters who had been there.

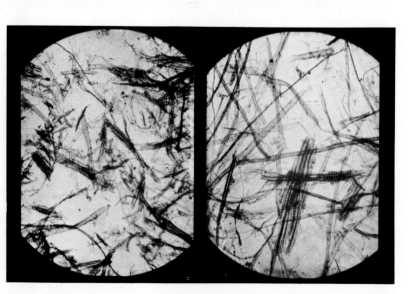

Left: photomicrographs of the "teleplasm" produced by Helen Duncan during a test seance. The teleplasm, on the left, is compared with a control sample of ordinary paper (60% chemical and 40% mechanical wood pulp). The fibers, medullary rays, etc. are identical in both photos.

"The World's Largest Seance"

raid may well have accelerated her death.

To Spiritualists it was a clear case of an entranced medium being injured by a sudden withdrawal of ectoplasm into her body. They reacted to Mrs. Duncan's death with a storm of protest. Hundreds of them contributed to a special fund to enable her husband to bring court proceedings against the police. On the advice of lawyers, however, the case was dropped. Today, Mrs. Duncan is regarded by most Spiritualists as a martyr. Many attribute the disappearance of physical phenomena to the fear of injury by mediums.

In the United States the legal position of mediums varies from state to state. There is no equivalent to the Fraudulent Mediums Act, although fraudulent psychics are open to prosecution in the same way as frauds in other spheres. In New York and California the courts are tough on mediums. To avoid prosecution, many adopt a religious title such as Reverend.

As a recognized denomination, American Spiritualism is small. The National Spiritualist Association includes about 200 churches with 5000 members, while the International General Assembly of Spiritualists has around 80 churches and 1200 members.

Britain, although a smaller country, has far more practicing Spiritualists. There are more than 500 Spiritualist churches, most of them belonging to the Spiritualists' National Union. This organization was founded in 1890 by Emma Hardinge Britten, one of Britain's earliest mediums and most active Spiritualist propagandists. Its main function is "to promote the advancement and diffusion of the religious philosophy of Spiritualism, on the basis of the Seven Principles." These

This series of photos was taken during the course of a modern Brazilian seance. A young woman medium apparently produced a complete materialized spirit. The arrows show where the beads were first materialized, and where they appeared on the fully materialized spirit's headdress.

Right: the medium was handcuffed inside a special barred cage.
Far right: the woman in trance begins to produce ectoplasm.

SPIRITUALISM TODAY

principles include such generally accepted beliefs as "the brotherhood of man" and "personal responsibility," along with more specifically Spiritualist tenets, such as "the Communion of Spirits and the Ministry of Angels."

A typical service in a Spiritualist church opens with a prayer by the chairman—not called Reverend in Britain—followed by hymns and more prayers, an address, and a demonstration of clairvoyance. The medium demonstrates his or her psychic talents by pacing the platform and selecting individuals in the audience to whom spirit messages are addressed. The quality of the clairvoyance at these public meetings varies greatly. At its worst it looks like a ludicrous guessing game, with the medium deliberately asking questions or discreetly fishing for information. At its best, as practiced by a gifted medium such as Ena Twigg, it yields some startlingly accurate information. There is no doubt that many people find such meetings satisfying. Every year on Armistice Day, thousands of people pack London's huge Royal Albert Hall to hear the top mediums convey messages from those who died in the two world wars.

This gathering, billed as "the world's largest seance," is organized by the Spiritualist Association of Great Britain. The SAGB is one of the largest Spiritualist organizations in the world. At its headquarters in London's fashionable Belgrave Square, it offers a wide range of activities including seances, lectures, and spiritual healing. The Association produces its own newspaper, publishes books, and sends mediums to the United States, Canada, and a number of European countries.

Although almost every country in the world has Spiritualist associations, Spiritualism has not elsewhere developed to the

Below left: the curtains are drawn over th cage, but the materialized figure appears and accepts a book as proof it is in fact material.

Below: the fully materialized figure appears outside the cage.

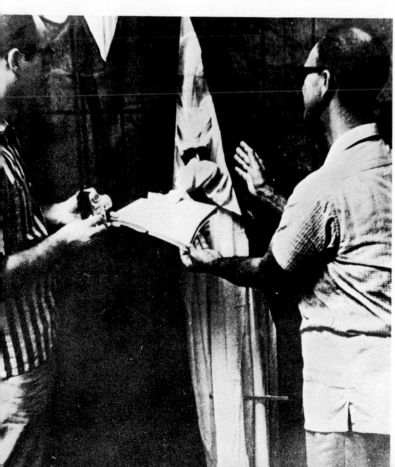

Psychic Surgery

same degree as in Britain and the United States. The exception is Brazil, where it is said to have some five million followers.

In Brazil, as in other South American countries and France, the popular form of Spiritualism is "Spiritism," a set of beliefs formulated by Allan Kardec. A Frenchman whose real name was Hippolyte Leon Denizard Rivail, Kardec began studying Spiritualism in its earliest days. He enlisted the help of 10 mediums in contacting spirits for answers to a wide range of questions. Kardec then distilled and systematized the answers, publishing them under the title *Le Livre des Esprits* (*The Book of Spirits*). The 1018 questions and answers in the book cover numerous subjects, from the creation to moral laws. Key passages in the book deal with the various realms of spirit, spiritual progression, and the belief in reincarnation. Not only are souls reborn, according to Kardec, but they also progress by being reborn on more advanced inhabited planets.

A major belief of Spiritism—or Kardecism as it is sometimes called—is that charity is essential for salvation, and the greatest act of charity is to bestow health. This can be achieved by co-operating with spirit entities having appropriate medical skills. This perhaps explains why Brazil, with its large number of Spiritists, is in the forefront of psychic healing.

There are several Brazilian Spiritist hospitals in which medical men and mediums work side by side. The largest of these is the 600-bed Porto Alegre Spirit Hospital, founded in 1926. Like all the other hospitals run by Spiritists, Porto Alegre specializes in the treatment of mental illness. According to Spiritism many disturbances of the mind are caused by spirit entities, and are best treated by trained mediums who can rid the afflicted patient of the obsessing spirit. The medical teams who work with the mediums in such hospitals do not have to subscribe to Spiritist beliefs, and practice orthodox medicine.

The treatment of the mentally ill also led to the founding of Palmelo, the only Spiritist community in the world. Located about 160 miles from Brazil's new capital of Brasilia, the Spiritist village started with one man, Jeronimo Candido Gomide. He built a hut on the site in 1925, and started treating the insane with Spiritist methods. Soon a small settlement grew up around him. Today the town of Palmelo has 2000 inhabitants, plus a fluctuating population of mental patients.

There is nothing startling or revolutionary about the Spiritist treatment of mental disorders. After all, many modern forms of psychotherapy could be described as spiritual healing even though the therapist does not believe the disorders come from spirit entities. But psychic surgery is another matter. In the last few years there have been reports from Brazil and the Philippines, another home of Spiritism, of seemingly miraculous operations performed by untrained people using makeshift instruments or, in some cases, their bare hands.

The most famous of these psychic surgeons was José Arigó, sometimes called "the surgeon of the rusty knife." Before his death in 1971 he operated on thousands of people, using unsterilized instruments such as kitchen knives and scissors. Most of the patients were cured or helped considerably, and there was not a single fatality despite the appalling conditions under

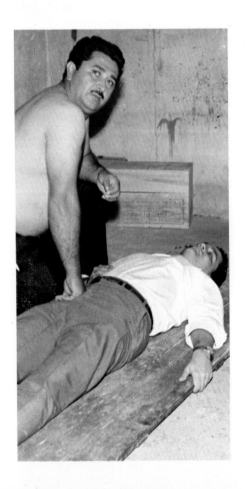

Below: the Brazilian healer José Arigó carrying out an eye operation on a patient. After a phenomenally successful career of psychic healing, Arigó was killed in a car crash in 1971.

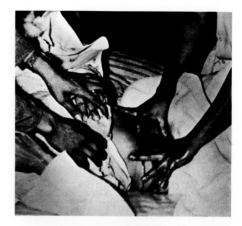

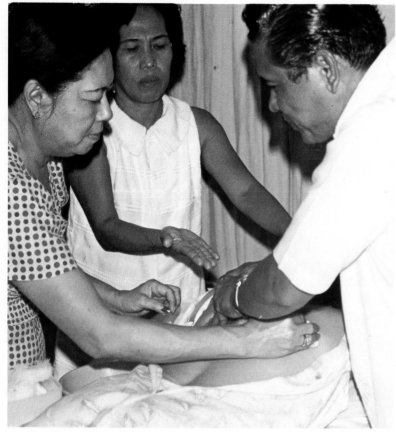

Above: Angelo, a psychic healer, shown working with two assistants on the back of a patient who has lung trouble. The location is Manila, the Philippines, which has now become another thriving center of psychic surgery and Spiritualist healing. There is a long history of faith healing in the Philippines, and today more than 400 healing centers allied with the Spiritualists exist throughout the islands.

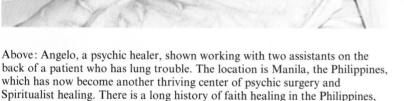

Right top to bottom: Tony Agpaoa, one of the most notable Filipino healers, operating on a malignant abdominal growth. The incision, made with bare hands, took only four seconds. The growth, about the size of an avocado stone, was pulled out, alcohol poured over the wound, and the incision closed. The abdomen, still blood-spattered, shows no scar.

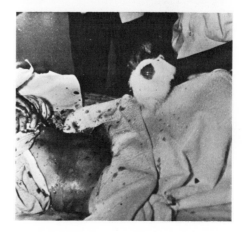

which he worked. Arigó was said to be controlled by "Dr. Fritz," a dead German surgeon. Whatever the source of Arigó's knowledge, his ability was astonishing. On one occasion a team of doctors studying Arigó presented him with 1000 patients to see if he could diagnose their illnesses. Without touching them, and taking on average just one minute to complete each consultation, Arigó made specific diagnoses and suggested appropriate treatment in each case. He used automatic writing to convey this information from Dr. Fritz. The doctors were able to confirm 550 of Dr. Fritz's diagnoses. The remaining 450 could not be confirmed because the team did not have on-the-spot resources to carry out tests, but in no case was the diagnosis or treatment discovered to be incorrect.

Dr. Fritz has never been identified, but another Brazilian

Above: Spiritualist healing British style. Harry Edwards is a well-known British healer who claims to have cured 10,000 patients in four years with the help of spirit guides, many of whom apparently had medical training during their life on earth. He says that Pasteur and Lister are two of them. Here, at a public demonstration of his powers, Harry Edwards calls for the to come forward.

Above right: Harry Edwards treating a patient suffering from back trouble by laying on of hands.

psychic surgeon, Lourival de Freitas, has a very famous control. This is the Roman emperor Nero, although he was not known for medical skills during his lifetime. A woman of Nero's court and a Japanese called "Sheka" also control de Freitas on occasion. The Japanese specializes in certain lung and bronchial operations.

De Freitas is vouched for by Anne Dooley, an English journalist and psychic researcher who suffered from a bronchial condition judged incurable by medical experts. Having watched de Freitas operate successfully on other people, Anne Dooley. decided to let him operate on her. She described the experience in the *Psychic* magazine of February 1973.

The operation began rather unfavorably with Nero controlling de Freitas and indulging in a long-winded attack on the press in general and on the patient in particular. Courageously the fully conscious reporter submitted to having her tonsils removed with a pair of scissors, and to having a cut made in her back. From this incision de Freitas withdrew a large clot of blood.

After a slightly painful but short convalescence, Anne Dooley returned to England and was examined at Greenwich Chest Clinic. The X-ray showed her to be normal.

Even more bizarre than this operation are some of the feats

of Philippine psychic surgeons. They work with their bare hands and seemingly open up bodies, remove diseased matter and growths, and mend the wounds.

Dr. Lyall Watson, a British scientist and writer who has watched these Filipino healers at work, offers an interesting hypothesis in his book *The Romeo Error*. While not dismissing the surgery itself as fraud, he believes that much of the blood in psychic surgery is window dressing to make observers believe that the bodies are actually being opened. Analysis of the blood in these operations has yielded some puzzling results. At times the blood is of the same type as the patient's, but at other times it belongs to a different blood group. Sometimes, it has proved to be animal's blood. Watson believes that the healers possess a form of materialization mediumship. He writes:

"I spent several days working with Josephine Sison . . . and saw her perform over 200 operations, about 85 percent of which involved materialization phenomena. At no time was I more than a foot away from her and not once while she worked did her hands move out of my sight, but she was able to produce bloodlike fluid from her fingertips whenever she pressed them against a patient's body. Sometimes the red liquid was accompanied by small pieces of tissue and on several occasions there appeared totally foreign objects. I saw her draw a rusty nail, two complete cobs, several large plastic bags, a film canister, three undamaged leaves still attached to a twig from a thorn bush, and a piece of jagged glass from the body surface of a series of patients. In every case the objects seemed to grow in the space between her fingers and the skin. I am totally convinced that no sleight-of-hand was involved and equally certain that these objects did not come from within the patients concerned. This leaves me with the following possibilities. Either I was deluded or being hypnotized (both unlikely explanations due to the fact that several of the operations in question were successfully filmed), or Sison is capable of bringing about controlled materializations."

Here we have the history of Spiritualism repeating itself: a scientist sets out to investigate strange and suspect phenomena, and ends up vouching for their authenticity. The reaction among Western Spiritualist healers to such gruesome surgery has been skeptical, and in some cases hostile. When Lourival de Freitas gave a demonstration of his methods before some British healers at the Spiritualist Association, he was prevented from continuing by the alarmed members of the audience.

The European spiritual healers, however, share with the psychic surgeons the belief that they are merely channels through which the spirits of doctors do the actual healing. Harry Edwards, possibly the world's most famous healer today, believes that a band of medical men—including Louis Pasteur and Lord Lister—direct his healing from the spirit world. "There is such a wide diversity of diseases healed," he says, "that each case must be a planned treatment. There must be an intelligence capable of truly diagnosing the cause of the sickness and possessing the knowledge how to apply the corrective forces necessary to bring about the healing. These healing intelligences must possess a superior knowledge to man. . . ."

Defense of Psychic Healing

Above: Edwards' technique, basically, consists of keeping his eyes shut to get attuned to his spirit guides, until he can feel the power flowing through his body. Then the healing can commence. He does no manipulation. Apart from the gentle laying on of hands, the most he does is a slight, rocking movement over the affected area of the patient.

Rosemary Brown

Below: Rosemary Brown with one of the scores she claims were dictated to her by the dead great masters of music. This particular piece, "Study in C♯ minor," was dictated by Chopin. Liszt, who is her spirit guide, has dictated more music to her than anyone else, and the closest runner-up is Chopin. Mrs. Brown, who is an untutored musician, writes: "Much of his new music is too difficult for me to play properly—I stumble through it, just getting some idea of how it should sound."

The supposed superior knowledge of spirits continues to be a hotly debated point between believers and skeptics. The communications received from spirits over the years have on the whole been banal and trivial. There have been cases of spirits apparently conveying detailed and accurate information, as in the R101 case, but even such messages as these do not necessarily support the idea of superior intellectual development on the "other side." In fact, communications allegedly received from the spirits of distinguished thinkers, such as scientists Thomas Henry Huxley and Sir Oliver Lodge, have been noticeably inferior to their earthly communications in both content and style.

While editor of the occult magazine *Tomorrow*, F. Clive-Ross was one of Spiritualism's sternest critics. He wrote in 1963 that one of the strongest arguments against Spiritualism was that little of significance had been communicated, "although the welter of rubbish has been stupendous." He went on to issue this challenge:

"According to Spiritualists the spirits of great composers also survive, and it should be a fairly simple matter to communicate some music. Cannot 'Silver Birch' [a then well-known spirit guide] ask Beethoven for a new symphony, Wagner for a new opera, or even an aria from Puccini, Verdi, Donizetti, Gounod, or Bellini? The great writers have been silent, so now let us see whether the great composers can do any better. Silver Birch enunciates long-winded platitudes readily enough, so here is his opportunity to produce something likely to convince a great many people of the truth of Spiritualism. It need not be anything very elaborate; just one of the latest compositions by any of these composers from the spheres where, the Spiritualists tell us, they continued to work and 'progress.'"

At the time this was published, newly widowed Rosemary Brown was struggling in poverty to bring up a young son and daughter. She had been psychic since childhood, and could remember a vision of an elderly gentleman who told her that one day he and other great composers would give her beautiful music, and teach her how to play it.

Years later she came across a picture of Franz Liszt, and recognized him as her mysterious visitor. In 1964 Rosemary Brown began to write music—not just simple tunes, but well-developed compositions in the styles of Liszt, Chopin, Debussy, Rachmaninoff, Brahms, Bach, and Beethoven. Most of these are piano pieces, though some are for orchestra. Having had only a few piano lessons, she finds some of the piano music too difficult to play herself. A recording, entitled "Rosemary Brown's Music" was released in 1970. On one side it features Mrs. Brown playing the simpler pieces; on the other side the renowned pianist Peter Katin plays the more complex music.

An observer who watched Rosemary Brown writing some of the music was amazed at the speed with which she wrote. She says that the music has already been composed when it is dictated to her. Some of the composers communicate in English but, she says, "Liszt tends to go off into a stream of German when excited—or French." The medium's schoolgirl French is barely adequate to understanding her French-speaking composers. When Chopin speaks Polish, she tries to write it down phonetically and gives it to a Polish friend to try to translate.

Reaction from the musical world has predictably been mixed. Many musicians have been greatly impressed with Rosemary Brown's works. Pianist Hephzibah Menuhin said: "I look at these manuscripts with immense respect. Each piece is distinctly in the composer's style." Composer Richard Rodney Bennet was more outspoken: "A lot of people can improvise, but you couldn't fake music like this without years of training. I couldn't have faked some of the Beethoven myself."

Nevertheless, some critics have found the music "less than the best" of which the composers were capable—often more characteristic of their early work than of their maturity. Spiritualists counter by saying that the point of the communication is not so much to add to the world's treasury of music as to give proof of survival. An introduction to the recording, supposedly dictated by the late musicologist Sir Donald Tovey, gave this view:

"In communicating through music and conversation, an organized group of musicians, who have departed from your world, are attempting to establish a precept for humanity, i.e., that physical death is a transition from one state of consciousness to another wherein one retains one's individuality. . . . We are not transmitting music to Rosemary Brown simply for the sake of offering possible pleasure in listening thereto; it is the implications relevant to this phenomenon which we hope will stimulate sensible and sensitive interest and stir many who are intelligent and impartial to consider and explore the unknown of man's mind and psyche. When man has plumbed the mysterious depths of his veiled consciousness, he will then be able to soar to correspondingly greater heights."

Spiritualism has come a long way from the rappings in the small cottage in Hydesville. Its manifestations in the modern world are extremely varied—from matter-of-fact messages through a fully conscious clairvoyant to gruesome operations by a psychic surgeon in trance. Healing in one form or another is an important part of Spiritualist activity in most countries, but apart from this common concern, the movement has little overall unity. An International Spiritualist Federation exists, but it has not been able to unite the movement. One dividing factor is whether or not mediums should take money for their services. Another is the belief in reincarnation, which is vital to Kardec's Spiritist school of thought but largely rejected in Europe and America. Some believers say Spiritualism is a religion, and others call it a way of life. Spiritualism, then, is thriving in disarray. And since it does not have a world leader— relying instead on the often conflicting teachings of spirit guides for its philosophy—the possibility of its ever growing into a world religion of major importance seems remote.

Spiritualists throughout the world have in common a belief in life after death, and a desire to demonstrate that many forms of communication with the world beyond are possible. To interested outsiders the question is: has sufficient evidence been amassed or are we still waiting for a communication that will decide the case once and for all?

Spirit Inspiration for New Music

Mrs. Rosemary Brown has been writing music since 1964 which, she claims, is dictated by the great musicians of the past. According to her, the spirit of the composer Franz Liszt first appeared to her when she was seven years old. In 1964 Mrs. Brown had an accident. Shortly afterward Liszt appeared and began to dictate music to her. Later Liszt introduced Chopin, Beethoven, Brahms, Bach, Debussy, Grieg, Rachmaninoff, and Stravinsky to Mrs. Brown, who took down their compositions as they dictated them. Many famous musicians have been impressed by the compositions. Others say that, though they are in the style of the great masters, they are not of the quality of their best compositions. One expert has suggested that Rosemary Brown belongs to "the type of sensitive whom frustration, often artistic, drives to the automatic production of material well beyond their conscious capacity."

Beethoven Writes a Tenth Symphony

The English medium Rosemary Brown has produced quantities of music she claims has been dictated to her by the great masters of music, who have chosen this way to prove that their spirits survive. One of her special favorites is Beethoven, and the two of them are engaged on a project that is taking years: the Tenth Symphony. It is an enormous choral work, like the great composer's Ninth Symphony.

In writing this new work Beethoven will be able to hear it, according to Rosemary Brown. In her autobiography *Unfinished Symphonies*, she says that his deafness is gone. "Those human ills and frailties disappear once we reach the other side," she writes. The spirit Beethoven is a less stormy person than he was in life, but he is still awe-inspiring. Rosemary Brown was so much in awe of him at first that little conversation took place. She received his music by a kind of telepathy, slowly catching his ideas in writing.

Now Beethoven works much more directly, dictating several bars for one hand, and then going back to fill in for the other. "After all," says the medium, "they know already what they are going to tell me to write, and it is simpler to keep to one line at a time."

Chapter 16
Sifting the Evidence

Are there any definite conclusions to be drawn about the world of spirits? Are there such things, and is it possible for living individuals to make conscious contact with apparitions of the dead? What messages do they have to convey to the living? Serious and dedicated investigators have spent years of their lives attempting to create an environment in which fraud and deceit were impossible—did they ever succeed? Are there communications which cannot be explained by natural means? What is the evidence? What can we say now about the relationship of the body and the spirit? Do we survive death?

Spiritualism has now been a flourishing belief for more than 125 years. From its noisy, melodramatic beginnings to its present mainly low-key manifestations, it has intrigued, baffled, convinced, and comforted millions of people, while many others have dismissed it as utter nonsense. If no longer news, it at least remains controversial.

If a person is a thoroughgoing skeptic, it is easy enough to refuse to consider the possibility that any part of the self survives bodily death—let alone communicates with the living. For one thing, such ideas seem to contradict present scientific knowledge. Moreover, a few of the more tawdry hoaxes perpetrated by some mediums will suffice to reinforce the cynic's belief that the whole Spiritualist case is a tissue of lies and delusions.

Those who start to examine Spiritualism objectively, however, will soon find themselves bewildered by conflicting evidence. They may be amused and disgusted in turn by the hoaxes and by the pathetic gullibility of some of the followers, but they may also discover cases that seem so genuine they are on the point of believing. Then they come across an explanation of how the material communicated could have been obtained by the medium either through telepathy with the sitter or from sources within the medium's subconscious mind. Once in a great while, they will find a case that seems inexplicable except in Spiritualist terms.

Logically, one such case is all that is needed. The American psychologist and philosopher William James made this point

Opposite: it all began in a small cottage in the town of Hydesville, New York, with two little girls and an unseen force trading raps. From that first communication believed to be with the spirit world, Spiritualism is now an idea encircling the globe.

"Never Detected in Fraud"

Below: Daniel Dunglas Home, the one medium who was never proved fraudulent in the physical phenomena he produced. He never tried materializations, but his levitations were legendary—and no one ever proved he was cheating.

when he said in a lecture: "To upset the conclusion that all crows are black there is no need to seek demonstration that no crow is white; it is sufficient to produce one white crow; a single one is sufficient." Once it is proved beyond the shadow of a doubt that in a particular case a communication or phenomenon originated from someone who has died, we have proof that survival is a fact. For convinced Spiritualists, the skies are full of white crows. For a skeptical investigator, such cases are so rare that he is more likely to file them away as "unsolved" rather than to accept them as proof of the existence of spirits.

Among the many physical mediums, the outstanding apparent white crow was D. D. Home. All of the others that were investigated—Mrs. Guppy, Florence Cook, Eusapia Paladino, Helen Duncan, to name a few—were caught in fraud, sometimes over and over again. The faithful would stoutly maintain that these mediums produced genuine phenomena as well, but for a critical investigator, their chronic cheating—often well planned in advance—casts strong doubt on the allegedly genuine occurrences. Not so in the case of D. D. Home. All psychic investigators acknowledge the fact that Home was never detected in fraud.

Time and time again in good light Home produced some of the most astonishing phenomena ever witnessed. The most thorough investigation of Home was done by Sir William Crookes, who also investigated Florence Cook and her materialized spirit Katie King. Crookes devised several tests for Home including a test of his power to make an accordion play by itself.

Crookes built a cage that was open at the top and bottom and would just fit under a table. He bought a new accordion to rule out the possibility of Home's using one of the self-playing models then available on the market. During the test seance, the cage was moved out from under the table and the accordion was placed inside it. The medium picked up the accordion at the opposite end to the keys, and held it with his thumb and middle finger. Adjacent sitters placed their feet on top of Home's, and the medium placed his free hand on the top of the table. The cage was moved back toward the table as far as Home's arm would permit. Soon the accordion began waving about curiously inside the cage. It played a few notes and then a simple tune. "But the sequel," reported Crookes, "was still more striking, for Mr. Home then removed his hand altogether from the accordion, . . . and placed it in the hand of the person next to him. The instrument then continued to play, no person touching it and no hand being near it."

An even more bizarre psychic concert by Home was reported by Lady Crookes, the wife of the scientist. During a seance held in a London house, she was sitting somewhat apart from the other sitters, facing them. Home, holding an accordion, stood in the doorway leading to the adjacent room. Then, according to Lady Crookes:

"The accordion was immediately taken from his hand by a cloudy appearance, which soon seemed to condense into a distinct human form, clothed in a filmy drapery, standing near Mr. Home between the two rooms. The accordion began to play (I do not remember whether on this occasion there was any recognized melody), and the figure advanced toward me till it almost touched me, playing continuously. It was semitransparent, and I could see the sitters through it all the time. Mr. Home remained near the sliding doors. As the figure approached I felt an intense cold, getting stronger as it got nearer, and as it was giving me the accordion I could not help screaming. The figure immediately seemed to sink into the floor to the waist, leaving only the head and shoulders visible, still playing the accordion, which was then about a foot off the floor. Mr. Home and my husband came to me at once, and I have no clear recollection of what then occurred, except that the accordion did not cease playing immediately. Mr. Serjeant Cox was rather angry at my want of nerve, and exclaimed: 'Mrs. Crookes, you have spoilt the finest manifestation we have ever had.' I have always regretted that my want of presence of mind brought the phenomena to so abrupt a termination."

On the face of it, we might conclude that Lady Crookes was deceived by her will to believe in supernormal phenomena. Likewise her husband, brilliant and honest scientist though he was, was a staunch Spiritualist. The other sitters were not necessarily trained observers. Might it not be, then, that their desire to believe in the supernatural, coupled with Home's charismatic personality, created a collective hallucination? Many sane and intelligent people have been known to hallucinate, and for several people to experience the same hallucination simultaneously is not unheard of, although rare.

The sheer bulk of the evidence in favor of Home, however, speaks strongly against hallucination. Dozens of witnesses independently left written testimony of astounding events apparently caused by Home. It was not uncommon for heavy pieces of furniture to rise several feet in the air, for example. One witness reporting such a case asserted that he had to use all his strength to push a levitated table back onto the floor. Perhaps

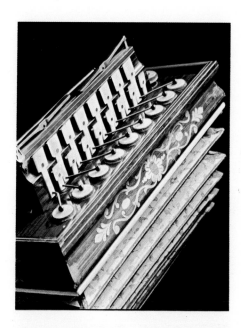

Above: Home's own accordion, which would play by itself during his seances. Sometimes music would even be heard when there was apparently no instrument present in the room at all.

Left: Home with his accordion. It played in spite of all the controls, including the special cage devised by Crookes to keep Home's hands and feet away from the instrument.

The Amazing Case of Stella C.

Below: the nurse Stella Cranshaw, known as Stella C. Although she was for a time a superb physical medium, she was barely interested in the phenomena she produced, and was unenthusiastic about psychical research. She did not appear to believe, personally, that the peculiar manifestations which had gone on in her vicinity since her childhood had anything to do with spirits. When she began the experiments, she was 21. During the five years that she was intermittently tested, her powers, and her interest, waned noticeably. After the last series of tests in 1928, she married, and gave up trying her unusual powers.

even more astonishing is the report that when tables moved about in the air, the objects lying on them remained undisturbed.

Less spectacular, but perhaps even more convincing for that very reason, were certain other experiments conducted by Crookes in which Home, by merely placing his fingertips in a glass of water resting on a board, was able to cause apparent weight fluctuations in the board. The fluctuations were measured by scales on which one end of the board was resting.

Such experiments convinced Crookes of the existence of a "new force" which Home possessed. Unfortunately, the scientists who were critical of Crookes' investigations and conclusions disdained to check his results with experiments of their own. Had they done so, they might have helped to establish without doubt Home's possession of supernormal powers. Even without their corroboration, however, Home's case continues to challenge the skeptics.

Though no other medium has demonstrated the powers of the new force in such a dramatic and colorful way, there have been some physical mediums whose manifestations have been subjected to rigorous tests. One of these was Stella Cranshaw, a young British nurse, usually referred to in research as Stella C. She was discovered in the 1920s by Harry Price, a well-known psychical researcher, to whom she reported during a conversation on a train that she sometimes experienced breezes in closed rooms, saw objects move apparently by themselves, and occasionally saw blue sparks—a very rare psychic phenomenon. She agreed to be investigated by Price and his team at the National Laboratory of Psychical Research in London. Price conducted several tests on Stella C. in the 1920s. They involved ingenious equipment and stringest controls. One piece of apparatus was a fraud-proof seance table. It consisted of two tables, one of which fitted inside the other. In the top of the inner table was a hinged trap door which could be opened only from the underside. Between the legs of the inner table was a shelf on which small musical instruments, such as a harmonica or a bell, could be placed. The sides of each table were enclosed with wooden trellises, and as an extra control, the legs of the inner table were wrapped with a length of gauze. The investigators thus made sure that no one could surreptitiously gain access to the objects inside the inner table.

Stella C. and the sitters sat around this table, two of the sitters holding her hands and feet. After she went into a trance, activity began to occur within the center table. The bell that had been put inside rang, and the harmonica therein played. Most remarkable of all, a red light flashed in the telekinetoscope, a device designed by Price. This was a sensitive piece of apparatus containing a battery and a small lightbulb that was turned on by pressing a telegraph key. To insure that the key could not be pressed by a person, Price covered it with a soap bubble and, to prevent the soap bubble from drying out and breaking, with a glass shade. After the seance the bubble was discovered still intact. The light had been turned on by some invisible force. This force that seemed to emanate from Stella C. was also capable of more vigorous activity. On one occasion it levitated the seance table, and at another memorable seance, it completely demolished the

table.

Was Stella C.'s power that of telekinesis—the movement of objects by an immaterial force? Telekinesis is a well-established psychic phenomenon that is thought by many modern scientists to account for a great deal of poltergeist activity. Most psychical researchers regard it as a power exerted by living humans rather than proof of the existence of spirits. It seems plausible that Home and Stella C. could have produced genuine physical phenomena through their own powers, and that spirits are not needed to account for them.

How do we account for materializations, though? Many cases can be dismissed as fraud, and many others as hallucinations. Even so, the subject has its baffling aspects. In 1929 and 1930, Harry Price conducted a series of seances in his laboratory with the Austrian medium Rudi Schneider. The medium was seated at a table with six observers including Price. All wore metallic gloves and shoes and touched the hands and feet of their neighbors. In front of each person was a red lightbulb, which remained lit as long as no one broke the circuit. If anyone were to remove his hand or foot, the light would go out. Price also searched Rudi before each seance. In spite of the rigid controls, Rudi time and again produced materialized hands and arms. Some of these limbs were only partial, missing the thumbs. At one sitting the observers saw a misshapen leg of a "pale chocolate color" emerge from the curtained cabinet and rock the table that stood in front of it.

Price's extensive notes on this series of seances constitute one of the most impressive documents on physical mediumship in the history of psychical research. But even these notes leave doubts. There is an allegation supported by photographic evidence that Rudi had one hand free during a seance in which, for some unknown reason, Price had not used the electrical control. Instead he had relied merely on holding Schneider's hands during the test. Price accused Rudi of fraud, and the whole investigation blew up in a personal quarrel.

Above left: the musical toys and instruments that were played by psychic forces at Stella C.'s experimental seances.

Above: the fraud-proof table made by H. W. Pugh. The center flap could be opened only from underneath. It did open several times during the seance, and two of the sitters, placing a silk handkerchief over the open flap, felt fingerlike forms moving under the handkerchief.

Below: the solid wood table that Stella C.'s forces once reduced to fragments.

Controlled Tests
by Harry Price

Right: the Austrian medium Rudi Schneider with Harry Price, demonstrating how electrical control functioned. The left arm of the end sitter was connected to the circuit by a metal plate screwed to the chair arm. In practice, the feet were not loosely slipped into the "socks" as here, but were tightly tied into place with special tapes.

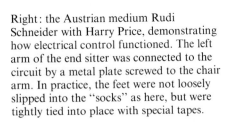

The materialization case rests on the existence or nonexistence of ectoplasm. This peculiar substance is believed by Spiritualists to issue from the mouth, pores, and other body openings of the medium. The psychical investigator Schrenck-Notzing pronounced it to be "a material, at first semifluid, which possesses some of the properties of a living substance, notably that of the power of change, of movement, and of the assumption of definite forms."

Dozens of investigators have testified to the reality of this substance, and to its ability to assume the appearance and texture of living flesh. Dozens of other investigations have discovered that ectoplasm consisted of chewed-up paper, cloth, and other materials regurgitated by the medium while apparently in a trance. The mysterious disappearance of materialization pheno-

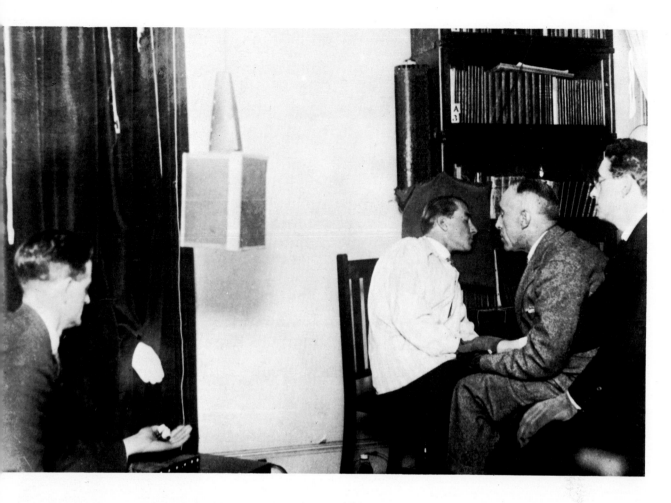

mena in the past few decades casts considerable doubt on the existence of this apparently miraculous substance.

With some relief one turns from ectoplasm to some of the more intellectual aspects of the survival question. For, irrespective of the reality or illusion of materialized limbs and flying tables, the central question is the possible existence of a personality independent of the body. If such a personality or mind, as distinguished from the physical brain, exists, its survival of death is logically not only possible but probable.

Most scientific evidence does not support such a theory. In his book *Psychical Research Today*, the psychiatrist and psychical researcher D. J. West cites the "evidence that our thoughts and feelings are entirely dependent upon the state of our brains. A deep anesthetic or a blow on the head will temporarily put an end to all mental activity. The administration of drugs that act upon the brain can cause confusion, change of mood, hallucinations, peculiar thoughts, delusions, and changes of character. Permanent changes of personality or destruction of faculties to the stage of idiocy are caused by disease, injury, or surgical operation. Where is the cherished independence of mind in the face of such evidence?"

This is a difficult question to answer. These facts cast serious doubt not only on the survival theory, but also on extrasensory perception, which is now a well-established phenomenon. If people can gain information that bypasses the normal sensory

Above: a reconstruction of the materialization of a hand from the cabinet while Schneider was under full control. Price is sitting in front of the medium. Price wrote about him: "Never, in the recorded history of any psychic, have phenomena been witnessed under such a merciless triple control of medium and before sitters of such repute."

media, then there must be something in the brain—subtler than any part or process yet detected—capable of transmitting and receiving such information. It could be that the permanent changes in personality caused by physical injury are only apparent changes, alterations of a superficial nature that do not affect the essential person, or soul.

Relevant to this question is the phenomenon of the OOBE, or out-of-the-body experience, reported by many people. These are experiences in which the person, usually lying unconscious, has a vivid impression of leaving his own body and looking down on it —or of traveling some distance away from it. Some of these experiences can be explained as hallucinations. In other cases, the things seen are later verified. An American woman named Mrs. Wilmot experienced an OOBE while sleeping restlessly because of worry about her husband, who was crossing the ocean in stormy weather. She seemed to leave her body, travel over the water, and alight on a steamer. She found her way to a cabin, entered, and saw her husband lying on his berth. Above him was a berth slightly set back in which another man was lying. She kissed her husband and left.

When she awoke Mrs. Wilmot made detailed notes of what she had seen, describing the cabin and the berth above her husband's. Later her description was found to be correct. Even more extraordinary, however, was the fact that, on the following morning at sea, Wilmot told witnesses he had seen a vision of his wife and that the vision had kissed him. That was not all: the cabin mate

Out-of-the-Body Phenomena

Precisely what ectoplasm looks like and behaves like appears to vary a bit between mediums, and even the same medium may discover that the manifestations appear to be different depending on his or her emotional state. If the ectoplasm is suddenly withdrawn back into the body of the medium—for example when a light is abruptly turned on—the medium is sometimes found to be bruised where the ectoplasm appeared to recoil with something like the force of a snapped elastic band. Of course, whether or not ectoplasm exists at all is a much disputed point. There is considerable proof that Helen Duncan's ectoplasm, for example, was yards of regurgitated cheesecloth, with the same frayed spots visible at each materialization.

Opposite: Kate Goligher, the Irish medium, levitating a table with the help of rodlike ectoplasm.

Left: Margery Crandon at a seance producing dark ectoplasm.

Complex Example of Telepathy

Below: William T. Stead, British editor and convinced Spiritualist. His automatic writing began with messages from a dead journalist friend, but he soon discovered he could receive messages from living friends as well. Oddly, the image of a sinking ocean liner occurred frequently in Stead's writings, and in 1893 he wrote a fictional story about the collision of a great liner with an iceberg in the Atlantic. Stead himself was on the maiden voyage of the ill-starred *Titanic*, and was one of the many drowned.

had also seen the woman and had teased Wilmot about his female visitor.

Whatever one may think of materializations and apparitions, the capacities of the human mind—particularly the subconscious mind—seem greater than we can account for by today's scientific knowledge. For example, consider the talents of William Stead, a British journalist of the 19th century. Stead had the gift of automatic writing and used this method to communicate with his living friends. It saved them from having to write letters to him, but they were not always happy about Stead having access to their secrets. Stead himself told this story of one such embarrassed correspondent:

"A friend of mine . . . had spent the weekend at Haslemere, 30 miles from London. She was to lunch with me on the Wednesday, if she had returned to town. On the Monday afternoon I wished to know about this, so taking up a pen I asked the lady mentally if she had returned home. My hand wrote as follows: 'I am sorry to say that I have had a most unpleasant experience, which I am almost ashamed to tell you. I left Haslemere at 2:27 p.m. in a second-class compartment in which were two women and a man. At Godalming the women got out and I was left alone with the man. He came over and sat by me. I was alarmed and pushed him away. He would not move, however, and tried to kiss me. I was furious and there was a struggle, during which I seized his umbrella and struck him with it repeatedly, but it broke, and I was afraid I would get the worst of it, when the train stopped some distance from Guildford. The man took fright, left me before the train reached the station, jumped out and took to his heels. I was extremely agitated, but I kept the umbrella.'"

Stead then continued: "I sent my secretary immediately to the lady's house with a note in which I expressed my regret for the assault she had suffered, adding, 'Calm yourself and bring me the man's umbrella on Wednesday.' She replied: 'I am sorry you have learnt of what happened to me, because I had decided not to speak of it to anyone; but the umbrella was mine, not his.'"

One of the most complex cases of telepathy ever recorded appeared at first to be a detailed message from a spirit. It took place during some sittings that Dr. S. G. Soal, a mathematician at London University, had with Mrs. Blanche Cooper in 1921–22. She was a direct voice medium who conversed normally with the sitter when the voice, which seemed to emanate close to her, was not speaking. The voice would seldom speak for more than a minute or two at a time, and there would sometimes be a pause for as much as a quarter of an hour before the communication would resume.

During one sitting Dr. Soal heard the voice of a man claiming to be a boyhood friend named Gordon Davis. Soal remembered him, but thought that he had been killed in World War I. The tone of Davis' voice and his characteristic speech mannerisms were more or less as Soal recalled them. Davis described various incidents from their schooldays and the circumstances in which they had last met. At the following seance, Davis showed concern for his wife and child and asked that a message of consolation be sent to them. Unfortunately, he was unable to give their address. At this point, one of Blanche Cooper's spirit guides took over and said that Davis was describing the house to her. "He says something about a funny dark tunnel—it's to do with the house."

The guide continued with the description mentioning "five or six steps and a half" to the door of the house. He said there was something resembling a verandah in front of the house, which was not on a "proper street" but on one that was "like half a street." He mentioned the letter "E" but seemed unable to determine its significance. Inside the house were some pictures of "glorious mountains and the sea," curious vases and saucers, two brass candlesticks on a shelf and "a black dickie bird" on the piano.

The earlier part of Davis' communication relating to his youth was already known to Soal, and could be explained as telepathy between sitter and medium. But the parts of the message relating to the house could not be confirmed immediately. If Soal could prove the description of the house to be accurate, the communication would presumably be evidence for survival, for only the deceased Gordon Davis could plausibly have imparted the information.

Three years after the seance Dr. Soal verified the description. Instead of proving life after death, however, the case raised more perplexing questions. To begin with, Davis was still alive. Dr. Soal found him living in Southend, a seaside town in Essex. His house was one of a row of houses on Eastern Esplanade (the "E's"), facing the sea ("half a street"; English usage considers a street to include the buildings on both sides). Six steps led up to the front door, but the bottom step was only a thin slab ("five or six steps and a half"). At regular intervals between the houses was a covered walkway ("funny dark tunnel") leading to the back garden. Across from Davis' house on the other side of the street was a seaside shelter ("something resembling a verandah"). Inside the house Soal found the pictures of mountains and sea, the two brass candlesticks, and a black figure of a bird sitting on the piano. In short, every detail communicated in the seance was correct except one: Davis was still alive.

The Gordon Davis case has a final strange twist to it that makes it even more astonishing. At the time Dr. Soal received the message, Davis was not living in Southend. He had inspected the house three days before the first communication, but he and his family did not move into it until nearly a year later. The furnishing of the house described in the seance had not been planned in advance by Davis, but had come about partly by chance.

It would seem from the evidence that Blanche Cooper's psychic faculty had been able to rummage in the subconscious mind of a man she did not know existed, and not only produce his voice and correct information about his past but also see the environment in which he would live in the future.

The feats of which the subconscious mind is capable—and the tricks it can play—are illustrated by another communication that Dr. Soal received through Mrs. Cooper. A communicator announcing himself as John Ferguson claimed to be a brother of James Ferguson, a former schoolfriend of Dr. Soal. John Ferguson gave an address, the date, place, and manner of his death, and a great deal of additional information. Soal did not remember that James Ferguson had a brother, but after each

Automatic Writing from the Living

Unlike most automatic writers, who received their messages from the spirits, the 19th-century British journalist William Stead got messages from the living—and saved them the bother of writing themselves. He would ask mental questions and his hand would write the answers automatically—sometimes learning more than the friends wanted him to.

Once he had arranged a lunch engagement with a woman who had been out of town over the weekend. He mentally inquired whether she had returned to London yet, and his hand wrote a long note. It described an unpleasant encounter she had had on the train. According to the message, she had found herself alone in a compartment with a strange man. He came over, sat close to her, and when she tried to push him away, attempted to kiss her. Struggling furiously, she thumped him with his umbrella, which broke. Then the train unexpectedly stopped and the man took flight.

When Stead sent his servant to his friend's house with a note condoling her on the assault, the woman was taken aback. She replied, "I had decided not to speak of it to anyone." She added, "The umbrella was mine, not his."

Above: Mrs. Blanche Cooper, who was the subject of investigation by Dr. Samuel Soal.

Below: Dr. Soal and his wife. Dr. Soal has studied many aspects of the paranormal for much of his career, and his series of seances with the medium Mrs. Blanche Cooper—which unquestionably produced evidence of some kind of psychic communication—are a remarkable episode in psychic research.

communication he speculated about the man's existence. He found that these guesses emerged as facts at the next sitting, and so, over a period of several weeks, the hypothetical John Ferguson, as visualized by Dr. Soal, confirmed the sitter's impressions through the medium.

On investigating, Soal discovered that John Ferguson did not exist, alive or dead, and that the details of his life and manner of death were therefore false. "It is interesting to note how rapidly John Ferguson disintegrated as a personality once his statements about himself had been disproved," wrote Soal. "For more than eight weeks he had been sustained by the emotional interest of the sitter, but immediately that interest had evaporated he became a confused and feeble ghost who disappeared almost as suddenly as he had come on the scene."

Probably the most common dramatization of the subconscious mind is the spirit control or guide. For the most part they are American Indians, Chinese philosophers, or anonymous monks. Most of them are patently the imaginings of the medium's subconscious, and yet they seem to play an important role in collecting and conveying supernormal evidence. The gifted medium Mrs. Leonore Piper, whom William James considered his "one white crow," had a succession of colorful spirit guides. They included an Indian girl with the unlikely name of "Chlorine," the English actress Mrs. Siddons, the poet Longfellow, and Johann Sebastian Bach. For most of her career Mrs. Piper's regular control was Dr. Phinuit, a French physician. His knowledge of medicine and command of French were minimal. Despite the obvious phoniness of her control, Leonore Piper produced some of the most convincing, well-documented communications in the history of Spiritualism. Later in her career Mrs. Piper's spirit guide was a known person, George Pelham. His repeated ability to correctly identify anonymous sitters unknown to Leonore Piper was strong evidence for his spiritual existence.

It is conceivable, of course, that Leonore Piper was gifted with extraordinarily acute ESP, and that she was able in some mysterious way to ferret out the sitter's correct identity. Such an explanation can be used to account for many presumed spirit messages.

What is needed to establish evidence for an afterlife that cannot be explained as telepathy or the workings of the subconscious is information that is not known by living people, or that appears to originate only with the communicator. The first requirement poses yet another problem. If the information is not known by living people, it has to be on record somewhere in order to be corroborated. Since some mediums have demonstrated the ability to read the contents of sealed envelopes, it becomes impossible to prove that recorded information in any form has not been inspected by the medium's psychic faculty. A typical example is the book test related by Sir William Barrett in his preface to the Reverend Drayton Thomas' book *Some New Evidence for Human Survival*. At a seance with Mrs. Gladys Osborne Leonard, Barrett received a message supposed to be from Frederick W. H. Myers, a former president of the SPR.

"There were some books on the right-hand side of a room

upstairs in your house in Devonshire Place. On the second shelf four feet from the ground, in the fourth book counting from the left, at the top of page 78, are some words which you should take as direct answer from him [Myers] to so much of the work you have been doing since he passed over."

Gladys Leonard asked for the name of the book, but the communicator was unable to give it. He said, however, that while "feeling" the books on the shelf, he got a sense of "progression," and that close to the text book were "one or two books on matters in which Sir William used to be very interested, but not of late years. It is connected with studies of his youth."

The medium had never visited Barrett's home, and the scientist had no idea what book was fourth from the left on the specified shelf. On returning home he found that it was George Eliot's *Middlemarch*. In the first line at the top of page 78 were the words "Ay, ay. I remember—you'll see I've remembered 'em all." Barrett regarded this quotation as singularly appropriate, for since Myers' death, much of Barrett's work had been concerned with the question of survival after death, and in particular whether the memories of friends continued once a spirit had left the body. Close at hand on the bookshelf were two volumes of *Heat and Sound* by Dr. John Tyndall, to whom Barrett had been an assistant when young. This may have been the reference to "studies of his youth."

It could be that Myers' spirit had somehow been able to study the books on Barrett's shelf, as claimed, or that Myers while alive had examined the books, and was now communicating what he remembered. Even so, many researchers would prefer to interpret this case and other such book tests as examples of clairvoyance on the part of the medium.

The most complex and perhaps most convincing evidence for survival is contained in what are known as the "cross-correspondences." These are an extensive collection of scripts taken in automatic writing by a group of women who came to be known as the "SPR Automatists."

Soon after the death of F. W. H. Myers in 1901, his friend Mrs. A. W. Verrall began receiving messages in automatic writing from a communicator claiming to be the spirit of Myers. Some of the messages were in Greek and Latin, though the standard of scholarship in these messages was inferior to that of both Myers and Mrs. Verrall. Then Mrs. Leonore Piper also began receiving automatic writing allegedly from Myers, containing references to topics appearing in Mrs. Verrall's scripts. Mrs. Verrall's daughter then began receiving scripts from Myers alluding to topics in the writings of both her mother and Mrs. Piper. A writer living in India and using the pseudonym "Mrs. Holland" also began receiving scripts from a communicator claiming to be Myers. He asked Mrs. Holland to send the scripts to Mrs. Verrall, and gave her the necessary address. Apparently doubting the accuracy of these instructions, Mrs. Holland sent the scripts to the SPR. There researchers found that the new scripts contained allusions to the other scripts already received.

Over some 30 years the SPR received thousands of pages of scripts from the automatists. Although the mediums realized that the messages might constitute proof that Myers had survived,

Unusual "Cross-Correspondences"

Below: Mrs Gladys Leonard became a celebrity when she made the first communication with Sir Oliver Lodge's son Raymond, who had been killed in World War I. She was also involved in a psychic experiment with Sir William Barrett in which the spirit of F. W. Myers, one of the founders of the Society for Psychical Research, led Barrett to a particular book he owned. Mrs. Gladys Leonard's powers were apparently heightened by the presence of her husband.

Do They Prove Life after Death?

they were unaware of the overall pattern of the communications. It was the researchers at the SPR, patiently combing through the masses of unrelated and often trivial material in the scripts, who detected the cross references and pieced together this intellectual jigsaw puzzle. Part of a quotation from the classics would be found in one script, another part in one of the other scripts, and the meaning behind the reference in still a third script. The related references would all appear within a fairly short time span.

Most of the messages are extremely complicated, containing roundabout and obscure literary allusions. An unusually simple example involved a laurel wreath. While in trance one day, Leonore Piper repeated the word "laurel" several times. The following day, again in trance, she was apparently controlled by the spirit of Myers and said, "I gave Mrs. Verrall laurel wreath." Examination of a script from Mrs. Verrall dated three weeks earlier revealed the phrases, "Apollo's laurel bough," "a laurel wreath," "corona laureata," and similar references. Three weeks after Mrs. Piper's trance utterances, Mrs. Verrall received a script containing these words, "Laurel leaves are emblem. Laurel for the victor's brow." The SPR investigators gradually came to the conclusion that the cross-correspondences might be part of a purposeful design on the part of Myers and, later on, of other departed psychical researchers who communicated scripts, to prove survival. There was no reference to such a plan in Myers' writings, but conceivably he could have devised it after death.

Other explanations for the cross-correspondences are discussed by H. F. Saltmarsh in his study *Evidence of Personal Survival from Cross-Correspondences*. He points out that in view of the character of the people involved and the 30-year span over which the correspondences occurred, "the hypothesis of fraud is so fantastic that it need only be mentioned to be dismissed." The possibility that corresponding quotations from classical sources should appear in these scripts at the same time by mere chance was "abstractly possible," but in his opinion had little to recommend it as a theory. The only alternative to the survival explanation is that the automatists had somehow established an extremely high level of ESP without realizing it, and were conveying messages to each other under the assumed personality of Myers.

In this case the ESP hypothesis is almost as great a strain on the reason as the belief that Myers and other spirits devised and communicated a long series of rather obscure messages as a means of signaling their continued existence. To some students of the cross-correspondences, the explanation of spirit communication is more plausible.

If we consider this case along with some of the other highly evidential cases such as the communication of data on the R101 disaster, we approach a situation in which the evidence for survival—slight though it is when weighed against our present scientific knowledge, and buried as it is in masses of phony evidence—becomes very convincing. For most people, however, absolute certainty about life after death is something that may be approached but never attained—at least not in our lifetime.

Opposite: a mezzotint by James Tissot of a double materialization he claimed to have witnessed at a seance. The girl had been dear to him in life, and he welcomed her reappearance as certain proof—to him at least—that she had survived the mysterious and inevitable passage through death.

Index

Picture Credits